African American Languag

M000204395

From birth to early adulthood, all aspects of a child's life undergo enormous development and change, and language is no exception. This book documents the results of a pioneering longitudinal linguistic survey, which followed a cohort of sixty-seven African American children over the first twenty years of life, to examine language development through childhood, adolescence, and early adulthood. It offers the first opportunity to hear what it sounds like to grow up linguistically for a cohort of African American speakers and provides fascinating insights into key linguistics issues, such as how physical growth influences pronunciation, how social factors influence language change, and the extent to which individuals modify their language use over time. By providing a lens into some of the most foundational questions about coming of age in African American Language, this study has implications for a wide range of disciplines, from speech pathology and education to research on language acquisition and sociolinguistics.

MARY KOHN is Associate Professor in English and director of the Chapman Center for Rural Studies at Kansas State University. Her work examines linguistic variation across the lifespan, youth language practices, and regional sound change. Her book *The Way I Communicate Changes But How I Speak Don't* is available through Duke University Press.

WALT WOLFRAM is William C. Friday Distinguished University Professor at North Carolina State University (NCSU) and has pioneered research on social and ethnic dialects for over sixty years. He has published more than 20 books and over 300 articles. The recipient of numerous awards, Dr. Wolfram was accepted into the American Academy of Arts and Sciences in 2019.

CHARLIE FARRINGTON developed the Corpus of Regional African American Language, in collaboration with Dr. Tyler Kendall. His numerous publications address regionality in African American Language, lifespan change, and sociophonetic variation.

JENNIFER RENN is Associate Research Scientist in the College of Education at Purdue University. Prior to joining Purdue, she was the Director of Linguistic and Cultural Diversity at the Center for Applied Linguistics in Washington, DC, where she directed the English for Heritage Language Speakers Program and worked in K-12 English language assessment research.

JANNEKE VAN HOFWEGEN's research focuses on understanding human behavior and stylistic expression through the lens of language and group/individual identity. Her research on lifespan change and sociophonetic variation among minority ethnic and LGBTQ communities has been published in *Language Variation and Change* and the *Journal of Sociolinguistics.*

African American Language

Language Development from Infancy to Adulthood

Mary Kohn
Kansas State University

Walt Wolfram
North Carolina State University

Charlie Farrington
University of Oregon

Jennifer Renn
Purdue University

Janneke Van Hofwegen
Google, Inc.

CAMBRIDGE
UNIVERSITY PRESS

University Printing House, Cambridge CB2 8BS, United Kingdom

One Liberty Plaza, 20th Floor, New York, NY 10006, USA

477 Williamstown Road, Port Melbourne, VIC 3207, Australia

314–321, 3rd Floor, Plot 3, Splendor Forum, Jasola District Centre,
New Delhi – 110025, India

79 Anson Road, #06–04/06, Singapore 079906

Cambridge University Press is part of the University of Cambridge.

It furthers the University's mission by disseminating knowledge in the pursuit of
education, learning, and research at the highest international levels of excellence.

www.cambridge.org
Information on this title: www.cambridge.org/9781108835947
DOI: 10.1017/9781108869607

© Mary Kohn, Walt Wolfram, Charlie Farrington, Jennifer Renn and Janneke Van
Hofwegen 2021

First published 2021

A catalogue record for this publication is available from the British Library.

ISBN 978-1-108-83594-7 Hardback
ISBN 978-1-108-79898-3 Paperback

Contents

Figures

Tables

Preface

It is sometimes difficult to recall what the research world was like at the inception of this longitudinal project in 1990. We contacted people on landline phones, recorded interviews on analog cassettes, transcribed language from foot-controlled machines, and coded the data by hand before storing it on CDs for analysis. The world of big data was only imagined, and the Internet was not yet accessible. In that world, a team of imaginative researchers at the Frank Porter Graham Child Development Institute envisioned a longitudinal study on African American children in the Central Piedmont region of North Carolina. From the rolls of children at preschool centers and other community organizations, eighty-eight healthy African American infants from six to twelve months of age were recruited from surrounding communities ostensibly to examine the impact of ear infections, among other factors, on speech development. The founding members of the team were Drs. Margaret Burchinal, Susan Zeisel, and Joanne Roberts, and their primary focus at the outset was on medical issues. As the study progressed, the emphasis shifted to a social concern with at-risk children, since over 70 percent of the original participants were defined as at risk by the operative definitions at that time. At that same time, the pioneering researchers saw the value of collecting linguistic data as a part of their study, so language samples and interviews were a part of the data from the initiation of the project. An interdisciplinary team was assembled, including a speech and language pathologist, sociologist, child psychologist, educator, and research designer and statistician. No linguists were on that team, and none of the authors of this book were a part of the original team. In fact, the first linguist to join the team was Walt Wolfram, when he was invited by the principal investigators in 1994 to serve on the team as a linguistic consultant. From that point forward, language variation over the lifespan became one of the dominant themes of the project, though researchers continued to investigate other social and educational issues over real time. The other authors of this book joined the team later, and they conducted a major portion of the research reported in this book. Mary Kohn and Walt Wolfram were primarily responsible for the introduction (Chapter 1) and conclusion (Chapter 9), as well as Chapter 2, along with Janneke Van Hofwegen. Wolfram and Van Hofwegen were responsible for the analysis in Chapter 3, which offers the rationale for and justification of the holistic measurement of dialect applied in some of the subsequent chapters. Mary Kohn was responsible for the research and writing of Chapter 4, which confronts the complexity of describing vowel variation and dialect in the early lifespan. Chapter 5, which focuses on the influence of caretaker's speech on children's early vowel systems, and Chapter 6, which examines the influence of peers on language variation, were researched and written primarily by Janneke Van Hofwegen. Chapter 7, which investigates stylistic variation in the early lifespan of African American speakers, and Chapter 8, which considers the influence of dialect on the standardized measurement of reading achievement, were based on research conducted by Jennifer Renn. Mary Kohn, Walt Wolfram, and Charlie Farrington fashioned the manuscript into a cohesive narrative and were responsible for preparing the final document for publication. The ordering of the authors reflects their involvement in the production of this manuscript, but the substantive contribution of each of the authors in research and earlier writing is fully and gratefully acknowledged. It goes without saying that this book is a team effort, from the initiation of the project to its publication three decades after its inception.

The result of this unprecedented collaboration by the overall team of researchers and by the linguistic collective provides the first comprehensive view of language development for the first twenty-one years in the lives of African Americans. The study offers the first opportunity to hear what it sounds like to grow up linguistically for a cohort of African American speakers. At the conclusion of the study in 2012, sixty-seven of the original eighty-eight young adults remained in the study. The retention rate of participants after two decades, in itself, is a stunning accomplishment.

Immense gratitude is due to the lead team of principal investigators who initiated the study, Drs. Burchinal, Roberts, and Zeisel. Their vision, imagination, and persistence in procuring funding sustained the project over the decades. Dr. Burchinal was accessible for consultation throughout the duration of the project and instrumental in the analyses in the early phases of the project. Dr. Roberts was central to all phases, from data collection to analysis, including the shift of project focus to language variation, until her untimely passing in 2008. We will be forever grateful for her leadership and engagement while she was with us and continue to feel the effects of her contributions in her absence.

The only member of the team who was actively engaged from the start to the finish of the project was Dr. Zeisel, and in many ways she was the human lynchpin of the entire project. She was the coordinator of the fieldwork and, in our opinion, was the most successful fieldworker we have ever witnessed. The retention rate above 75 percent for a two-decade study of this type was absolutely amazing – and unprecedented, given the demographic profile of the community. She did it with her deep commitment to the community and participants. She kept in touch with the participants throughout their involvement in the project, visiting the children at school and home, attending graduations, and becoming a genuine friend of the families who were a part of the study. Indeed, our greatest gratitude for the completion of the study is due to her. Dr. Zeisel's fieldwork coordination deserves to be the model for longitudinal studies.

Of course, many other people were involved in this study, far too many to recall even a majority of them. For example, each semester, linguistic and speech and language pathology students at the University of North Carolina at Chapel Hill would help transcribe and code data. With the exception of a few of them who are now established professionals in their own right, we can't recall them. A cohort of other researchers and professors, such as Sandra Jackson, most recently of North Carolina Central University, and J. Michael Terry of the University of North Carolina at Chapel Hill, conducted and published significant research on particular topics using these data that complements the research reported here. We apologize that we cannot name all of those who contributed in so many ways. Unfortunately, there have been so many and the time span so long that we simply cannot resurrect all of the names. But this does not mitigate our indebtedness to them. From start to finish, this has been a collaborative, interdisciplinary effort. That is the only way to conduct this kind of research over a couple of decades.

A number of research grants and different agencies have graciously funded this effort, notwithstanding the deferment of our publication of substantive results. Initial funding came from a series of grants from Maternal and Child Health Bureau MCJ-370599, MCJ-379154, MCJ-370649, R40 MC 00343, and R40MC05488-01, US Department of Health and Human Services. Later funding came from NSF Grant No. BCS-0843865 and BCS-0544744, as well as an NSF RAPID grant BSC-1129778 that provided funding for the collection of data during the postsecondary phase of data collection.

The result of this monumental project provides a unique glimpse into what it means to mature from a linguistic perspective, particularly in terms of a vernacular variety of English. The research reported within these pages represents the cumulative efforts of a host of researchers, family members, and children who worked together to create a once-in-a-lifetime opportunity to examine the human condition with respect to language development for the first two decades of their lives. As we listen to these children grow from babies to adults in their own voices and unique styles, we hope to provide a lens into some of the most foundational questions about coming of age in African American Language.

Abbreviations

AAL	African American Language
AAVE	African American Vernacular English
AAVS	African American Vowel System
AIC	Akaike Information Criterion
BIC	Bayesian Information Criterion
CAT	Communication Accommodation Theory
CDS	Child-Directed Speech
cfpu	children's DDM frequency per utterance
CMC	computer-mediated communication
CPRS	Child–Parent Relationship Scale
CVS	California Vowel Shift
DELV-S	Diagnostic Evaluation of Language Variation – Screening Test
DDM	Dialect Density Measure
ED	Euclidean Distance
FPG	Frank Porter Graham Study
fpu	features per utterance
HBCU	Historically Black College or University
HOME	Home Observation for Measurement of the Environment
ICC	intraclass correlation coefficient
LAGS	Linguistic Atlas of the Gulf States
LANE	Linguistic Atlas of New England
MAE	Mainstream American English
mfpu	mother's DDM frequency per utterance
MIBI	Multidimensional Inventory of Black Identity
MLU	mean length of utterance
NSF	National Science Foundation
pICC	partial intraclass correlation coefficient
SALT	Systematic Analysis for Language Transcription
SSRS	Social Skills Rating System

SVS	Southern Vowel Shift
TVS	Third Vowel Shift
VDM	vowel dispersion measure
VL	vector length
VSA	vowel space area

1 Coming of Age in African American Language

1.1 Introduction

All speakers of language take a journey in developing linguistic competence. Along this path, one observes the unfurling of linguistic developmental processes, the encouraging voices of family and friends, the challenges, and the decisions that allow a speaker to move from baby talk to an ever-changing linguistic repertoire through childhood, adolescence, and adulthood. Speakers often take this path for granted as they recount the footsteps that carried them into adulthood. But for the linguist these data are precious and rare. Even as the field of sociolinguistics compiles new longitudinal corpora and utilizes heritage recordings to conduct real-time studies of language change, studies that extend through childhood and adolescence have been limited to a handful of case studies.

Individual stories reveal how development, changing environments, and situational factors all influence linguistic behavior. They allow us to follow the story of Foxy Boston as she moves from a dynamic teen to a professional adult (Rickford and Price 2013). Or, we can watch two boys from the North of England adapt to new communities, new professions, and changing roles in life (Sankoff 2004). These individual stories demonstrate the flexibility, innovation, and accommodation of a single human negotiating their linguistic landscape. Case studies provide deep insight into the human condition. But these stories cannot be generalized to a larger population. So, while individual stories enrich our understanding of what it means to grow up from a linguistic perspective, they remain rare, and they remain individual narratives.

What could a chorus of individuals tell us? What would we find if we could follow whole cohorts of children as they go from babbling babies to trendy teens and accomplished adults? A significant longitudinal corpus of child and adolescent and early adult speech could reveal typical paths of language socialization, illuminating whether hypothesized developmental trajectories authentically represent observed linguistic behavior. We can, for example, discern if entrance to public schools influences speech patterns in predictable ways, or whether the onset of adolescence predicts innovative linguistic stylizations. We can document the extent to which individuals and cohorts modify their speech upon leaving school to enter the workforce or enroll in institutions of higher learning. This wealth of information has the potential to confirm or alter sociolinguistic theory related to topics ranging from language change to the stylization of language.

Despite the great potential of such rich data, there are practical reasons why such studies are so rare. Recruitment, retention, transcription, and data curation over an expanded period frustrate attempts to carry on such large-scale longitudinal research. A project requires levels of coordinated administrative and research staff with the foresight to manage data collection over the course of decades and transformed technology, to say nothing of funding rarely available for such long-term linguistic research. Under these conditions, it is not surprising that large-scale longitudinal linguistic research appeared to be out of reach.

Lacking the resources to conduct longitudinal studies, cornerstone linguistic theories of language socialization for individuals, as well as language change for communities, have rested upon cross-sectional evidence where cohorts of different ages are compared as a proxy for change over time. Much can be learned utilizing cross-sectional designs where data collected at a single time point from cohorts of different ages are compared to estimate the direction and speed of language change. But cross-sectional data cannot track paths through life stages, leaving the natural road from childhood acquisition to adult sociolinguistic competence obscured and indirectly pieced together. Without longitudinal research, the actual process of linguistic development from childhood through adolescence remained largely a source of conjecture among linguists. In this context, the Frank Porter Graham project reported in this book emerges as an invaluable, unique resource for the study of lifespan change, development, and language socialization.

The story of the Frank Porter Graham study (FPG) begins in Chapel Hill, North Carolina, in 1990 at the Frank Porter Graham Child Development Institute, where eighty-eight healthy African American infants were recruited from surrounding communities to examine the impact of ear infections, among other factors, on speech development. While this initial effort had a primary medical focus, Drs. Margaret Burchinal, Susan Zeisel, and Joanne Roberts, the founding members of the project, saw the value of the linguistic data collected as a part of their efforts. And so a collaboration among researchers in a range of disciplines and, most importantly, the families of the children themselves was formed. The result of this unprecedented collaboration is a study that provides the first comprehensive view of language development for the first twenty-one years of life. With sixty-seven young adults remaining in the study as of the last data collection time point in 2012, FPG gives us the first opportunity to hear how it sounds to grow up linguistically for a cohort of speakers.

This book provides a glimpse into what it means to mature from a linguistic perspective, particularly in terms of a vernacular variety of English. The research reported within these pages represents the cumulative and collaborative efforts of a host of researchers, family members, and children who worked together to create a once-in-a-lifetime opportunity to examine the human condition with respect to language development for the first two decades of their lives. As we listen to these children grow from babies to adults in their own voices and unique styles, we hope to provide a lens into some of the most foundational questions in our field:

• In what ways do life stages correlate with linguistic behavior? Are there predictable points of change?
• How dynamic are individual voices as they grow from infants to adults? Do we see temporal points of stability and variability?
• Can we establish predictable paths of language socialization?

The social lives of the children who led us down this path are a crucial component of the story that follows. Arguably, no social factor is more salient in the United States than race. As African American children growing up in the Southern United States, factors such as the acquisition of African American Language (AAL), the impact of segregation on language, code-switching, and access to literacy are all part of this story. This additional layer invites a number of questions we would be remiss not to address:

• What community, social, and personal factors influence the use of AAL?
• How do ethnolects interact with predominant regional varieties over the lifespan?
• Does the use of vernacular AAL predict literacy skills and educational achievement over time?

Throughout this book, we will wander down the developmental paths that the FPG participants so generously shared with us in search of the answers to these questions.

1.2   The Significance of Longitudinal Research

In the absence of longitudinal studies, cross-sectional studies, that is, the study of data collected at one time point from participants of different ages, emerged as the best alternative to observing language change. Within the field of acquisition, cross-sectional studies provide a glimpse into how individuals develop language, as younger children are compared to their older peers as evidence of how a child might change as they grow. Sociolinguists primarily use cross-sectional designs to estimate community-level language change. Often referred to as the apparent-time method, seniors may be compared to middle-aged and younger cohorts to infer how communities might change over time. Linguists have long noted the confounds of such an approach, with potential cohort effects or age-grading changes associated with certain life stages, leading to false assumptions of stability or change (Bailey et al. 1991; Sankoff 2004; Wagner 2012b). The fact that allied fields such as sociolinguistics and language acquisition approach cross-sectional designs with such different interpretive aims speaks to the difficulty in utilizing cohort comparisons to estimate language change. How can cross-sectional studies estimate change for both an aggregate community and particular individuals within the community?

Real-time studies, or studies that gather data from the same participants at different time points to track change over time, can clarify whether differences between cohorts are likely due to individual change, community change, or a combination of the two as data collected from distinct time periods are compared for evidence of community change. Indeed, sociolinguistic literature on real-time studies often touts the ability to test hypotheses based on apparent-time evidence as one of the main advantages of these studies (Labov 1994; Sankoff 2004; Wagner 2012b). Labov's (1963) revolutionary introduction of the apparent-time model set a precedent for utilizing heritage data to verify hypotheses about community change. In his study of Martha's Vineyard, Labov relied on Linguistic Atlas of New England (LANE) data to verify whether generational differences in pronunciation reflected community change, where vowels of interest changed within each new generation, or age-grading, where individuals might change their pronunciation as they age. The role of real-time data in sociolinguistic analyses has thus been a central component of the field from the very first studies of variation and change as many studies in sociolinguistics continue to look for real-time evidence to verify whether changes found in cross-sectional data are more likely to be due to age-grading or change occurring at the community level. But individual speakers are lost in the crowd, since such studies cannot trace whether particular speakers within these age cohorts change over time, and interpretations can sometimes be elusive. In follow-up studies of Labov's study on Martha's Vineyard four decades later, different researchers came to quite contrary interpretations about whether the phenomenon he uncovered was actually a progressive sound change or a temporary reversal of a change that would be suspended (Pope 2002; Blake and Josey 2003).

Although comparisons between cross-sectional studies with heritage recordings, like Labov's study using LANE, can strengthen conclusions based on cross-sectional research, such differences in data collection and analysis can produce ambiguity and inference about change for the particular group members. Trend studies, which examine different subjects in a community at different points in time, address these issues by designing consistent methodologies to collect comparable speech samples across time. These studies attempt to resample populations selecting for specific criteria to identify whether community changes advance over time. Holding data collection techniques constant, these studies provide an additional layer of rigor for verifying community change that may be missing from studies that rely solely on the apparent-time construct. Henrietta Cedergren was one of the first scholars to utilize this method in her study of *ch* lenition in Panamanian Spanish. Fifteen years after finding an adolescent lead for this variable, Cedergren resampled the population between 1982 and 1984 (Cedergren 1987). The adolescent lead remained, even as the sound change had advanced by 10 to 15 percent per age group. This pattern suggested that the original apparent-time adolescent lead documented in 1973 represented not only community-level change, with the sound change advancing generally within the community, but also a certain amount of individual dynamicity. Findings such as these would suggest that the apparent-time method may underestimate the extent of change as individuals may increase their use of innovative variants as they age, shifting their linguistic behavior in the direction of community change. Though trend studies may suggest that individuals are dynamic, these studies cannot document the extent to which individuals within a community change. Such conclusions are based on inference, rather than direct observation.

Panel studies supplement cross-sectional and trend studies by placing the focus of analysis on the individual. These studies sample the same individuals as they age, thus establishing trajectories of change for each member in the study. Panel studies often cover shorter time spans than cross-sectional or trend studies but contain much larger amounts of data for each participant. Multiple time points are a crucial component of panel studies so that researchers can identify whether trajectories exhibit directionality, or whether differences between points represent fluctuations that do not lead to permanent change. In fact, more than two time points are necessary in order to qualify as an authentic longitudinal study.

Gillian Sankoff and her colleagues' work on Montreal French illustrates why linguists need to pay attention to individuals, even when focusing on community change. Depending on the variable under analysis, speakers were found to move both in the direction of community change, indicating that apparent time would underestimate the actual extent of community change (Sankoff, Blondeau and Charity 2001), and counter to community patterns of change, indicating that apparent-time models might overestimate total levels of community change (Sankoff and Wagner 2006). In this context, the value of understanding individual patterns of linguistic behavior cannot be underestimated. If linguists are able to identify the circumstances under which individuals are likely to progress in the direction of community change, stay stable, or retract from community change, the apparent-time hypothesis can be applied with more rigor and precision.

When studying community change, the dynamic individual is a problem to be overcome rather than embraced. However, more and more linguistics scholars turn to this individual dynamicity as the focus of inquiry. Studies of style-shifting, age-grading, and accommodation all track the ordered hetero-geneity of individual dynamicity. Panel studies form the backbone of these conversations. When individuals are tracked over time, linguists can examine how changing social factors influence the behavior of their participants. Using longitudinal data, studies demonstrate how interlocutors influence linguistic behavior (Rickford and McNair-Knox 1994), how changing schools or com-munities can lead to change (Sankoff 2004; Carter 2007; Cukor-Avila and Bailey 2011), how gender can influence lifespan trajectories of change (Eisikovits 1998), or even how social network factors or social aspirations can correlate with patterns of change (Moore 2004; Wagner 2008). The import-ance of panel studies thus extends beyond testing the apparent-time hypothesis by allowing linguists to closely examine what makes individual linguistic behavior dynamic.

The more that linguists learn about how and why individuals may change their linguistic behavior over time, the more that general observations about these changes can be made. These generalizations provide a foundation for understanding how language may interact with the unique social circumstances of different life stages. For example, entrance to school marks the transition from early childhood to middle childhood, so this particular life stage is associated with institutions that fundamentally alter a child's social network. Similarly, retirement, associated with more advanced aging, can lead to wide-spread changes in social networks, routines, and behaviors. Many scholars have called to theorize the role of life stages in linguistic behavior as it is assumed that common social circumstances associated with moving between different life stages are likely to influence speech (Hockett 1950; Chambers 1995, 2003; Eckert 1997; Kerswill and Williams 2000; Labov 2001; Cheshire 2005; Foulkes and Docherty 2006; Woolard 2011; Wagner 2012b). While cross-sectional data allow for comparisons across age groups, panel data allow linguists to document what kinds of changes individuals make as they pass from one life stage to the next, providing measurable and observable evidence to support the theorization of how life stages influence linguistic behavior.

Each technique, whether cross-sectional, trend, or panel, provides a piece of the puzzle for understanding how dynamic individuals fit within community change. However, only panel studies place the focus on individual dynamicity. At the same time, only panel studies with multiple temporal data points (rather than two points) can provide authentic insight into the dynamic nature of longitudinal progression of an individual. The envelope for inquiry becomes greatly expanded when linguists track individual behavior incrementally at multiple points over time, opening up the opportunity to explore a host of factors ranging from micro and situational changes, such as how changes in interlocutors or speech tasks influence speech, to large-scale changes, such as how life stage, community, or school changes influence behavior. The more dynamic the linguistic behavior an individual is likely to display, the more important longitudinal analyses become. Indeed, longitudinal studies would be pointless if individual stability is assumed. For this reason, childhood and adolescence should be an obvious focus for such studies. As those who focus on language acquisition already know, there is no time considered more dynamic for language than the transitions across the first twenty years of life. Accordingly, longitudinal analysis is particularly critical for these earliest life stages.

1.3   Childhood and Adolescent Studies in Sociolinguistic Research

Childhood is a dynamic life stage characterized by rapid changes intimately connected to social context and developmental processes, a fact driving those who research language acquisition. Within this subdiscipline, longitudinal studies have been central to our understanding of typical and atypical development (Miller and Ervin 1964; Bloom 1970; Brown 1973). But due to a focus on early acquisition, these studies tend to track children to the point of early elementary school, about age six years, stopping at that point. By contrast, sociolinguists have directed their attention on teens due to their linguistic creativity, their assumed vernacularity, and the possibility that adolescents may play a crucial role in sound change (Eckert 1997; Labov 2001), while, with some notable exceptions, largely ignoring sociolinguistic variation during early and middle childhood. Unlike the field of language acquisition, panel studies have been much more limited and rare in sociolinguistics (Wagner and Buchstaller 2017).

Due to the difficulty of tracking teens across an extended time period, sociolinguistic research on adolescence either tends to employ cross-sectional designs or focuses on ethnographic studies conducted over the course of a year or two at most (e.g., Habick 1993; Eckert 1997; Eisikovits 1998; Fought 1999; Wagner 2008, 2012a; Bucholtz 2011; Carter 2013). Using these techniques, linguists have made huge strides in understanding language acquisition and stylization. And yet this split focus, with acquisitionists tracking early development and sociolinguists documenting adolescent innovation, leaves critical gaps in the field. How do individuals transition from childhood to adolescence? What is the role of middle childhood in the acquisition of style and language change? In what ways do acquisition and social variation interact? These kinds of questions can only be answered using panel studies that span early childhood, adolescence, and adulthood. The FPG study unites these two subfields by tracking the path from childhood to adulthood, documenting as the linguistic individual negotiates their surroundings and adapts to their environment. While we view these paths through the lens of variationist analysis and composite, scalar analysis, the FPG study is interdisciplinary in nature, granting insight into acquisition, development, and educational performance, among other disciplines. For now, we turn to some of the key questions that have placed adolescence at the center of the sociolinguistic field to demonstrate why such work is so critical to the field.

1.3.1   The Story of Teens

Teens have a special place in sociolinguistics as linguists and laypersons alike assume that teenage stylizations have the potential to reshape and pave the road to language change (Chambers 1995; Eckert 1997; Labov 2001). For linguists, these hypotheses are based on the appearance of "adolescent peaks" in a number of studies, in which the speech of adolescents stands out as more innovative and/or vernacular than their younger or older cohorts. These peaks have been found in a number of studies including research on sound change in Philadelphia (Labov 2001), Panama (Cedergren 1987), and morphosyntactic change in Toronto (Tagliamonte and D'Arcy 2009), just to name a few. Why would teens stand out as more innovative? Labov (2001) suggests that this peak is more than just an anomaly. Instead, he is among those who believe that this trend reflects the future of the language, the eventual majority pattern. How do teens come to be out in front of these changes? Why are adults and children left behind? And, most importantly, what are the factors that prompt these changes to begin with?

Under Labov's (2001) account, children move away from parental models when entering school. Once children are exposed to a wider social network, they begin emulating the speech patterns of those who slightly outrank them: the older kids in the school. Over the years, they increment forward, moving closer and closer to their target models, only to surpass them. In other words, teens lead sound change simply because they've had more time to reshape their speech in ways that make them stand apart from their younger siblings and parents. The youngest children remain closer to the parental models because they have not had the opportunity to reshape their language to the same extent.

Evidence for adolescent innovation largely comes from cross-sectional studies. But adolescent peaks are ambiguous and difficult to confirm without the support of real-time studies. While teens may use newer or more vernacular forms as part of their adolescent identities, there is no guarantee that individuals won't adjust their linguistic performance as they adapt to new cultural circumstances and develop their sense of style. So, just as children of the 1990s shed their JNCO jeans, they also fled from uptalk. As noted before, age-grading raises problems for the way linguists interpret adolescent peaks in cross-sectional data. Do these peaks represent a temporary change, or a change that will affect generations to come? Panel studies that follow individuals over time are able to test whether changes observed in cross-sectional studies continue to advance or disappear when adolescents toss certain variants aside as juvenile or faddish.

1.3.2   Middle Childhood

While previous studies provide convincing evidence that teens do, in fact, deserve our attention, there is additional motivation to investigate younger age groups. Like the middle child in a large family, middle childhood has mostly been ignored by sociolinguists, so that characterizations of this life stage generally rely on a handful of participants, if included at all in studies. Yet, based on Labov's (2001) theory of incrementation, middle childhood is precisely the period when individuals start modifying their speech away from parental models. This hypothesis finds support in the few studies that do focus on middle childhood and preadolescence. For example, Habib (2014) demonstrates in a study of more than fifty Syrian children, age 6 to 18 years, that preadolescent participants most actively utilized linguistic resources for identity construction, as 8-year-old boys turned to local variants to construct a more masculine identity. This work supports Eckert's hypothesis that preadolescence may be a crucial point for linguistic stylization, as the preadolescent girls in her study skillfully demonstrate through the incorporation of innovative linguistic features in their emerging preteen stylizations (Eckert 2011). While teens may stand out the most in cross-sectional studies, sitting at the peak of vernacularity, middle childhood may be the point when individuals start erecting the mountain, creating paths toward the innovations that will set these children apart from their parents as they reach adolescence. Even if change may stabilize in late adolescence, children get the ball rolling.

The little evidence that exists for middle childhood suggests that the transition from home to school may trigger language change and encourage new patterns of linguistic stylization. To fully understand how childhood fits in the linguistic lifecycle of an individual, however, more studies need to track how children move from early acquisition (Roberts 2002; Smith, Durham, and Fortune 2007), where they transition to school networks and, subsequently, find new linguistic role models (Kerswill and Williams 2000), before becoming trend-setting preteens (Eckert 2011). The FPG project is the first project that follows a large cohort of children through this process, not only offering insight into the neglected life stage of middle childhood but also providing evidence for how transitions between childhood and adolescence impact linguistic behavior.

1.3.3   Emerging Adulthood

Because transitions between life stages offer important insights into how individuals linguistically navigate the social changes associated with entering a new life stage, the transition from adolescence to adulthood also marks a potentially critical moment for linguistic development. New demands associated with entering the workforce, new contacts formed in universities, or newfound mobility sparked through military deployments or work-related relocations all set the stage for individual linguistic change. Unlike middle childhood, plenty of eighteen- to twenty-two-year-olds have been included in sociolinguistic studies over the years, but the importance of this momentous period has been lost as these individuals are often dumped into cross-sectional age bins spanning a decade or more. Recent studies on emerging adulthood, as this life stage has come to be called (Arnett 2000), demonstrate that this transition deserves the kind of scrutiny that adolescence has received in the past. These studies indicate that emerging adulthood is associated with modifications in linguistic behavior, particularly for individuals who hold non-local aspirations or who experience contact with speakers of other dialects in educational or work settings (De Decker 2006; Evans and Iverson 2007; Wagner 2008; Bigham 2012; Prichard and Tamminga 2012). The initial waves of research indicate that transitions between life stages can offer valuable insight into when, to what extent, and in what ways individuals adjust their speech when faced with new social dynamics.

The dynamicity across early childhood, adolescence, and emerging adulthood documented in short-term longitudinal studies and cross-sectional research all indicate that these life stages would benefit from more extended longitudinal analysis. To fully understand how adolescence impacts language, linguists must observe the ways in which children transition into adolescence and emerge on the other side. Indeed, there is strong evidence that middle childhood and emerging adulthood deserve more attention from linguists, as both may improve current understanding of how sound change advances, and the ways in which life stages correlate with linguistic change. Because FPG is a panel study that traverses infancy to early adulthood, this study can identify individual trajectories of change through these critical life stages, establishing trajectories for each individual in the study. Theoretically, these trajectories are necessary to validate Labov's adolescent-centric model of language change, as well as Eckert's theories of the impact that life stages have on linguistic stylization. From an applied perspective, linguists can also examine the ways in which surrounding social factors associated with distinct life stages, such as entrance into school or the workforce, or individual goals and aspirations, impact the ways in which individuals transition through these life stages. Both theoretical and applied perspectives demonstrate how critical long-term and large-scale panel research is for these life stages. As the FPG study will illustrate, such research has the opportunity to greatly advance current understanding of how individuals develop linguistic repertoires and move through a complex linguistic landscape.

1.4 Ethnolinguistic Variation across the Lifespan

There is additional motivation to study ethnolinguistic variation across childhood and early adulthood, particularly for AAL. Unlike European American English varieties, child vernacular AAL has been a cornerstone of sociolinguistic research due to an assumed link between the well-documented education achievement gap and home language use (Rickford 1999). It is no coincidence that early research into the variety was funded by the US Office of Education, with specific interest in the relationship between African American Vernacular English (AAVE) and school performance (Labov et al. 1968; Baratz and Shuy 1969; Fasold and Wolfram 1970; Wolfram 1971). This work has continued to develop over the years, prompting research into the intersection between reading and AAVE use (Labov, Gadsden, and Wagner 1995; Craig and Washington 2006; Van Hofwegen and Stob 2012), effective teaching strategies (Rickford and Rickford 1995; Sweetland 2006; Wheeler 2016), and vernacular AAL language acquisition (Green 2011; Newkirk-Turner, Oetting, and Stockman 2014; Green and White-Sustaita 2015). An assumed relationship between adolescence and vernacularity has prompted numerous investigations into teenage stylization and AAL (e.g., Labov 1965; Baugh 1983; Rickford 1999), as well as a handful of longitudinal case studies tracking AAL use during adolescence and adulthood (Baugh 1996; Cukor-Avila 2002; Cukor-Avila and Bailey 2011; Rickford and Price 2013). This handful of studies indicates that speakers of AAL modify the extent to which they use vernacular features as they age. These studies additionally provide evidence for the ways in which social structures and linguistic stylization interact over time, from the broad influence of overarching institutional structures to the in situ influence of interlocutors and stylization.

For example, Cukor-Avila and Bailey (2011) track the ways in which changing school structures and parenting models influence trajectories of use for AAL features and innovative quotatives, documenting in real-time how changing school demographics introduced the use of quotative *be like* into the speech of adolescents in their study. These trends provide additional evidence for patterns observed in cross-sectional data in which school demographics correlate with student participation in sound systems associated with the predominant population in a given educational institution (Kohn 2017). Case studies, such as Rickford and McNair-Knox's (1994) famous "Foxy Boston" study, also shed light on how developing roles may influence the use of an ethnolect for certain variants but not others. Rickford and Price (2013) attributed a decline of vernacular AAL morphosyntactic variants in their participants' speech to the influence of workplace expectations, adult responsibilities, and motherhood. However, a similar shift in vocalic variants was not observed, with participants showing little change for their vowel systems. Such research indicates the need to explore both macro and individual factors that may influence linguistic behavior, while also serving as a reminder that linguistic variants may show distinct paths of change over time.

These studies indicate that changes associated with distinct life stages have the potential to influence participation in ethnolectal variants in distinct ways for a myriad of reasons. Varying levels of segregation experienced in school, work, and social environments, choices to navigate linguistic prejudice in the educational system, the work place, or broader society, or changing social and/ or familial roles, all have the potential to lead to variable participation in an ethnolect over the lifespan. It bears repeating that whenever individual dynamicity is found, studies that track individuals over time are best equipped to document why and how individuals modify their linguistic behavior. However, the potential social impact of such research is even more critical given the real-world impact of linguistic prejudice (Rickford and King 2016) and possible links with academic performance.

1.5   History of the FPG Project

The FPG project stands as an unprecedented research undertaking within the field of sociolinguistics, providing the only large-scale multi-decade study of AAL that spans childhood, adolescence, and emerging adulthood. The study began in 1990 at the University of North Carolina, Chapel Hill, when eighty-eight African American children were recruited as infants from the Piedmont region of North Carolina. With a mean age of 8.1 months, ranging from 6 to 12 months, the majority of children were in the babbling stage at the time of recruitment. By the time of the last data collection point in 2012, some participants were having their own babbling babies, some had entered college, others found places in the workforce, and all were laying the foundations for their lives as adults. The scope of such a project cannot be understated, as participants actively contributed their time and their voices for over twenty years of their lifespan. The researchers who worked with participants were thus able to capture snapshots of each child as they moved from baby, to toddler, to child, to teen, to adult making their own decisions about parenthood, work, and education.

The goals, data collection protocol, and funding streams have developed and changed over time as the focus of the study has shifted. The study began to examine a number of factors, including the role of Otitis Media on language acquisition, as well as the effects of early educational interventions, social, and psychological factors on cognitive development, language acquisition, and school performance (Burchinal et al. 1996). Given these goals, four main criteria guided initial recruitment: all participants were required to be African American, none could have genetic disorder or other serious complications at birth, all must have a healthy birth weight (greater than 2,500 grams), and all were recruited from nine local childcare centers. Upon entry into the study, 71 percent of participants came from families living below the poverty level according to federally defined guidelines. Additionally, the majority came from households that posed risk factors for school success. So, for example, the majority of mothers were young, single, and many had not completed high school at the time of their child's birth. These selection criteria provide a level of homogeneity to the initial sample as all participants come from a similar geographic area and share ethnicity, and most come from similar socioeconomic backgrounds.

Because of the interdisciplinary nature of the study, a number of measures related to home and school environments were tracked at regular intervals, particularly during the early years of the study. Home environment characteristics were collected, including measures of language stimulation, responsivity, cognitive stimulation, and emotional support. School characteristics were also documented, including level of poverty within the school district and racial composition of the school, as obtained from the National Center for Education Statistics (Snyder and Hoffman 2003). These surveys and evaluations added a layer of context to the linguistic data collected, allowing researchers to identify the influence of home and school environmental factors on speech. In addition, from age 4 years until the 5th grade, about age 10 years, participants were administered a battery of standardized literacy and language tests annually, providing the opportunity to evaluate academic performance. Finally, and most importantly for the purposes of linguistic research, informal interactions between caregivers and participants were recorded from about 24 months to age 9 years. Early funding for the project was provided by the Maternal and Child Health Bureau (MCJ-370599, MCJ-379154 & MCJ-370649, R40MC-00343), due to the initial medical focus of the study. A number of studies on early cognitive development, the impact of childcare (Burchinal et al. 2000), the influence of family support (Burchinal et al. 1996), and environmental risk factors (Burchinal et al. 2000) on language development were published from this initial wave of research.

As the project progressed, the linguistic value of the study became increasingly apparent. As such, both data collection protocols and funding streams evolved to accommodate the linguistic focus of the study. Starting in the sixth grade, or about age 12 years, each participant recruited a friend into the study. In addition to doubling the sample size, this provided the opportunity to record interactions between peers. Additional language tasks were introduced to the protocol, including designs to elicit both formal and informal speech. These tasks were adjusted over the years to be age-appropriate, as will be discussed in Chapter 2. School factors such as level of poverty and racial make-up continued to be collected, and the level of poverty in the home environment was also tracked. A selection of standard-ized literacy and academic tests continued to be collected. However, add-itional measures, such as a racial centrality survey, were also developed and added to the data collection protocol. The latter half of the study was funded by the National Science Foundation (NSF BCS-0544744; BCS-1129778) due to the primarily linguistic focus of this stage of research. This latter stage of the project has resulted in several comprehensive studies of the development of AAL on a variety of linguistic levels and social factors ranging from the influence of physical growth on acoustic correlates of pronunciation (Kohn and Farrington 2012; Kohn and Farrington 2017), to studies of the acquisi-tion of style-shifting (Renn 2007; Renn 2010), to the impact of AAL on educational testing (Renn and Terry 2009), to evaluations of age-grading (Van Hofwegen and Wolfram 2010).

The final stage of data collection occurred in 2012 when the participants were, on average, 20 years old. Although the majority of participants started out in similar socioeconomic circumstances, each member of the study shaped their own path in life, with some attending college, some starting families, some entering the workforce, and others moving away. Despite these challenges, more than sixty-seven of the original eighty-eight participants participated in the final interview. In addition to a formal and informal language task, participants were able to reflect on their experience in the project, as well as their feelings regarding language use and language change during this period. Many participants fondly recalled snack time, story time, and playing games with Susan Zeisel, field coordinator through-out the entire study, and other researchers in the project, speaking to the level of commitment of both the investigators and the participants to the project as a whole.

The size and depth of the corpus at this time is nothing short of astonishing. The database includes the speech of two generations, numerous speech record-ings over the course of 18 years for sixty-seven of the eighty-eight original participants, a cohort of peers at three additional time points, standardized testing information, demographic information, social network information, family and teacher questionnaires, participant reflections on ethnicity, hopes, dreams, expectations, and language use. In the subsequent years, a host of linguists has dug through this treasure trove, often working as a team to discover what the stories of more than sixty-seven children can teach us about life, language, and change.

1.6   Book Outline

This book compiles the shared lessons learned from more than twenty-six years
of work on the FPG project. We take both a holistic and particularized approach
to the data, analyzing a range of linguistic and social variables to provide an
overarching picture of how children change the way they speak over the course
of their lifespan.

We begin, in Chapter 2, by addressing what it means to measure a moving
target. Specifically, we evaluate the interaction of physical development and
language acquisition processes on linguistic behavior, especially for the earliest
years of data collection. First, we outline the ways in which data collection
evolved to meet the developmental level of the participants over the course of
the study, cataloging the variety of data collection techniques that occurred at
each data collection point. We then present evidence for the influence of
physical and developmental factors on early speech production in the study.
Analyses of vowel production confirm patterns observed in cross-sectional
studies for the ways in which vocal tract anatomy affects formant production
over time. A study of constraints on copula absence indicates a shift from
universal developmental constraints to dialect-specific constraints over the first
four years of development. This chapter offers valuable insights to the potential
and pitfalls of examining early childhood variation, not only illustrating how
developmental processes interact with social variation, but also providing
advice for those who wish to attempt such work in cross-sectional or longitudinal studies.

Chapter 3 documents trajectories of change over time for morphosyntactic
and consonantal variation. This chapter addresses questions of vernacular
optimization, identifying the way in which participants modify their use of
vernacular AAL as they move through childhood, adolescence, and adulthood.
These trajectories are tracked using a variety of metrics, ranging from traditional variation analysis of select variables including copula absence, third
person singular -*s* absence, and variation in "ing", to composite assessments
measuring a range of AAL morphosyntactic variables. This chapter illustrates
widespread patterns of age-grading with peak vernacular use in the adolescent
years and subsequent declines in emerging adulthood, providing insight into
patterns of age-grading for AAL previously hypothesized in cross-sectional
studies and case studies.

Chapter 4 addresses changes to the vowel system over time. Although vowel
variation has been a cornerstone focus for analysis in European American
varieties, demonstrating ongoing sound changes throughout the United
States, variation in AAL vowels has received less attention and practically no
attention in terms of their change over the lifespan. This chapter examines how
the local stable AAL system interacts with ongoing sound changes identified

among European Americans in the region. Unlike morphosyntactic variation, patterns of change appear idiosyncratic, indicating greater community stability over the lifespan and confirming patterns observed in case studies such as Rickford and Price (2013). This chapter indicates differential patterns of change for distinct linguistic subsystems over the lifespan. In addition, these documented trajectories of vocalic variation provide key insights into interpreting apparent-time peaks for vocalic variation in communities undergoing sound change.

Chapters 5 and 6 turn to external factors ranging from correlations with caretaker speech and peer speech, and community and school segregation with participation in AAL. A range of psychosocial measures are evaluated within these chapters, including racial centrality, social networks, stress levels, social skills, self-esteem, and perceived relationships with friends. Within the context of these many psychosocial metrics, the strong correlation between community and school segregation and the use of AAL features over the lifespan provides key evidence that spatial segregation is the most important predictor of AAL use.

Chapter 7 examines style-shifting and language interaction over the lifespan. Beginning with the acquisition of style-shifting, we demonstrate that the formality of an interaction does not influence use of AAL until after age 6 years, indicating that style-shifting is a linguistic skill acquired in middle childhood. We then turn to issues of accommodation, examining correlations between mother and child AAL use, as well as peer-to-peer accommodation levels. This chapter holds key insights into the acquisition of style-shifting and patterns of accommodation over the lifespan.

Chapter 8 considers the correlation between AAL use and scores of different components of a standardized reading test, The Woodcock-Johnson Test of Cognitive Abilities, focusing on three sections related to reading: (1) Letter-Word Identification, (2) Comprehension, and (3) Word Attack Skills. As with other studies on AAL and literacy conducted as a part of the FPG project (Van Hofwegen and Stob 2011; Terry, et al. 2010), the results indicate an inverse relationship between literacy and AAL use, thus suggesting an effect related to the use of AAL. However, a number of mitigating effects exist, and participants who show greater code-switching abilities tend to achieve higher scores on these sections.

In the concluding chapter, we review how the FPG project presents an unparalleled view into the linguistic lives of children and adolescents as they establish their own paths toward adulthood. This book offers a unique journey through this process, illustrating how development, linguistic structures, social structures, and the social conditions surrounding individuals all play a role in paving these paths. The insights offered by these journeys not only expand our understanding of sociolinguistic behavior over the lifespan, but provide a critical interpretive lens to complement and, at times, counter the more common cross-sectional analyses that have dominated sociolinguistics over its first half-century of development.

References

Arnett, Jeffrey J. 2000. Emerging adulthood: A theory of development from the late teens through the twenties. *American Psychologist* 55(5): 469–480.

Bailey, Guy, Tom Wikle, Jan Tillery and Lori Sand. 1991. The apparent time construct. *Language Variation and Change* 3(1991): 241–264.

Baratz, Joan and Roger W. Shuy (eds.). 1969. *Teaching Black Children to Read*. Arlington, VA: Center for Applied Linguistics.

Baugh, John. 1983. A survey of Afro-American English. *Annual Review of Anthropology* 12(1): 335–354.

Baugh, John. 1996. Dimensions of a theory of econolinguistics. In Gregory Guy, Crawford Feagan, Deborah Schiffrin, and John Baugh (eds.), *Towards a Social Science of Language: Papers in Honor of William Labov*, 397–419. Amsterdam: John Benjamins.

Bigham, Douglas. 2012. Emerging adulthood in sociolinguistics. *Language and Linguistics Compass* 6(8): 533–544.

Blake, Renée and Meredith Josey. 2003. The /ay/ diphthong in a Martha's Vineyard community: What can we say 40 years after Labov? *Language in Society* 32(4): 451–485.

Bloom, Lois. 1970. *Language Development: Form and Function in Emerging Grammars*. Cambridge, MA: MIT Press.

Brown, Roger. 1973. *A First Language: The Early Stages*. Cambridge, MA: Harvard University Press.

Bucholtz, Mary. 2011. *White Kids: Language, Race, and Styles of Youth Identity*. Cambridge: Cambridge University Press.

Burchinal, Margaret R., Joanne E. Roberts, Steve Hooper, and Susan A. Zeisel. 2000. Cumulative risk and early cognitive development: A comparison of statistical risk models. *Developmental Psychology* 36(6): 793–807.

Burchinal, Margaret R., Joanne E. Roberts, Laura A. Nabors, and Donna M. Bryant. 1996. Quality of center child care and infant cognitive and language development. *Child Development* 67(2): 606–620.

Burchinal, Margaret R., Joanne E. Roberts, Rhodus Riggins, Susan A. Zeisel, Eloise Neebe, and Donna M. Bryant. 2015. Relating quality of center-based child care to early cognitive and language development longitudinally. *Child Development* 71(2): 339–357.

Carter, Phillip. 2007. Phonetic variation and speaker agency: Mexicana identity in a North Carolina middle school. *University of Pennsylvania Working Papers in Linguistics* 13(2): 1–14.

Carter, Phillip M. 2013. Shared spaces, shared structures: Latino social formation and African American English in the U.S. south. *Journal of Sociolinguistics* 17(1): 66–92.

Cedergren, Henrietta. 1987. The spread of language change: Verifying inferences of linguistic diffusion. In P. Lowenberg (ed.), *Language Spread and Language*

Policy: Issues, Implications and Case Studies: Georgetown University Round Table on Language and Linguistics, 44–60. Washington, DC: Georgetown University Press.

Chambers, J.K. 1995. *Sociolinguistic Theory: Linguistic Variation and Its Social Significance*. Oxford: Blackwell.

Chambers, J.K. 2003. *Sociolinguistic Theory: Linguistic Variation and Its Social Significance*. Oxford: Blackwell.

Cheshire, Jenny. 2005. Age and generation-specific use of language. In Ulrich Ammon, Norbert Dittmar, and Klaus J. Mattheier (eds.), *Sociolinguistics: An Introductory Handbook of the Science of Language and Society*, 1552–1563. Boston/Berlin: Mouton de Gruyter.

Craig, Holly K. and Julie A. Washington. 2006. *Malik Goes to School: Examining the Language Skills of African American Students from Preschool-5th Grade*. Mahwah, NJ: Lawrence Erlbaum Associates.

Cukor-Avila, Patricia. 2002. She say, she go, she be like: Verbs of quotation over time in African American Vernacular English. *American Speech* 77(1): 3–31.

Cukor-Avila, Patricia and Guy Bailey. 2011. The interaction of transmission and diffusion in the spread of linguistic forms. *University of Pennsylvania Working Papers in Linguistics* 17(2): 39–49.

De Decker, Paul. 2006. A real-time investigation of social and phonetic changes in post-adolescence. *University of Pennsylvania Working Papers in Linguistics* 12(2): 65–76.

Eckert, Penelope. 1997. Age as a sociolinguistic variable. In Florian Coulmas (ed.), *The Handbook of Sociolinguistics*, 151–167. Oxford: Blackwell.

Eckert, Penelope. 2011. Language and power in the preadolescent heterosexual market. *American Speech* 86(1): 85–97.

Eisikovits, Edina. 1998. Girl-talk/boy-talk: Sex differences in adolescent speech. In Jennifer Coates (ed.), *Language and Gender: A Reader*, 45–58. Sydney: Australian Professional Publications.

Evans, Bronwen and Paul Iverson. 2007. Plasticity in vowel perception and production: A study of accent change in young adults. *Journal of the Acoustical Society of America* 121(6): 3814–3826.

Fasold, Ralph W. and Walt Wolfram. 1970. Some linguistic features of Negro dialect. In Ralph W. Fasold and Roger Shuy (eds.), *Teaching Standard English in the Inner City*, 41–86. Washington, DC: Center for Applied Linguistics.

Fought, Carmen. 1999. A majority sound change in a minority community: /u/-fronting in Chicano English. *Journal of Sociolinguistics* 4(1): 5–23.

Foulkes, Paul and Gerard Docherty. 2006. The social life of phonetics and phonology. *Journal of Phonetics* 34(4): 409–438.

Green, Lisa J. 2011. *Language and the African American Child*. Cambridge: Cambridge University Press.

Green, Lisa J. and Jessica White-Sustaita. 2015. Development of variation in child African American English. In Sonja Lanehart (ed.), *The Oxford Handbook of African American English*, 475–491. Oxford: Oxford University Press.

Habib, Rania. 2014. Vowel variation and reverse acquisition in rural Syrian child and adolescent language. *Language Variation and Change* 26(1): 45–75.

Habick, Timothy. 1993. Farmer City, Illinois: Sound systems shifting south. In Timothy Frazer (ed.), *"Heartland" English: Variation and Transition in the American Midwest*, 97–121. Tuscaloosa, AL: University of Alabama Press.

Hockett, Charles. 1950. Age-grading and linguistic continuity. *Language* 26: 449–459.

Kerswill, Paul and Ann Williams. 2000. Creating a new town koine: Children and language change in Milton Keynes. *Language in Society* 29: 65–115.

Kohn, Mary Elizabeth. 2017. (De)Segregation: The impact of de-facto and de-jure segregation on African American English in the New South. *Proceedings from LAVIS IV: Language Variety in the South*. Chapel Hill, NC: UNC Press.

Kohn, Mary Elizabeth and Charlie Farrington. 2012. Evaluating acoustic speaker normalization algorithms: Evidence from longitudinal child data. *The Journal of the Acoustical Society of America* 131(3): 2237–2248.

Kohn, Mary Elizabeth and Charlie Farrington. 2017. Longitudinal sociophonetic analysis: What to expect when working with child and adolescent data. In Suzanne Evans Wagner and Isabelle Buchstaller (eds.), *Using Panel Data in the Sociolinguistic Study of Variation and Change*, 122–154. New York: Routledge.

Labov, William. 1963. The social motivation of a sound change. *Word* 19(January): 273–309.

Labov, William. 1965. Linguistic research on the non-standard English of Negro children. In A. Dore (ed.), *Problems and Practices in the New York City Schools*, 110–117. New York: New York Society for the Experimental Study of Education.

Labov, William. 1994. *Principles of Linguistic Change: Internal Factors. Vol. 1*. Cambridge: Blackwell.

Labov, William. 1995. Can reading failure be reversed? A linguistic approach to the question. In Victoria Gadsden and Debora. Wagner (eds.), *Literacy Among African-American Youth: Issues in Learning, Teaching, and Schooling*, 39–68. Cresskill, NJ: Hampton.

Labov, William. 2001. *Principles of Linguistic Change: Social Factors. Vol. 2*. Oxford: Blackwell.

Labov, William, Paul Cohen, Clarence Robins and John Lewis. 1968. *A Study of the Non-Standard English of Negro and Puerto Rican Speakers in New York City*. Report on cooperative research project 3288. New York, NY: Columbia University.

Miller, Wick and Susan Ervin. 1964. The Development of Grammar in Child Language. *Monographs of the Society for Research in Child Development* 29(1): 9–34.

Moore, Emma. 2004. Sociolinguistic style: A multidimensional resource for shared identity creation. *Canadian Journal of Linguistics* 49. 375–396.

Newkirk-Turner, Brandi L., Janna B. Oetting and Ida J. Stockman. 2014. BE, DO, and modal auxiliaries of 3-year-old African American English speakers. *Journal of Speech, Language, and Hearing Research* 57(4). 1383–1393.

Pope, Jennifer. 2002. The Social History of a Sound Change on the Island of Martha's Vineyard, Massachusetts: Forty years after Labov. Unpublished M.A. dissertation. Edinburgh, UK: University of Edinburgh.

Prichard, Hilary and Meredith Tamminga. 2012. The impact of higher education on Philadelphia vowels. *University of Pennsylvania Working Papers in Linguistics* 18 (2): 87–95.

Renn, Jennifer E. 2007. *Measuring Style Shift: A Quantitative Analysis of African American English*. M.A. Thesis. Chapel Hill, NC: University of North Carolina at Chapel Hill.

Renn, Jennifer E. 2010. *Acquiring Style: The Development of Dialect Shifting among African American Children*. Ph.D. Dissertation. Chapel Hill, NC: University of North Carolina at Chapel Hill.

Renn, Jennifer E. and J. Michael Terry. 2009. Operationalizing style: Quantifying the use of style shift in the speech of African American adolescents. *American Speech* 84 (4): 367–390.

Rickford, John R. 1999. *African American Vernacular English: Features, Evolution, Educational Implications*. Malden, MA: Wiley-Blackwell.

Rickford, John R. and Sharese King. 2016. Language and linguistics on trial: Hearing Rachel Jeantel (and other vernacular speakers) in the courtroom and beyond. *Language* 92(4): 948–988.

Rickford, John R. and Faye McNair-Knox. 1994. Addressee- and topic-influenced style shift: A quantitative sociolinguistic study. In Douglas Biber and Edward Finegan (eds.), *Sociolinguistic Perspectives on Register*, 235–276. New York/Oxford: Oxford University Press.

Rickford, John R. and MacKenzie Price. 2013. Girlz II women: Age-grading, language change and stylistic variation. *Journal of Sociolinguistics* 17(2): 143–179.

Rickford, John R. and Angela E. Rickford. 1995. Dialect readers revisited. *Linguistics and Education* 7(2): 107–128.

Roberts, Julie. 2002. Child language variation. In J.K. Chambers, Peter Trudgill, and Natalie Schilling-Estes (eds.), *The Handbook of Language Variation and Change*, 333–348. Oxford: Blackwell.

Sankoff, Gillian. 2004. Adolescents, young adults, and the critical period: Two case studies from "Seven Up." In Carmen Fought (ed.), *Sociolinguistic Variation: Critical Reflections*, 121–139. Oxford: Oxford University Press.

Sankoff, Gillian, Helene Blondeau and Anne Charity. 2001. Individual roles in a real-time change: Montreal (r->R) 1947–1995. In Hans van de Velde and Roeland van Hout (eds.), *'r-atics: Sociolinguistic, Phonetic and Phonological Characteristics of /r/*. Bruxelles: ILVP.

Sankoff, Gillian and Suzanne Evans Wagner. 2006. Age-grading in retrograde movement: The inflected future in Montreal French. *University of Pennsylvania Working Papers in Linguistics* 12(2): Article 16.

Smith, Jennifer, Mercedes Durham and Liane Fortune. 2007. "Mam, my trousers is fa'in doon!" Community, caregiver, and child in the acquisition of variation in a Scottish dialect. *Language Variation and Change* 19(1): 63–99.

Snyder, Thomas D. and Charlene M. Hoffman. 2003. *Digest of Educational Statistics, 2002*. Washington, DC: National Center for Educational Statistics.

Sweetland, Julie. 2006. *Teaching Writing in the African American Classroom: A Sociolinguistic Approach*. Ph.D. dissertation. Palo Alto, CA: Stanford University.

Tagliamonte, Sali A. and Alexandra D'Arcy. 2009. Peaks beyond phonology: Adolescence, incrementation, and language change. *Language* 85(1): 58–108.

Terry, J. Michael, Randall Hendrick, Evangelos Evangelou, and Richard L. Smith. 2010. Variable dialect switching among African American children: Inferences about working memory. *Lingua*, (*120*): 2463–75.

Van Hofwegen, Janneke and Reuben Stob. 2011. A longitudinal analysis of the relationship between reading and AAE vernacularity. Paper presented at *New Ways of Analyzing Variation* 40. Washington, DC: Georgetown University.

Van Hofwegen, Janneke Van and Reuben Stob. 2012. The gender gap: how dialect usage affects reading outcomes in African American youth. Paper presented at *the Linguistic Society of America* 2012 Annual Meeting, Portland, OR, January 5–8.

Van Hofwegen, Janneke and Walt Wolfram. 2010. Coming of age in African American English: A longitudinal study. *Journal of Sociolinguistics* 14(4): 427–455.

Wagner, Suzanne Evans. 2008. *Language Change and Stabilization in the Transition from Adolescence to Adulthood.* Ph.D. dissertation. Philadelphia, PA: University of Pennsylvania.

Wagner, Suzanne Evans. 2012a. Real-time evidence for age grad(ing) in late adolescence. *Language Variation and Change* 24(2): 179–202.

Wagner, Suzanne Evans. 2012b. Age grading in sociolinguistic theory. *Linguistics and Language Compass* 6(6): 371–382.

Wagner, Suzanne Evans and Isabelle Buchstaller (eds.), 2017. *Using Panel Data in the Sociolinguistic Study of Variation and Change.* Routledge Studies in Language Change Series. New York: Routledge.

Wheeler, Rebecca. 2016. So much research, so little change: Teaching Standard English in African American classrooms. *Annual Review of Linguistics* 2(1): 367–390.

Wolfram, Walt. 1971. Black and White speech differences revisited. In Walt Wolfram and Nona H. Clark (eds.), *Black-White Speech Relationships*, 139–161. Washington, DC: Center for Applied Linguistics.

Woolard, Kathryn. 2011. Is there linguistic life after high school? Longitudinal changes in the bilingual repertoire in metropolitan Barcelona. *Language in Society* 40(5): 617–648.

2 The Analysis of Sociolinguistic Change over the Lifespan

2.1 Introduction

How does a researcher assess change to a linguistic system when individuals are constantly in motion, changing alongside their ever-evolving world? Developmental trends, individual interactional and stylistic stances, changing social class, evolving social networks, personal goals, and changing familial roles are just some of the variables that complicate the interpretation of change across time for language use in general, and even more so for children. At the same time, researchers must consider what linguistic variables or subsystems are most appropriate to include in longitudinal studies. A myriad of potential variables extending across the levels of language organization are available for consideration. The sheer scope and depth of data that can potentially be acquired in terms of linguistic variation, social variation, and developmental change are both a strength and a challenge for longitudinal research. While much can be learned applying traditional analysis techniques to longitudinal data, new analytical approaches are a necessary supplement to fully realize the explanatory potential hidden within the rich information preserved in these recordings.

The approach to the description of language variation developed over the last half century has focused on systematic variation under the construct of the linguistic variable (Labov 1966, 1969), a convenient abstraction that includes allo-variants within a structural set of some type (Wolfram 1993). So, for example, *–ing fronting* may be studied by comparing velar realizations ([iŋ] as in *swimming*) to alveolar realizations ([in] as in *swimmin'*), syllable-coda cluster reduction is examined by finding the proportion of reduced clusters (e.g., *col'* for *cold*) to full clusters, or vowel pronunciations within a phonological set may be compared in terms of their formant frequencies. The increasing description of language variation over real time has, for the most part, continued the scrutiny of particular structural variables, often providing detailed descriptions of several variables over time (Sankoff and Blondeau 2007; Sankoff and Wagner 2011; Wagner 2012a, 2012b). These studies have identified a range of differences between variables in terms of change over time as well as within the lifespan of speakers, with some variables showing predictable patterns of change associated with age-grading, while others remain relatively stable. Such an approach thus offers important detail and insight about the progression of age-graded and real-time language change for selected structural features.

At the same time, Guy (2014) notes that the particular variables at the foundation of the variationist paradigm are simply "the individual bricks that together build the structure of the lect – the coherent 'unified whole.'" Myopic focus on single-set variables adds great understanding about the details of systematic variability for the chosen variables, but focus on the variable trees may also obscure an important view of the sociolinguistic forest. To build on Guy's metaphor, language varieties are not a bunch of bricks simply thrown in a pile; they are cemented together in a way that builds the unique structure of a language variety. The overall configuration of a language variety is as essential as – and complements – the description of particular variables.

As longitudinal studies become more common in the field of sociolinguistics, researchers have begun to establish methodological protocols to address the challenge of establishing methods that consider global patterns of change, the forest as opposed to the trees (Buchstaller and Evans Wagner 2017). These protocols have proven necessary to analyze a host of non-linguistic variables as they relate to language change. Global linguistic measures facilitate the exploration of social factors: when the number of linguistic variables can be reduced, the researcher has the opportunity to identify meaningful trends over the course of the lifespan. Within this chapter, we describe the methodological tools with which we attempt to provide both a global description of language variation, alongside more particularized and nuanced assessments, to fully capture when and why individuals change their linguistic behavior over time. Under this model, we emphasize the need to view language as a system by moving beyond individual variables to more fully characterize the ways in which individual linguistic features move in tandem across the lifespan. An overall set of features or a "composite index" is one such tool. As we demonstrate subsequently, this measure may provide context for more nuanced traditional variation analyses – and additional analytical power. Through the establishment of global linguistic variables described in this chapter, we thus gain the analytical tools to more thoroughly assess the influence of both social and developmental factors on language change across the lifespan.

2.2 Individual Variables and Composite Indices

The composite index is an attempt to provide an overall picture of a variety by including a comprehensive set of structural traits associated with that variety rather than its particularized traits. While current variationist approaches have been limited to particular variables, other approaches to data, including linguistic data, may use more holistic-oriented, composite indices, or at least a mixture of overall indices and the measurement of particular structures. For example, overall measurements are routinely used for language in allied fields such as speech and language pathology, foreign language assessment, and proficiency in English. We argue, and hope to demonstrate in this analysis, that holistic data can be useful in the examination of longitudinal language change and variation, and the approach we take utilizes both composite indices as well as individual variables in an effort to capture trajectories of language change over the lifespan. On one level, we propose that linguists working in the longitudinal paradigm consider using a "big" variable – one that is commensurate with the bigness of the data. A composite index is one such variable.

Notwithstanding the utility of variable-by-variable analysis, we argue that some broader social and educational issues cannot be addressed without appealing to a more comprehensive profile of the linguistic system, for example, the social consequences of dialect discrimination and the correlation of educational achievement with dialect use. These kinds of broad-based concerns are applicable to any language variety, but particularly critical in the examination of AAL given concerns with overall dialect use and a broad range of educational issues (cf. Jencks and Phillips 1998) between whites and non-whites for well over a half-century now. The big picture of social subordination and educational inequality related to dialect use remains in sharp focus a half-century later.

In the following section, we describe how a composite index, namely the *Dialect Density Measure* (DDM), has been used to assess the development of AAL across the lifespans of the many African American children participating in the FPG longitudinal study. We will use this index, along with other measures where appropriate, to address in subsequent chapters an array of questions pertaining to language use and development, educational achievement, style-shifting, and caregiver and peer interactions.

2.3   A Composite Index: The Dialect Density Measure (DDM)

For valid reasons, linguists and sociolinguists are cautious about assessing dialect use in terms of an overall dialect measure, particularly with respect to a variety such as AAL. In fact, the theoretical and operational definition of vernacular AAL remains an open, controversial issue (Morgan 2002; Makoni et al. 2003; Wolfram 2007, 2015; Lanehart 2015) after over a half-century of descriptive scrutiny. One of the recurrent criticisms of descriptions of vernacular AAL is its reduction to a simple inventory of independent traits (Labov 1998; Terry 2004; Green 2011). Furthermore, not all structural traits are equally weighted in marking socioethnic varieties; for example, the use of invariant *be* (e.g., *my ears be itching*) or completive *done* (e.g., *they done messed up again*) might be much more socially marked than syllable-coda cluster reduction (e.g., *wes' en'*) or unstressed *-ing* fronting (e.g., *,-in* for *-ing* in *swimmin'*) in indexing vernacularity or ethnicity. And, of course, many traits associated with AAL are shared with other varieties, including different vernaculars and Mainstream American English. Finally, there is the issue of variability in describing vernacular structures, since variation studies for a half-century now have recognized that social differentiation is often determined not by the discrete use or nonuse of variants but by the relative frequency with which particular variants are used by particular groups (e.g., Labov 1966; Wolfram and Fasold 1974; Tagliamonte 2006, 2011). Given such issues, it is understandable that sociolinguists have resisted attempts to reduce the assessment of vernacular dialect to a unitary score on a dialect scale.

Despite the valid cautions about using inventories of features, there appears to be heuristic, analytical justifications for characterizing dialect use in terms of an overall dialect ranking. As noted, scalar indices of language proficiency are commonly used in allied fields of language acquisition and foreign/other language study where it is expedient to assess speakers in terms of overall language proficiency. Thus, the reduction of language proficiency in a non-native language to a scalar index is common in foreign language assessment (Durán 1988; Bachman and Palmer 2008), and such testing is sometimes even mandated by federal law. Further, the assessment of children's native language development is typically measured on such scales in the field of speech and language pathology with good construct and concurrent validity (Kelley, Jones, and Fein 2003). For some analytical and descriptive purposes, it thus appears that prudently constructed, unitary indices of language use may provide valid information about the relative use of a designated language variety, particularly as its use correlates with various social and educational factors. Furthermore, in everyday interaction, most people's judgment of dialect along a vernacular-standard continuum is guided by holistic perceptions of language variety rather than the particular features of dialect composition (Preston 1996; Preston and Niedzielski 2000).

For more than a decade, language researchers of AAL in allied disciplines have relied on metrics that reduce assessment to a singular, scalar score that has construct validity and high reliability (Seymour, Roeper, and De Villiers 2003; Craig and Washington 2004, 2006). The so-called DDM (Oetting and McDonald 2001, 2002; Craig and Washington 2006; Renn 2007, 2010) utilized here is a token-based measurement index. In this measure, a set of dialect traits extracted from the canonical descriptions of AAL (e.g., Labov et al. 1968; Wolfram 1969; Wolfram and Fasold 1974; Baugh 1983; Rickford 1999; Green 2002) is compiled and language samples are coded for the incidence of these features per utterance or word. In the version of the

DDM used by Renn (2007, 2010) and Van Hofwegen and Wolfram (2010), forty-four features were coded: forty-one morphosyntactic and three phonological (see Appendix).

The DDM was developed originally by Craig and Washington (2006) in consultation with AAL linguistic experts; it was revised by linguists Walt Wolfram and J. Michael Terry for Renn's research (2007, 2010) to exhibit categories and features that more accurately reflected the linguistic status of the inventory of structures. This inventory expanded the set of morphosyntactic features; at the same time, it was more limited in terms of its phonological structures, so that only three were included in the set. When the DDM inventories of Craig and Washington (2006) were applied to the examination of stylistic variation for 112 Grade 6 (age 11–12 years) subjects in two contextual situations (Renn 2007), the DDM developed by Craig and Washington (2006) and the revised one offered in Renn (2007) showed extremely high reliability ($r = 0.99$), suggesting concurrent and content validity for the measure. The predominance of morphosyntactic features in this measure shows an obvious bias toward the role of grammatical features in marking AAL dialect use. Morphosyntactic features are considered to be stronger markers of vernacular dialect use than phonological ones, though Thomas (2007) suggests that phonetic cues actually may be stronger than grammatical features in the perceptual identification of AAL speakers.

Research on the application of the DDM (Oetting and McDonald 2002; Craig and Washington 2006; Renn 2007; Van Hofwegen and Wolfram 2010; Van Hofwegen 2015a, 2015b) has indicated that it can be useful as a measure of overall AAL use, particularly if combined with the application of other complementary analyses that include type-based and frequency-based methods (Oetting and McDonald 2002; Van Hofwegen and Wolfram 2010). In fact, the triangulation of token-based, type-based, and relative-frequency-based analyses of data from these studies provides important empirical justification for the validity of composite indices while, at the same time, revealing some of their limitations.

2.4   Analytical Potential of the DDM

The first and most obvious advantage offered by the DDM is that it provides a "snapshot" glimpse of the dialect usage of a speaker in a given speech sample. Given the inventory of AAL structures, an analyst can tabulate how many AAL features per communication unit of speech are produced for any speaker in any sample – regardless of relative differences in talking time – and get a *features per utterance* (fpu) score or a *features per word* (fpw) score. An example of a transcript with DDM codes is presented subsequently. Here, feature codes are listed in brackets (see Appendix). If the communication unit does not have any DDM features, it is given a [OOO] code.

> P Oh, respect for other/s [OOO].
> P In my house don't nobody have no respect [NEG].
> P Well we do have respect for each other [OOO].
> P But it/'s[XIT][XCO] time/s when people don't have respect for each other.
> P Like go/ing[NAS] in my room when I/'m not there.
> P Touch/ing[NAS] my stuff.
> P Read/ing[NAS] my letter/s.
> P Listen/ing[NAS] on my phone call/s.
> 1 What I think ya'll should do <is[XCO] have a little> house meeting[NAS].
> P I should get a cell_phone [OOO].
> 1 A house meeting[NAS].
> 1 (Like) go in the living[NAS] room, sit down.
> 1 You, your momma, your sister, your (little co*) your little niece and you [OOO].
> 1 Just go sit down and talk about everything[XNA] [OOO].
> 1 Like (um) momma, I can/'t take anymore [OOO].
> 1 Everybody keep/*3s go/ing[NAS] in my stuff.
> 1 I need my privacy [OOO].
> 1 I need (to 1*) my own lock on my door [OOO].
> 1 So nobody don't go in my room while I/'m not there [NEG].
> 1 I need my privacy to myself [OOO].

This method of using a feature per communication unit of speech measure controls for length of the language sample and results in a continuous measure. Table 3.1 in Chapter 3 illustrates the DDM scores for one child in the FPG longitudinal sample at seven points in his life.

DDM scores can be calculated for one speaker across many time points in their life, as in Table 3.1 found in Chapter 3, or many speakers at one point in their lives. For longitudinal studies, though, the DDM's obvious utility is that it can reflect language use for many speakers at many points in their lives. Thus, Figure 3.1 in Chapter 3 depicts the DDM scores for thirty-one FPG longitudinal children, providing a useful visual display of the various trajectories of AAL usage in this particular population. DDM trajectory analysis allows us to answer the question of when the minimal and optimal times are for each speaker as well as prominent trends in the trajectory of the sample through the statistical smoothing of trajectory trend lines.

To address the DDM's relative lack of nuance for assessing individual feature trajectories over the lifespan, it is also possible to conduct comple-mentary analyses to support and triangulate the DDM's role as an overall language index. In Chapter 3, we construct a type-based analysis of AAL that focuses on different types of AAL features represented in a sample as opposed to the frequency of AAL tokens. A speaker may, for example, show a high incidence of AAL tokens per word or communication unit in their token-based DDM, but it is possible that this may be due to a limited number of AAL structures used more frequently, thus potentially skewing the representation of vernacular AAL. Type-based profiles of AAL may operate in tandem with, or independent from, token-based accounts (Oetting and McDonald 2002), but in some current studies, type-based tabulations are employed along with token-based metrics (Oetting and McDonald 2002; Van Hofwegen and Wolfram 2010). As we demonstrate in Chapter 3, we consistently found that higher DDM scores correlate significantly with higher numbers of feature types, supporting the idea that the DDM is an appropriate reflection of general usage of AAL.

Another complementary analysis is the consideration of the relative frequency of selected dialect variants in relation to the potential cases where they might occur, following the traditional variationist paradigm (Cedergren and Sankoff 1974; Tagliamonte 2006, 2011). Thus, we can employ the traditional multivariate logistic regression via the Goldvarb tool (Sankoff, Tagliamonte, and Smith 2005) or the statistical program R to show the factor weights for each of these variables plotted over time. This analysis can then be aligned with the DDM trajectory analysis to show favoring effects at various age points in the subjects' speech. We demonstrate in Chapter 3 that, with some small individual differences, the parallel in trajectories is striking.

The triangulation of different types of analyses of structural features set forth here provides an important vantage point that combines the complementary perspectives of token-based, type-based, and variationist analytical traditions within linguistics and sociolinguistics to reliably reflect overall patterns of use as well as the use of particular structures in AAL. Especially when testing the reliability of a new composite index, we recommend conducting triangulations of this sort. For one thing, if a type-based analysis does not align with a token-based (composite) analysis, there may be an imbalance in the representativeness of the features that comprise the composite index. For the FPG project, in particular, this suite of findings has revealed the complementary utility of both composite and structurally specific analyses in the assessment of longitudinal language development, underscoring the need for analytical and descriptive triangulation in providing an authentic picture of longitudinal language change in the lifespan of both AAL and other language varieties. While the fact remains that the DDM is a composite of many well-documented AAL features, and not an exhaustive inventory of all features of the language variety, the analyses empirically establish that it is valuable as a global assessment of AAL usage across the lifespan.

As we have shown, a composite index score like the DDM can be used by itself as a means of tracking trajectories of language use across the lifespan of individuals. In addition, due to its unidimensional scalar nature, the DDM score can also be used productively as a dependent variable in statistical analysis, with the goal of discerning how other factors influence its patterns of change, not only in terms of overall trajectory shape, but also on the relative magnitude of change in the trajectory. Longitudinal data must be handled carefully in statistical analysis (Singer and Willett 2003). Not only are the particular variables nested within speakers, but they are also nested within time points, so multilevel regression analysis, which incorporates both fixed and random effects, is a necessary statistical tool. Additionally, as the FPG studies have shown, change trajectories are often far from linear. In the case of nonlinear trajectories, polynomial functions must also be incorporated into the regression modeling. For the FPG DDM data specifically, a cubic function was needed to account for the predominant trajectory trend – the roller-coaster shape.

In the FPG study, the vast array of psychosocial, demographic, and academic measures gathered for each of the longitudinal subjects has provided an ideal dataset for addressing many of the big-picture questions posed at the outset of this section. How might a speaker's ethnic identity and the prevalence of African Americans in their community affect their usage and development of AAL? Using the DDM as a dependent variable in multilevel mixed regression, we have assessed the effects of independent factors such as speakers' ethnic identity (*Multidimensional Inventory of Black Identity,* centrality scale, Sellers et al. 1997), the quality and ethnic make-up of social contacts, and the percentage of African Americans in the school. What about a speaker's family/home environment that might impact their AAL usage over time? To address this, we have incorporated factors like relationship quality with parents (*Child-Parent Relationship Scale,* Pianta 1992), the presence of (another) significant caregiver in the home, family income, mother's education, and mother's AAL use. Finally, how might the speakers' individual psychological and social characteristics affect AAL usage? Using the DDM score as a dependent variable, we've incorporated individual personal and psychological factors such as speakers' gender, stress levels (*Holmes-Rahe Social Readjustment Scale,* Holmes and Rahe 1967), social skills (*Social Skills Rating System,* Gresham and Elliott 1990), self-esteem (*HARE General and Area-Specific Self-Esteem Scale,* Hare 1985), and perceived relationship quality with friends (*Friendship Quality Questionnaire,* Parker and Asher 1993). Amazingly, for all this wealth of psychosocial data on the FPG longitudinal speakers, none of these factors have significantly predicted longitudinal change patterns in AAL usage. Rather, speaker age continues to be the most powerful factor in predicting longitudinal trends. From these results, we have not concluded that external factors do not affect the change trajectory of AAL usage across the early lifespan. Instead, it is likely that other factors in the developmental process, which are not accounted for in the psychosocial measures tested so far, play a role.

Not only can the DDM score itself be informative for tracking the trajectories of change across the lifespan of individuals, but it can be used for comparing speech patterns in different settings. In Chapter 7, we follow up on Renn (2010) to examine the differences between language samples from formal and informal contexts between the time of early schooling and in early adolescence. In this way, she used the DDM score as not only a snapshot of a speaker's dialect usage at a point in time, but also *in different contexts at that point in time.* In work reported in Chapter 6, we use the DDM as a dependent variable for conducting *dyadic analysis,* investigating the extent to which two speakers in an interaction accommodate to each other (cf. Communication Accommodation Theory, for example, Giles 1973, 2008) in their AAL usage, and in Chapter 5, we use the DDM for a dyadic analysis on the mother–child interactions at ages 6–9 years, in which children did not accommodate to their mothers.

For other questions of change across the lifespan, a composite index score can be used as an independent (predictor) variable. For example, in Chapter 8, we investigate whether vernacular language use (i.e., relative DDM scores) contributed to academic achievement in the FPG sample, including a longitudinal study of reading achievement (i.e., Broad Reading cluster scores from the *Woodcock-Johnson Revised (WJ-R) Tests of Achievement,* Woodcock and Johnson 1989) from five time points from age 6 through 15 years. In the study, the WJ-R reading score was the dependent variable, while DDM score was a predictor/independent variable alongside other factors.

Regardless, whether a variation study is synchronic or diachronic, cross-sectional or longitudinal, the FPG studies have illustrated the efficacy of a composite index for addressing big-picture questions of language use in a variety of contexts. Many of the analyses reported in this project could have been conducted with a single linguistic variable as the dependent or outcome variable instead of a composite index like the DDM. Indeed, as we have shown in the variation analysis conducted as triangulation, looking at trajectory patterns for individual variables can be informative, particularly when it comes to questions of acquisition or age-grading. But, the central issue remains: what big-picture questions can an individual variable analysis address? Data that are longitudinal in nature are so rare because they are difficult to attain and maintain. Thus, when a longitudinal dataset has been gathered, a unique opportunity arises for addressing large-scale issues that are not possible to address in other types of studies. Variationists who have access to longitudinal data may feel reluctant to supplement or replace the analytical tools that have been so productive for them in synchronic and apparent time studies, but we have shown how composite indices can have great utility for longitudinal analysis.

A language variety is more than a set of isolated structural features, and overall indices of language use offer an essential descriptive profile that complements and enhances other data description methods. Composite indices can be constructed carefully, tested for reliability, and utilized alongside complementary analyses. As such, they can be valid and reliable methods for measuring overall language based on current inventories and sub-inventories of structural linguistic traits. We have found a composite index to be heuristically useful – and analytically felicitous – in correlating dialect use with a full range of social, developmental, and educational factors. Accordingly, we conclude that variationists should engage with big variables such as composite indices and big datasets such as longitudinal studies. In the "big data" era, longitudinal studies are only going to become more prolific and easier to manage.

2.5   Sounds as Systems

Broad indices are not a replacement for traditional variationist analyses, but, rather, a tool that can provide a backdrop against which such detailed research can be evaluated, as well as a heuristic overview that adds to our understanding of the ways in which social and physical factors influence variation and change. Such tools afford a lens to view variables in tandem, thus providing a way in which to conceptualize individual variables as a related system. In some ways, sociophonetic studies have been more readily disposed to zoom out to the level of system than morphosyntactic research, looking at the forest of vowels as a whole. Descriptions of sound changes have long made reference to sound systems as linked structures, so that movements of individual vowels are often theorized as connected. Even the terminology used to describe sound change places emphasis on the vowel space as a system, with sound change metaphorically described as chain shifts, in which one move triggers related changes (Labov 1991).

Notwithstanding this structural heritage, similar to morphosyntactic variation, much longitudinal research on vowel variation focuses on one or two variables. Moving targets attract attention, so that researchers often choose to examine variables that are undergoing change within the community. These decisions can lead to misleading estimations of how much individuals alter their speech during their lifespan, as well as missed opportunities to explore the social or linguistic contexts that keep some parts of a system stable even as other components undergo change. Attention to the full shape of vowel systems, as well as the relative distribution of vowels within the system, encourages researchers to avoid cherry-picking variables that are likely to show change. To continue the metaphor, this approach allows researchers to gain insight into how individual vocalic "trees" fit into and work together to create the overall landscape of the vowel space forest.

When researchers focus on a broad distribution of vowel classes, they have the opportunity to examine vowel space areas. Studies that include vowel space area (VSA) measures illuminate how physical and developmental characteristics related to biological sex and age influence the overall size and configuration of the vowel space, as well as the extent to which components within the vowel space change in relationship with each other over time. In this way, VSA serves as a "big picture" composite variable that facilitates longitudinal research, especially when such research includes distinct developmental stages. Despite these advantages, the overall size and shape of the vowel space has remained remarkably neglected as a potential variable of interest within sociolinguistic studies in general, and longitudinal studies in particular. With this in mind, our analysis of vowel variation begins by considering VSA over time, as introduced in this chapter, and concludes with an analysis of a broad range of vowel variables as presented in Chapter 4.

2.5.1   Composite Measure of Vowel Space

While some early pioneering research in sociophonetics included general descriptions of overall vowel shapes (Habick 1993), vowel dispersion measures remain underutilized within linguistics as a whole, partly due to the aforementioned tendency to focus on one or two vowel variables at a time. Still, the descriptive utility of VSA measures has attracted the attention of researchers in allied fields such as acquisition and speech pathology. In speech pathology, researchers collect data from normally developing children, as well as those with disordered speech, to establish vowel dispersion measures as a clinical diagnostic tool (Vorperian and Kent 2007; Flipsen and Lee 2012). Researchers who focus on development and aging, particularly for the very young and very old, have found that VSA shows important and predictable shifts over the lifespan (Rastatter et al. 1997; Vorperian and Kent 2007). Such research may be important for the field of sociolinguistics, not only for determining best practices for comparing acoustic data across age groups, but also for consideration of how changes across age groups might possibly contribute to observed sociolinguistic patterns such as adolescent leads in sound change (Labov 2001).

Analysis of vowel space shape and size may also inform studies of style. Phonologists have utilized dispersion measures as a correlate of attention to speech, with more expanded vowel spaces correlating with careful speech (Lindblom 1990). These findings have contributed to studies of gender, sexuality, and language which illustrate how VSA may come to be associated with speaker style. So, for example, several US studies find that smaller vowel spaces associated with hypo-articulation may be indexical of heteronormative masculinity while more expanded vowel spaces associated with careful speech are found to index femininity and/or gay male personae (Pierrehumbert et al. 2004; Munson et al. 2006; Heffernan 2010). Although relationships between individual vowel measures continue to dominate sociophonetic literature, it is clear that vowel dispersion measures offer additional insight into both social and developmental trends in language.

Given this context, several considerations motivate the inclusion of vowel dispersion measures in longitudinal research on vowel variation. Aging significantly impacts the shape and size of the vowel space, as do stylistic factors such as attention to speech. Further, as we'll discuss subsequently, an exploration of the vowel space as a whole can assist researchers in selecting appropriate normalization techniques by allowing researchers to identify appropriate anchor vowels to determine the vowel space periphery or to use as reference points for vowels undergoing change. Consideration of these factors prior to the analysis of individual vowels can capture overarching developmental trends, offer visual confirmation of group similarities and differences, and prevent normalization errors.

2.5.2   Measures of Vowel Dispersion

Studies that consider overall vowel spaces generally follow two analytical approaches: those that identify a vowel space area through calculating the geometric area of the vowel space, and those that measure vowel dispersion by calculating the distance of peripheral vowels from the center of the vowel space. Early studies in particular frequently calculated vowel space areas by using peripheral vowels to characterize the vowel space as a quadrilateral or triangle (Higgens and Hodge 2002; Vorperian and Kent 2007; Flipsen and Lee 2012). The vowel space area can then be calculated using the formula for identifying the area of an irregular quadrilateral (see Formula 2.1) or triangle (see Formula 2.2). The total area of the vowel space can then be compared across speakers, styles, or developmental stages.

Formula 2.1 Calculation for a quadrilateral vowel space assuming /i/, /æ/, /u/, and /ɑ/ are peripheral

$$VSA = \frac{1}{2}\Big((F2_{/i/} * F1_{/æ/} + F2_{/æ/} * F1_{/a/} + F2_{/a/} * F1_{/u/} + F2_{/i/} * F1_{/u/}) - (F1_{/i/} * F2_{/æ/} + F1_{/æ/} * F2_{/a/} + F1_{/a/} * F2_{/u/} + F1_{/i/} * F2_{/u/}) \Big)$$

Formula 2.2 Calculation for a triangular vowel space area assuming /i/, /u/, and /ɑ/ are peripheral

$$VSA = \frac{1}{2}\left((F2_{/i/} - F2_{/u/}) * (F1_{/a/} - F1_{/i/})\right)$$

Another approach calculates the overall dispersion of peripheral vowels from the central tendency of the vowel space. This approach, known as the vowel dispersion measure (VDM), does not rely on the assumption that vowel spaces will share the same geometric configuration across populations or age groups, but still provides a single numeric value that can be compared across groups. This measure averages the Euclidean distance (ED) of peripheral vowels from a central tendency in the vowel space. The ED is the distance between two points on a plane and is calculated using Formula 2.3. Figure 2.1 provides a visual representation in which BEET, BAT, BOT, and BOAR tokens have

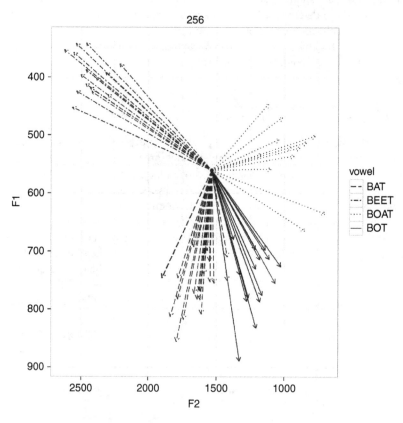

Figure 2.1 Visualization of VDM. Image from Kohn and Farrington (2017: 107)

been chosen as representative peripheral vowels and each line represents the ED of each peripheral vowel from the central tendency of the vowel space.

Calculation of the VDM can be broken down into three steps: first, the central tendency of the vowel space must be calculated (see Formula 2.3); then, the ED for each peripheral vowel must be calculated (see Formula 2.4); finally, the grand mean of these values is calculated to derive the VDM (see Formula 2.5).

Formula 2.3 Calculation of the central tendency of a vowel space, where *i* represents the highest and most fronted vowel in the vowel space, *a* represents the lowest vowel in the vowel space, and *u* represents the most backed vowel in the vowel space. Note that due to language and dialect variation, the exact phonemic categories of these vowel classes will vary.

$$C = \frac{(F1_i + F1_a)}{2}, \frac{(F2_i + F2_u)}{2}$$

Formula 2.4 Calculation of the ED between the central tendency (a) and the vowel token in question (b) on the F1 and F2 planes.

$$ED = \sqrt{(a_{f2} - b_{f2})^2 + (a_{f1} - b_{f1})^2}$$

Formula 2.5 VDM as a calculation of the grand mean of ED values as grouped by phonemic class. In this example, /i/, /a/, /æ/, and /o/ before /ɹ/[1] are the four peripheral classes considered. The mean of each is added together and divided by the total number of phonemic classes considered, in this case four phonemic classes are considered in this calculation.

$$VDM = \frac{\mu_{ED(i)} + \mu_{ED(a)} + \mu_{ED(æ)} + \mu_{ED(oɹ)}}{4}$$

While comparisons of VSAs and VDMs based on peripheral vowel productions have been fruitfully applied in studies restricted to a single dialect group, comparisons across dialect groups may sometimes be misleading. Differences in vowel configurations across dialect groups can lead to differences in VSA that are unrelated to either development or articulatory factors such as attention to speech. For example, the extreme back vowel fronting observed in the California Vowel Shift leads to a quadrilateral vowel space characterized by a relatively narrow width as the back of the vowel space is underutilized. If such a vowel space is compared to a variety that does retain backed pronunciations, differences in VSA may be related to dialect differences, rather than reflect development or articulatory patterns (Clopper 2009).[2]

---

[1] Pre-rhotic /o/ is utilized in this calculation as /o/ in other environments frequently undergoes fronting in American English (Thomas 2001; Labov, Ash, and Boberg 2006). In non-rhotic environments, /o/ would not provide a reliable estimate of the back of the vowel space.

[2] Fox and Jacewicz (2017) additionally illustrate that VSAs are ineffective at capturing dialect differences as the majority of cross-dialectal differences emerge from the way the working vowel space is utilized, rather than the shape of the working vowel space.

Care should be taken when selecting vowels to include in dispersion or VSA measures to avoid such methodological pitfalls.

2.6   Age- and Sex-Related Patterns in Vowel Spaces

Cross-sectional data has indicated that there are age- and sex-related trends in the overall size of the vowel space such that size decreases with age, and male vowel spaces undergo greater reduction than female vowel spaces (Vorperian and Kent 2007; Flipsen and Lee 2012). These changes occur as a result of physical changes to vocal tract morphology and articulatory issues such as a lack of fine motor control in young children (Pettinato et al. 2016). Yet, because of the nature of cross-sectional studies, cohort effects cannot be ruled out. Longitudinal studies have the opportunity to verify such trends by exploring intra-speaker change over time. However, few such studies exist, and those that do focus on short time frames (McGowen et al. 2014).

We turn to the speech of 20 children from the FPG corpus to identify developmental trends in vowel space reduction over the course of four time points from ages 10 to 20. We additionally include data from an additional time point at age four for participants who produced sufficient speech samples for analysis at this time point. Of the twenty participants, ten produced enough data to be normalized and analyzed at age four. Results from this analysis were first reported in Kohn and Farrington (2017) where we additionally examined changes to corner vowel F1 and F2 over time. Figure 2.2 presents vowel quadrilaterals calculated from grand means of the vowel classes BEET, BAT, BOT, and BOAR across five time points for males and females. These quadrilaterals provide evidence of the dramatic change that occurs between ages ten and fourteen for both males and females. Each group undergoes a substantial decrease in the overall VSA as formants shift back and up over time.

Changes to male vowel spaces appear more extreme than those observed among the female cohort due to the impact of puberty on vocal tract morphology (Fitch and Giedd 1999). This difference may be compounded by stylistic factors, such as the reduction of vowel space associated with the performance of masculine identity (Heffernan 2010).

VSA measures can then capture the total extent that individuals change over time to establish typical benchmarks for clinical or descriptive purposes. Figure 2.3 displays changes across time among the FPG cohort examined for VSA. Individual trends follow group trends, with the largest decreases occurring between ages 10 and 14 years, and with male VSAs reaching smaller sizes than females by age 16 years. For the majority of speakers, vowel spaces are smallest at age 14 years before rebounding to a slightly larger size at later time points. These patterns confirm cross-sectional studies, which have suggested that adolescent vowel spaces are slightly smaller than adult vowel

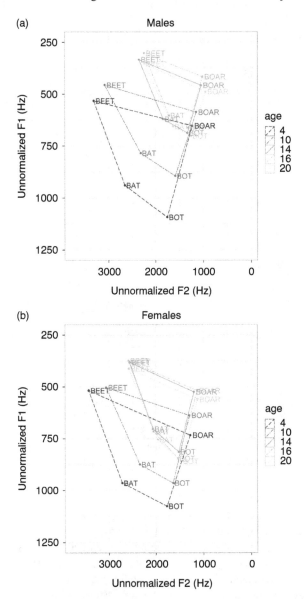

Figure 2.2 Vowel space quadrilaterals across five time points for twenty speakers, ten females and ten males, at five time points. Image from Kohn and Farrington (2018: 104–105).

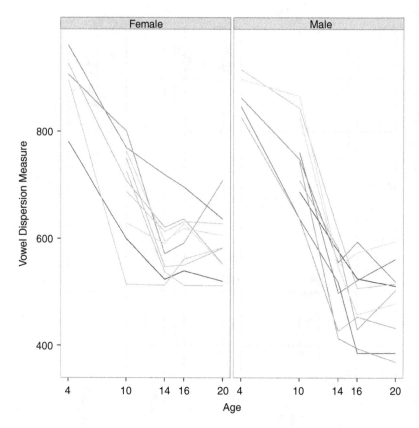

Figure 2.3 VSA measures across five time points for twenty speakers, ten females and ten males, at five time points. Image from Kohn and Farrington (2017: 109).

spaces (Lee et al. 1999), a pattern that may have intriguing implications for the mechanisms by which adolescents lead sound change (Labov 2001).

Longitudinal data and composite measures thus capture systemwide changes associated with development and style. The dramatic changes observed between ages ten and fourteen indicate that differences in formant values across time points will largely be attributed to developmental issues. While it is important to document these changes, sociolinguists are more concerned with differences across time points that reflect stylistic choices or social influences. To assess the extent to which children modify their vowel pronunciation for social purposes as they age, it is necessary to first account for developmental differences by normalizing formant values.

2.7   A First Step to Normalization

An initial examination of the overall shape and size of the vowel space provides a strong empirical platform for choosing normalization techniques. Within sociolinguistics, the goal of normalization is to eliminate acoustic correlates of physical differences while preserving socially significant distinctions in pronunciation. Normalization is a critical first step in comparing formant measures for vowels across speakers as, without normalization, statistical comparisons of formant values would be uninterpretable due to physiological noise.[3] Increased overlap in vowel spaces across sex and age are often viewed as a measure of successful normalization (Clopper 2009).

The most successful normalization techniques for child and adult data reduce physiological noise in formant values by establishing a unified central value for each speaker, essentially aligning the center of vowel spaces for all speakers (Kohn and Farrington 2012). Both Lobanov (1971) and Nearey (1978), two of the most common normalization techniques in the field, accomplish this task by subtracting the mean formant value across all vowels for a speaker from individual vowel tokens, so that vowels closer to the center of the vowel space will have smaller values.[4] This technique centers the data, as is common in studies that employ statistical analysis.

In theory, normalization techniques such as Lobanov's (1971) z-score normalization include information from all vowel classes to identify the central tendency of the vowel space; but, in practice, scholars tend to choose a small number of peripheral vowel classes. This selection process can introduce error into the normalization procedure as vowel classes that are peripheral for one group may not be peripheral for others. For example, in the California Vowel Shift (CVS), BOT classes are not always the lowest vowel class in the vowel space. Instead, BAT frequently is lower. Similarly, BOAT and BOOT are no longer peripheral due to back vowel fronting. If a researcher normalizes data using these vowel classes, assuming their peripherality, data will not be comparable with dialects that maintain BOT as the lowest vowel in the vowel space. So, for example, normalized vowel spaces for older generations that predate the CVS will not be comparable to younger speakers because the normalization technique will underestimate the size of the younger speakers' vowel spaces.

Two different approaches can prevent this type of normalization error. First, an examination of full vowel spaces will allow researchers to select

---

[3] Although, see Nycz (2011) for a method that incorporates mixed effects as a substitution for traditional normalization techniques.

[4] The techniques differ in that Nearey (1978) log-transforms values as a first step to normalization, mimicking non-linear perception scales, while Lobanov (1971) additionally normalizes the range of the vowel space by dividing by the standard deviation of the full vowel space as a final step to normalization.

truly peripheral vowels for the normalization procedure. For example, to account for the tendency of BOAT to undergo fronting in American English, the normalization technique we applied to the FPG data utilizes pre-rhotic BOAT, which resists fronting as a representative back vowel. This allows us to have a more accurate representation of the back of the vowel space. Alternatively, researchers can create average values based on peripheral vowel values without accounting for vowel class. This technique is more feasible with increased automation of vowel extraction, but was not feasible with the FPG corpus as automatic extraction of child data has not yet been tested. Regardless, researchers decrease the chance of normalization errors when they consider the vowel space as a whole before selecting a normalization procedure.

Measures of overall vowel space size and shape thus complement analyses of individual vowels in a number of ways. These metrics grant insight into typical development, as illustrated by predictable changes to vowel space size across childhood and adolescence. They also provide an opportunity to consider style, as reduced or expanded vowel spaces may gain indexical meanings in certain social groups. Finally, these broad overviews allow researchers to choose appropriate techniques to compare data across developmentally distinct periods. The consideration of vowel space areas and full vowel spaces provides an important launching pad for investigation of changes to individual vowel classes.

2.8   Conclusions

As longitudinal studies become increasingly more common, new tools and approaches will be necessary to meet the unique demands of these temporally expansive datasets. The FPG project offers both a wealth of information, as well as the challenge to effectively explore this information. Innovation has been a necessary component of our analysis, as the uniqueness of the database required us to find ways to identify trends over time. The broad-lens approaches that we have adopted provide context for more traditional variationist research. In some cases, such as the VDM, these approaches document developmental shifts, allowing researchers to characterize typical change over adolescence, as well as control for such variation to explore changes in linguistic style over time. In other cases, such as the DDM, these holistic measures provide a snapshot that can be utilized as a dependent variable in the assessment of social factors on language change. As the following chapters illustrate, we have been able to unlock a wealth of information about language use throughout childhood and adolescence by pairing traditional variationist analysis with the more global assessments presented in this chapter.

References

Bachman, Lyle F. and Adrian S. Palmer. 2008. *Language Assessment in the Real World*. Oxford: Oxford University Press.

Baugh, John. 1983. *Black Street Speech: Its History, Structure, and Survival*. Austin, TX: University of Texas Press.

Buchstaller, Isabelle and Suzanne Evans Wagner. 2017. Using panel data in the socio-linguistic study of variation and change. In Suzanne Evans Wagner and Isabelle Buchstaller (eds.), *Panel Studies of Variation and Change*, 1–18. New York: Routledge.

Cedergren, Henrietta and David Sankoff. 1974. Variable rules: Performance as a statistical reflection of competence. *Language* 50(2): 333–355.

Clopper, Cynthia G. 2009. Computational methods for normalizing acoustic vowel data for talker differences. *Linguistics and Language Compass* 3(6): 1430–1442.

Craig, Holly K. and Julie A. Washington. 2004. Grade-related changes in the production of African American English. *Journal of Speech, Language, and Hearing Research* 47(2): 450–463.

Craig, Holly K. and Julie A. Washington. 2006. *Malik Goes to School: Examining the Language Skills of African American Students from Preschool-5th Grade*. Mahwah, NJ: Lawrence Erlbaum Associates.

Durán, Robert. 1988. Validity and language skills assessment: Non-English background students. In Howard Wainer and Henry I. Braun (eds.) *Test Validity*, 105–127. Hillsdale, NJ: Lawrence Erlbaum.

Fitch,W. Tecumseh and Jay Giedd. 1999. Morphology and development of the human vocal tract: A study using magnetic resonance imaging. *Journal of the Acoustical Society of America* 106(3): 1511–22.

Flipsen, Peter. and Sungbok Lee. 2012. Reference data for the American English acoustic vowel space. *Clinical Linguistics and Phonetics* 26(11–12): 926–933.

Fox, Robert Allen and Ewa Jacewicz. 2017. Reconceptualizing the vowel space in analyzing regional dialect variation and sound change in American English. *Journal of the Acoustical Society of America* 142(1): 444–459.

Giles, Howard. 1973. Accent mobility: A model and some data. *Anthropological Linguistics* 15(2): 87–105.

Giles, Howard. 2008. Communication accommodation theory: "When in Rome." or not! In Leslie A. Baxter and Dawn O. Braithwaite (eds.) *Engaging Theories in Interpersonal Communication: Multiple Perspectives*, 161–173. Los Angeles, CA: Sage.

Green, Lisa J. 2002. *African American English: A Linguistic Introduction*. Cambridge: Cambridge University Press.

Green, Lisa J. 2011. *Language and the African American Child*. Cambridge: Cambridge University Press.

Gresham, Frank M. and Elliot, Stephen N. 1990. *Social Skills Rating System (SSRR)*. Circle Pines, MN: American Guidance Service.

Guy, Gregory R. 2014. Bricks and bricolage. Paper presented at *New Ways of Analyzing Variation* 43, October, Chicago, IL.

Habick, Timothy. 1993. Farmer City, Illinois: Sound systems shifting south. In Timothy Frazer (ed.), *"Heartland" English: Variation and Transition in the American Midwest*, 97–121. Tuscaloosa, AL: University of Alabama Press.

Hare, Bruce R. 1985. The HARE General and Area-specific Self-esteem Scale. Unpublished manuscript. Stony Brook, NY: State University of New York, Stony Brook.

Heffernan, Kevin. 2010. Mumbling is macho: Phonetic distinctiveness in the speech of American radio DJs. *American Speech* 85(1): 67–90.

Higgins, C. M. and M. M. Hodge. 2002. Vowel area and intelligibility in children with and without dysarthria. *Journal of Medical Speech-Language Pathology*, 10(4): 271–277.

Holmes, Thomas H. and Richard H. Rahe. 1967. The social readjustment rating scale. *Journal of Psychosomatic Research* 11(2): 213–218.

Jencks, Christopher and Meredith Phillips (eds.). 1998. *The Black-White Test Score Gap*. Washington, DC: The Brookings Institution.

Kelley, Elizabeth, Garland Jones, and Deborah Fein. 2003. Language assessment in children. In Michel Herson and S.R. Beers (eds.), *Comprehensive Handbook of Psychological Assessment Vol. 1: Intellectual and Neuropsychological Assessment*, 191–215. New York: Wiley.

Kohn, Mary Elizabeth and Charlie Farrington. 2012. Speaker normalization: Evidence from longitudinal child data. *Journal of the Acoustical Society of America* 131(3): 2237–2248.

Kohn, Mary Elizabeth and Charlie Farrington. 2017. Longitudinal sociophonetic analysis: What to expect when working with child and adolescent data. In Suzanne Evans Wagner and Isabelle Buchstaller (eds.), *Using Panel Data in the Sociolinguistic Study of Variation and Change*, 122–152. London/New York: Routledge.

Labov, William. 1966. *The Social Stratification of English in New York City*. Washington, DC: Center for Applied Linguistics.

Labov, William. 1969. Contraction, deletion, and inherent variability of the English copula. *Language* 45(4): 715–762.

Labov, William. 1991. The three dialects of English. *New Ways of Analyzing Sound Change*, 1–44. San Diego: Academic Press.

Labov, William. 1998. Co-existent systems in African American Vernacular English. In Salikoko S. Mufwene, John R. Rickford, Guy Bailey and John Baugh (eds.), *African American English: Structure, History, and Use*, 110–153. London/New York: Routledge.

Labov, William. 2001. *Principles of Linguistic Change: Social Factors. Vol. 2. Language in Society*. Oxford, UK: Blackwell.

Labov, William, Sharon Ash, and Charles Boberg. 2006. *The Atlas of North American English: Phonetics, Phonology and Sound Change: A Multimedia Reference Tool*. Berlin, Germany: Mouton de Gruyter.

Labov, William, Paul Cohen, Clarence Robins and John Lewis. 1968. *A Study of the Non-standard English of Negro and Puerto Rican Speakers in New York City*. Final report, Cooperative Research Project 3288. 2 vols. Philadelphia, PA: U.S. Regional Survey.

Lanehart, Sonja L. (ed.). 2015. *The Oxford Handbook of African American Language*. Oxford, UK: Oxford University Press.

Lee, Sungbok, Alexandros Potamianos, and Shrikanth Narayanan. 1999. Acoustics of children's speech: Developmental changes of temporal and spectral parameters. *Journal of the Acoustical Society of America* 105(3): 1455–1468.

Lindblom, Björn. 1990. Explaining phonetic variation: A sketch of the H&H theory. In W. J. Hardcastle and A. Marchal (eds.), *Speech Production and Speech Modelling*, 403–439. Dordrecht, the Netherlands: Kluwer Academic.

Makoni, Sinfree, Geneva Smitherman, Arnetha F. Ball, and Arthur K. Spears (eds.). 2003. *Black Linguistics: Language, Society, and Politics in Africa and the Americas*. New York: Routledge.

McGowen, Rebecca, Richard McGowen, Margaret Denny, and Susan Nittrouer. 2014. A longitudinal study of very young children's vowel production. *Journal of Speech, Language, and Hearing Research* 57(1): 1–15.

Morgan, Marcyliena. 2002. *Language, Discourse, and Power in African American Culture*. Cambridge, UK: Cambridge University Press.

Munson, Benjamin, Elizabeth C McDonald, Nancy L Deboe, and Aubrey R White. 2006. The acoustic and perceptual bases of judgments of women and men's sexual orientation from read speech. *Journal of Phonetics* 34(2): 202–240.

Nycz, Jennifer. 2011. *Second Dialect Acquisition: Implications for Theories of Phonological Representation*. Ph.D. Dissertation. New York: New York University.

Oetting, Janna B. and Janet L McDonald. 2001. Nonmainstream dialect use and specific language impairment. *Journal of Speech, Language, and Hearing Research* 44(1): 207–223.

Oetting, Janna B. and Janet L. McDonald. 2002. Methods for characterizing participants' nonmainstream dialect use in child language research. *Journal of Speech, Language, and Hearing Research* 45(3): 505–518.

Parker, Jeffry G. and Steven R. Asher. 1993. Friendship and friendship quality in middle childhood: Links with peer group acceptance and feelings of loneliness and social dissatisfaction. *Developmental Psychology* 29(4): 611–621.

Pettinato, Michèle, Outi Tuomainen, Sonia Granlund, and Valerie Hazan. 2016. Vowel space area in later childhood and adolescence: Effects of age, sex and ease of communication. *Journal of Phonetics* 54: 1–14.

Pianta, Robert E. 1992. *Child-Parent Relationship Scale*. Unpublished measure. Charlottesville, VA: University of Virginia.

Pierrehumbert, Janet, Tessa Bent, Anne Bradlow, Benjamin Munson, and J. Michael Bailey. 2004. The influence of sexual orientation on vowel production. *Journal of the Acoustic Society of America* 116 (4): 1905–1908.

Preston, Dennis R. 1996. Where the worst English is spoken. In Edgar Schneider (ed.), *Focus on the USA*, 297–360. Amsterdam: Benjamins.

Preston, Dennis R. and Nancy Niedzielski. 2000. *Folk Linguistics*. Berlin: Mouton de Gruyter.

Rastatter, M., R. McGuire, J. Kalinowski, and A. Stuart. 1997. Formant frequency characteristics of elderly speakers in contextual speech. *Folia Phoniatrica et Logopaedica* 49(1): 1–8.

Renn, Jennifer E. 2007. Measuring style shift: A quantitative analysis of African American English. Unpublished Master's thesis. Chapel Hill, NC: University of North Carolina at Chapel Hill.

Renn, Jennifer E. 2010. *Acquiring Style: the Development of Dialect Shifting among African American Children*. Ph.D. Dissertation. Chapel Hill, NC: University of North Carolina at Chapel Hill.

Rickford, John R. 1999. *African American Vernacular English: Features, Evaluation and Educational Implications*. Malden/Oxford: Blackwell.

Sankoff, David, Sali A. Tagliamonte, and E. Smith. 2005. Goldvarb (Version 3.0b3) [Computer Program]. Last accessed March 31, 2008, at http://individual.utoronto.ca /tagliamonte/goldvarb.html

Sankoff, Gillian and Hélène Blondeau. 2007. Language change across the lifespan /r/ in Montreal French. *Language* 83(3): 560–88.

Sankoff, Gillian and Suzanne Evans Wagner. 2011. Age grading in the Montréal French future tense. *Language Variation and Change* 23(3): 275–313.

Sellers, Robert M., Stephanie J. Rowley, Tabbye M. Chavous, J. Nicole Shelton, and Mia A. Smith. 1997. Multidimensional Inventory of Black identity: A preliminary investigation of reliability and construct validity. *Journal of Personality and Social Psychology* 73(4): 805–815.

Seymour, Harry N., Thomas Roeper, and Jill De Villiers. 2003. *Diagnostic Evaluation of Language Variation*. Chicago, IL: Pearson.

Singer, Judith D. and John B. Willett. 2003. *Applied Longitudinal Data Analysis: Modeling Change and Event Occurrence*. Oxford: Oxford University Press

Stewart, William A. 1968. Continuity and change in American Negro dialects. *The Florida FL Reporter* 6: 14–16, 18, 30.

Stockman, Ida. J. and Anna Fay Vaughn-Cooke. 1989. Addressing new questions about black children's language. In Deborah Schiffrin and Ralph W. Fasold (eds.), *Current Issues in Linguistic Theory 52*, 275–300. Philadelphia, PA: John Benjamins.

Tagliamonte, Sali A. 2006. *Analysing Sociolinguistic Variation*. New York/Cambridge, UK: Cambridge University Press.

Tagliamonte, Sali A. 2011. *Variationist Sociolinguistics: Change, Observation, Interpretation*. Malden/Oxford: Wiley-Blackwell.

Terry, J. Michael. 2004. *On the Articulation of Aspectual Meaning in African American English*. Unpublished Ph.D. dissertation. Amherst, Massachusetts: University of Massachusetts Amherst.

Thomas, Erik R. 2001.*An Acoustic Analysis of Vowel Variation in New World English*. Durham, NC: Duke University Press.

Thomas, Erik R. 2007. Phonological and phonetic characteristics of African American Vernacular English. *Language and Linguistics Compass* 1(5): 450–75.

Van Hofwegen, Janneke. 2015a. Dyadic analysis: Factors affecting African American English usage and accommodation in adolescent peer dyads. *Language and Communication* 41: 28–45.

Van Hofwegen, Janneke. 2015b. The development of African American English through childhood and adolescence. In Sonja L. Lanehart (ed.), *The Oxford Handbook of African American Language*, 454–74. Oxford, UK: Oxford University Press.

Van Hofwegen, Janneke and Walt Wolfram. 2010. Coming of age in African American English: A longitudinal study. *Journal of Sociolinguistics* 14(4): 27–52.

Vorperian, Houri K. and Ray D. Kent. 2007. Vowel acoustic space development in children: A synthesis of acoustic and anatomic data. *Journal of Speech, Language, and Hearing Research* 50(6): 1510–1545.

Wagner, Suzanne Evans. 2012a. Real-time evidence for age grad(ing) in late adolescence. *Language Variation and Change* 24(2): 179–202.

Wagner, Suzanne Evans. 2012b. Age grading in sociolinguistic theory. *Language and Linguistic Compass* 6(6): 371–82.

Wolfram, Walter A. 1969. *A Sociolinguistic Description of Detroit Negro Speech*. Washington, DC: Center for Applied Linguistics.

Wolfram, Walt. 1993. Identifying and interpreting variables. In Dennis R. Preston (ed.), *American Dialect Research*, 193–221. Philadelphia/Amsterdam: John Benjamins.

Wolfram, Walt. 2007. Sociolinguistic myths in the study of African American English. *Language and Linguistics Compass* 1: 292–313.

Wolfram, Walt. 2015. The sociolinguistic construction of African American Language. In Sonja L. Lanehart (ed.), *The Oxford Handbook on African American Language*, 338–52. Oxford: Oxford University Press.

Wolfram, Walt and Ralph W. Fasold. 1974. *The Study of Social Dialects in the United States*. Englewood Cliffs, NJ: Prentice Hall.

Woodcock, Richard W. and M. B. Johnson. 1989. *Woodcock-Johnson Tests of Achievement: Standard and Supplemental Batteries*. Allen, TX: DLM Teaching Resources.

3 Profiles of Change

The Early Lifespan of African American Language

3.1 Introduction

Speaker 1058 was raised in Durham, North Carolina. By her post-high school interview, she was attending North Carolina Central University, a large Historically Black College and University (HBCU) in Durham, NC. Growing up attending schools with predominantly African American student populations, 1058 discussed the importance of AAL at that time, stating that taking AAL out of the classroom is the same as taking diversity out of the classroom. Yet, 1058 is deeply aware that she changes how she speaks in different situations. Part of this change she associates with the process of growing up: "Really, if you're a freshman in college and you're still talking like you're in middle school. [...] it's a problem." Indeed, when examining her speech across the FPG Project, speaker 1058 shows a dramatic increase in her vernacular variables in the sixth and eighth grade, while dramatically decreasing her use of such variables in the tenth grade. While this pattern makes intuitive sense, how common is this trajectory of linguistic behavior?

Linguists have long hypothesized that the cultural process of aging includes predictable cycles of linguistic behavior (Hockett 1950). The cultural influence of life stages on language variation is frequently cited as an explanation for the use of more or less vernacular structures of English at various stages, contrasting the teenaged years with childhood and adulthood (Chambers 2003; Eckert 1997). As previewed in Chapter 1, longitudinal research into shifting and stable linguistic variables helps elucidate the relationship between life stages and community variation, as trajectories of variability across the lifespan cannot be attributed simply to ongoing language changes over time. Clearly, there are changes related to the lifespan of individuals, both as individuals and as community group members. Notwithstanding a recent uptick of interest within sociolinguistics in studies of language change over the lifespan, longitudinal studies remain relatively rare and exceptional.

3.2 The Linguistic Lifespan

The interaction of language with social structures over the lifespan is dynamic and intersectional. Institutions such as school, work, and family structures produce environments in which gender, age, social segregation and social interaction correlate with social and linguistic behavior at various life stages. Although theorization about psychosocial development in linguistic behavior has circulated for some time, the study of life stages in language variation represents a more recent and important development within the field of socio-linguistics; one that first developed with the recognition that adolescent culture does not exist as an imperfect imitation of adult systems, but rather, emerges within the social and developmental contexts of this life stage (Eckert 1989).

An understanding of the interaction between age and linguistic behavior is intimately related to the cultural processes of development and aging in the broadest sense, which is why panel studies have emerged as a crucial test case for such theories. As noted in Chapter 1, panel studies consist of two or more interviews of the same individuals over a span of time, thus providing informa-tion on change (Sankoff 2005), both for individual speakers and communities of speakers. For the most part, the majority of what is known about linguistic change across middle childhood and adolescence comes from apparent time or from case studies over a limited period. While these studies provide informa-tion on the interaction between development, aging, and linguistic behavior across the lifespan, there is no substitute for the insight that can be gained by following groups of individuals through the developmental and social experi-ences of growing up in progressive temporal increments (Sankoff 2004; Wagner 2012a). Only panel studies can empirically establish that individuals show linguistic stability or change across the lifespan and only studies that include more than two temporal data points can reveal how change correlates with progression through life stages.

How do individuals linguistically transition between life stages? Does real-time data provide evidence to indicate that the linguistic life stage of adoles-cence stands apart from other life stages? If so, are such behaviors restricted to certain linguistic structures? Are there limits to language change across the lifespan? These and many other questions emerge in considering language change through the lifespan.

3.3 Evidence for Life Stages

Evidence from apparent time and adolescent panel studies, ethnographic stud-ies of child and adolescent linguistic behavior, adult panel studies, and dialect acquisition studies all contribute to the conversation of whether there are typical and predictable patterns of change and constraints across early child-hood and adolescence. Evidence from ethnographic studies of adolescent speech suggests that teens may follow different linguistic trajectories for some variables depending on their engagement with adolescent social structures (Eisikovits 1998; Moore 2004) and the nature of the linguistic structure (Kohn 2013).

The majority of what is known about linguistic development through childhood and adolescence has emerged from apparent-time data investigating stable morphosyntactic and consonantal variation or sound changes in progress. In the traditional sociolinguistic study, evidence comes from studies with participants from a wide age range, typically including children from about age 10 through the elderly (Labov 1966, 2001; Wolfram 1969; Wolfram and Christian 1975; Trudgill 1974; Macaulay 1977; Cameron 2005) and ethnographic studies that hone in on specific life stages (Brice-Heath 1983; Mendoza Denton 2008). Research from apparent-time studies indicates that individuals in different life stages use stable vernacular morphosyntactic features and incoming changes to different degrees. Starting with a developmental stage where the child acquires linguistic variants closely aligned with parental models (Roberts 1994, 1997, 2002; Foulkes and Docherty 2006; Smith, Durham, and Fortune 2007), apparent-time evidence and short-term real-time evidence suggests that children begin to diverge from parental models as they gain exposure to peer models in elementary school (Kerswill and Williams 2000, 2005). Several scholars suggest that this process of divergence continues incrementally across childhood, peaking in the adolescent years as teens seek to establish autonomous identities from both adults and children (Labov 1964, 1972, 2001; Cheshire 1987, 2005; Eckert 1997, 2000, 2011). As teens transition toward adulthood, they are described as attenuating their use of vernacular variables, moving toward adult norms (Labov 2001). Attenuation of variables undergoing a change in progress may occur, but to a lesser extent (Cedergren 1987). Often, young adults' orientations toward marketplace pressures are cited as instigating this shift, and sometimes a similar shift back to more vernacular behavior has been predicted for retirees who no longer experience the pressure of conforming to linguistic marketplace pressures (Chambers 1995, 2003; Eckert 1997).

3.3.1   Age-Grading: Evidence from Generational and Panel Studies

Studies that focus on developmental or cultural aspects of variation across childhood and adolescence are typically limited to a narrow age range. Most studies of language variation that focus on younger speakers address the question of how and when children acquire variable forms (e.g., Foulkes and Docherty 2005; Roberts 1997, 2002; Smith et al. 2007) or how they acquire primary structures associated with particular dialect varieties (e.g., Stockman and Vaughn-Cook 1989; Seymour and Roeper 1999; Green 2011). Accordingly, they tend to be limited to the early stages of development through the first six years. Interest in adolescent speech typically explores engagement in identity work that may correlate with more innovative or vernacular speech (Eckert 1997, 2000, 2011), or how adolescent linguistic behavior reflects and interacts with social structures specific to both the age group and the local context of the group in question (Habick 1993; Bucholtz 1999; Fought 2003; Moore 2004; Mendoza-Denton 2008), limiting studies to the secondary school years while ignoring childhood and earlier adolescence. Until recently, the category of emerging adulthood following secondary school has been lumped in with either adolescence or adulthood, but recent research demonstrates that the transitional nature of this life stage has important implications for language change across the lifespan as well (Bigham 2008, 2012; Wagner 2008; Prichard and Tamminga 2012). These studies provide a complementary assessment of the linguistic influence of life stages when compared to the panel studies and large generational comparisons.

Interest in how and when children acquire variable speech patterns has led to the growth of early childhood research from a sociolinguistic perspective. Data from Child-Directed Speech (CDS) indicate that children are exposed to socially meaningful variation at the earliest stages of acquisition, and analysis of child speech for these earliest time periods indicates close alignment with parental models for socially salient variables (Kerswill and Williams 2000; Roberts 2002; Foulkes, Docherty, and Watt 2005; Smith et al. 2007). Longitudinal (Callahan-Price 2011) and apparent-time analyses of language acquisition indicate that developmental constraints on variation cede to linguistic constraints found in the larger adult population during the preschool years (Roberts 1994, 1997; Foulkes et al. 1999). Research into middle childhood illustrates a shift toward peer models, with schools serving as an important location for social contact (Kerswill and Williams 2000).

Beyond the acquisition of variation in early childhood, analysis of middle childhood speech provides evidence that the transition between infancy at home to childhood and toward adolescence at school correlates with the reorganization of variation based on peer models (Kerswill and Williams 2000). While middle childhood is clearly an important time in the linguistic lifecycle for moving away from parental models and learning sociolinguistic-ally meaningful variation in the context of the peer group, the emphasis in sociolinguistic analysis has been placed on early acquisition, adolescent vari-ation, or the presumably stable adult system. Because middle childhood lan-guage, between 7 and 11 years, represents a relatively intact structural system with developing social components, this particular time period deserves greater attention from linguists interested in how the linguistic individual progresses through the lifespan.

While there are few apparent-time studies addressing the transition from childhood to adolescence, Eckert notes that this stage is likely a crucial one in the development of the linguistic individual: " … it is in this early social order that kids' sociolinguistic competence expands to engage with the wider social world" (Eckert 2011: 86). Eckert's initial investigations of preadolescent speech suggest that innovative vowel variation, for example, including advanced variants of Californian vowels undergoing a change in progress, is one tool that preadolescents draw upon to establish their social orders.

In their study of 4, 8, and 12 year olds at Milton Keynes, Kerswill and Williams (2000) focused on children as the promoters of koineization, a process of rapid dialect change that occurs in dialect contact environments, but their results speak to the importance of life stage variation as well. For all of the variables, the children avoided salient regional markers and were more homogenous than the adults who hailed from various dialect regions.

3.3.2   Adolescence and Teenagers

Studies of adolescent culture suggest that the importance of establishing an identity within the context of peer culture leads to extensive identity work performed through linguistic variation during this life stage (c.f. Eckert 1989, 2000; Eisikovits 1998; Habick 1993; Bucholtz 1999; Fought 2003; Moore 2004; Mendoza-Denton 2008). Because of this identity work, many teens take the lead in adopting vernacular and innovative forms, and ethnographic- ally defined emic categories are shown to be better predictors of variation vis-á- vis adult social class categories at this stage in the lifecycle. These studies identify the cultural mechanisms behind patterns identified in generational studies. How do children linguistically become adolescents?

By adolescence, emergent social systems identified in preadolescence appear firmly integrated so that teen social orders have fully developed groups with corresponding linguistic divisions. So, for example, both Eckert (2000) and Habick (1993) found that teens who oriented away from institutional organizations, nicknamed "burnouts" in both studies, had more advanced instantiations of sound change compared to the more conservative teens in each community. From a dialect accommodation/resistance perspective, Fought (1999) identified gang affiliation as a better predictor of resistance to back vowel fronting than class background for a group of Latino students in California, a region where back vowel fronting is rigorous and widespread for the predominant regional variety.

Frequently the construction of these teen cultural practices involves the incorporation of new or more advanced linguistic variants, or vernacular variants into the linguistic repertoire. Yet, not all teens actively engage in these kinds of practices, as Bucholtz (1999) illustrates in her analysis of high school nerd girls who resist Californian back vowel fronting (a change in progress), along with other sociolinguistic and social markers of main- stream teens.

Socially conditioned patterns of age-grading have been observed for adolescents as illustrated in Eisikovits's (1998) analysis of adolescent speech in Australia and Moore's (2004) study of teens in the northwest of England. Eisikovits (1998) identified different trajectories of change for females and males during adolescence as female panel participants reduced their use of stable non-standard morphosyntactic and consonantal features, such as vernacular past tense realizations, over the course of the study while male participants either maintained or increased the use of these same features. Eisikovits suggested that the girls and boys in her study had different cultural expectations for maturation, leading to distinct patterns of language change across adolescence.

Parallel to these findings, Moore (2004) followed a group of girls over the course of two years. She found that age-grading patterns corresponded to the development of group identities, with girls who developed into a social group known as "Townies," a group identified by engagement in "risky" behaviors, demonstrating an increase in *were* leveling (e.g., *I/you/(s)he/we/you/they were there*), tag questions, and negative concord over the two-year span. This pattern contrasted with girls who associated with the "Popular" category, a group that refrained from the more rebellious behaviors of the "Townies." Overall, the Populars demonstrated less extreme increases in non-standard linguistic behavior over the course of the two-year study. Findings like these highlight how a group's orientation to the cultural context influences life stage patterns. While large-scale, life stage studies may identify dominant trajectories of linguistic change, there are likely to be sub-patterns related to such choices.

Even as children grow up within the context of dominant discourses of what it means to be a teenager, it is unlikely that all children will progress in a uniform fashion through this period in life. While generational studies cited earlier offer evidence that teens strengthen innovative changes and frequently have higher rates of stable vernacular features, we may ask whether this pattern is pervasive among teens or restricted to those who engage in the kind of oppositional identity work found in situations described by Eckert.

3.3.3   Early Adults

As noted by Deser, " … if Labov believes that the child is likely to undergo radical language change in her preadolescent (as well as adolescent) years, then isn't it also quite possible that a further series of changes might occur in the adult years where other goals such as career and employment come into play?" (Deser 1990: 35). Interviews with post-high school subjects in the 18- and 25-year-old age range are not uncommon in the field of sociolinguistics, but they frequently are lumped into broader age categories. There is reason to believe, however, that the transition from high school to post-high school merits further investigation, especially within the changing context of a post-industrial society where post-high school education, multiple career changes and moves, extended dependence on parental support, and delayed introduction into typical cultural markers of adulthood such as marriage and child-rearing are common (Arnett 2001). This is precisely the kind of observation that drives the most recent research into life stages as linked to lifespan change and language change in general (Bigham 2012).

Wagner's (2008) analysis of Philadelphia women transitioning between high school and post-high school is particularly relevant for the current study because the analysis includes both stable consonantal variables for twenty-two participants and vocalic variables that are changes in progress for a subsample of nine participants at two time points. Class differences in age-grading emerged for the stable phonological variables (ING) and interdental fricative stopping, with only the highest socioeconomic group showing a decline in non-standard variants between high school and college.

Because modern instantiations of post-high school culture lend themselves to intense dialect contact situations found in institutions such as universities and the military, Bigham (2012) suggested that a focus on this life stage can provide insight into patterns of diffusion. He explored accommodation during emerging adulthood using word list data for southeastern Illinois students attending a university with both southeastern Illinois students and students from the Chicago area with the Northern Cities Vowel Shift (NCS). He used apparent-time data from teens enrolled at a local high school as a comparison to the southern Illinois college students. The southern Illinois college students showed evidence of accommodation toward NCS norms, although patterns of accommodation varied among participants.

Individual orientation toward the community in question during emerging adulthood may also play a role in predicting participation in local sound changes, as demonstrated in Prichard and Tamminga's (2012) study of Philadelphia vowel systems. Speakers who did not pursue higher education or who attended locally oriented institutions were more likely to exhibit diagnostic local features including the split short-*a* system and a raised BOUGHT class. Speakers who attended nationally oriented institutions did not exhibit these local features, and speakers who attended regionally oriented institutions had an intermediate distribution. Without longitudinal data, however, it is unclear whether these participants altered their linguistic behavior during emerging adulthood or entered this stage of life with the vowel system intact.

Several important themes emerge from this new body of work. First, cultural shifts experienced by emerging adults are likely to be as significant, if not more significant, than those experienced by preadolescents moving toward adolescence. Second, heightened mobility during this life stage produces a situation where dialect contact is highly likely for many individuals. Finally, identity work likely plays an important role in the outcomes of such contact such that individuals will show change if negative stigma makes such change socially desirable. However, the trajectories of change may differ.

3.3.4 Change in Adulthood

Change in adulthood can be facilitated by a number of factors. One of the factors uncovered by some studies indicates that variable structures are more likely to change than categorical structures (Nahkola and Saanilahti 2004; Sankoff and Blondeau 2007). This finding is not surprising as such changes represent a shift in frequency rather than the acquisition of a new form. Change for vocalic variation across the lifespan has received less attention, but vocalic variation across the lifespan appears much more restricted than segmental or morphosyntactic changes (Wagner 2008, see Chapter 4). In a panel and trend study of the variation of (r) undergoing a change in progress in Montreal French by Sankoff and Blondeau (2007), they found that change for panel members was restricted to midrange users of the two variables, illustrating that variable speakers can shift rates of variation. With one exception, all those who demonstrated change shifted in the direction of the community change in progress. These findings illustrate a consistent pattern of later-in-life change for a consonantal feature undergoing a change in progress when speakers show variable productions at the initial time point. Nahkola and Saanilahit (2004) identified similar patterns for both morphosyntactic and phonological features in their panel study of twenty-four Finnish speakers interviewed twice during a span of ten years. Categorical speakers tended to remain categorical, while variable speakers tended to change in the direction of community change.

The findings raise several questions about linguistic stability and assumptions of change. Will patterns identified in two-time-point studies continue upon expected trajectories with more temporal data points, or will individuals exhibit non-monotonic change? Does group stability mask individual variation? Will stable variables that display salient regional or ethnic patterns display similar noisiness or will they be subject to age-grading? Some variables may be more likely to experience change than others, and the explanations may include social, individual, and cognitive bases. The current research suggests that, despite the importance placed on childhood and adolescence in sociolinguistic studies, change is ongoing in adulthood as well.

Linguistic plasticity is also one of the factors that may determine whether, when, or how speakers change through the lifespan. In this area, the majority of research has focused on Second Language Acquisition (SLA), with a focus on whether a critical period exists for language learning. Evidence indicates that the ability for speakers to acquire a second language structure correlates with the speaker's age, age of exposure in the second language, the linguistic level and complexity of the target structure, and the relationship of the incoming structure to structures already present within the L1 system, among other factors.

Within variation studies, linguistic plasticity is relevant to the acquisition of another dialect, and the examination of what types of linguistic structures that individuals modify across the lifespan, as well as how such modification occurs. Younger speakers tend to show more change than older individuals, and the nature of the linguistic structure may influence the ease of acquisition. Sociocognitive factors such as the saliency of the feature (Trudgill 1986) and the speaker's orientation toward the sociolinguistic indexing of the variable also come into play (Giles and Coupland 1991). Our study approaches the question of linguistic plasticity from the perspective of lifetime change for a number of variables in a social setting so we can consider the types of linguistic structures involved.

3.4   Change in the Early Lifespan of African American Language

Issues and questions raised in the previous sections provide the framework for the longitudinal study of AAL over the first two decades of life. The study of AAL over the past half-century has fueled a number of empirically unresolved questions about its development and change from the onset of language to early adulthood and beyond. Is there a period in the life cycle when the vernacular structures are most likely to be evidenced, and if so, when? How much variation in vernacular usage may be demonstrated from childhood through adolescence and through adulthood, and do children show similar or different trajectories of vernacular dialect development and change over time? A number of linguistic studies (e.g., Labov et al. 1968; Wolfram 1969; Fasold 1972; Rickford 1999) have considered the correlation of age with vernacular dialect variables, but questions have persisted since the early descriptive studies. Furthermore, traditional sociolinguistic studies such as those cited earlier start only after language development is mostly complete, at around age 10. On the other hand, studies of developing African American speech typically end before this age period (e.g., Stockman and Vaughn-Cook 1989; Seymour and Roeper 1999; Craig and Washington 2006; Green 2011), thus offering mutually exclusive datasets. In this context, several different hypotheses have been offered about the optimal development of African American speakers.

Stewart (1965, 1968) and Dillard (1972) maintained that the optimal period for vernacular use was the preschool, post-developmental childhood years, before the contamination of vernacular forms from exposure to prescriptive school norms. Stewart (1968: 4) observed that:

The older non-standard (and sometimes even creole-like) dialect features remained in use principally by younger children in Negro speech communities – being learned from other young children, to be given up later in life when "small-boy" talk was no longer appropriate.

Stewart (1965: 16–17) notes that "the consistent use of basilect patterns, even in predominantly lower-class neighborhoods, is largely restricted to young children," and Dillard (1972: 236) observes that "[t]he comparatively archaic character of the speech of the younger children always those who are beyond the stage of language acquisition, of 'learning to talk' – is sociolinguistically perhaps the most exciting factor in Black English." The early childhood basilectal hypothesis set forth by Stewart and Dillard, interpreted as a developmental view of the creole-origin hypothesis of AAL (Stewart 1967, 1968; Dillard 1972), was based largely on first-hand ethnographic, anecdotal observation rather than a systematic longitudinal study or cross-sectional study of children and adolescents at different age levels.

The position of Craig and Washington (2006) four decades later, based on a cross-sectional survey of school children from preschool (ages 3–4) through Grade 5 (about age 10), similarly concludes that vernacular AAL use is optimal in the preschool, post-developmental stage, though it is not linked to a creole remnant as in the case of Stewart and Dillard's hypothesis. With the onset of schooling, speakers progressively reduce their vernacular feature use in Kindergarten (about age 5 years) through Grade 5. The first stage in vernacular recession takes place during Grade 1 (about age 6 years), followed by a reduction in vernacular language features in Grade 3 (about age 8 years) and 4 (about age 9 years). Craig and Washington (2006: 51) note that:

Production rates for AAL features decrease with increases in grade. With longer systematic exposure to SAE [Standard American English], on average students reduce the frequency with which they use AAL features in school contexts. This is manifested as a dialect shift at first grade for spoken discourse and at third grade for reading aloud.

Craig and Washington focus on language in school, finding that moderating effects such as discourse type (e.g., narrative description, spontaneous speech) and demographic variables (community, socioeconomic status, gender) correlate with the vernacular reduction trajectory from Kindergarten through Grade 5. While both Stewart and Dillard and Craig and Washington indicate that younger speakers at the onset of formal schooling tend to use a higher incidence of vernacular structures than their older cohorts, there are important differences in language context, methods of data collection, assumptions about language development, and the implications of their respective studies for interpreting language change during the childhood-adolescent lifespan of the AAL speaker. Craig and Washington (2006) rely, for the most part, on a canonical set of adult vernacular AAL features culled from the expansive descriptions of adult AAL that have been compiled over the last half-century (e.g., Labov et al. 1968; Wolfram 1969; Fasold 1972; Baugh 1983; Rickford 1999; Green 2002), with a recognition of limited traits that might be endemic to childhood AAL (Washington and Craig 2002; Craig et al. 2003), whereas Stewart (1965, 1968) and Dillard (1972) tend to focus on more divergent, disputably creole-like features of AAL associated with childhood AAL.

Furthermore, as noted, Craig and Washington focus on vernacular language use in the context of school whereas Stewart and Dillard focus on naturalistic language use in neighborhood interactions. And Craig and Washington rely on systematically recorded language data for a large number of subjects whereas Stewart and Dillard are content with informal observations of language use in the natural context of home or neighborhood. Notwithstanding these different types of studies and datasets conducted almost a half-century apart, they converge in their conclusion that early childhood is the optimal period for vernacular AAL use.

Lisa Green's *Language and the African American Child* (2011) offers a radically different approach to the development of AAL, focusing on the acquisition of vernacular forms by 3–5-year-olds in Louisiana. Using both spontaneous and structurally elicited forms, she views AAL as a complex system not reducible to a set of individual and independent features. In this context, she shows how the tense-aspect system is acquired over a time that extends beyond the preschool phase; in fact, many of the aspectual structures are not fully in place in early preschool development so that speakers would not realize optimal vernacular AAL in preschool.

An alternative hypothesis for optimal vernacular AAL use is offered by Labov (1964), who notes that there is an accelerating trend in the development of vernacular features during adolescence that reaches a plateau during the teenage years. Labov (1964: 91) asserts that "in the pre-adolescent years, from roughly ages five to twelve, the child learns the use of the local dialect in a form consistent with that of his [sic] immediate group of friends and associates." According to Labov, this is a stage when the influence of parents is submerged under the influence of the peer group. With respect to vernacular AAL, Labov et al. (1968: 4) note that "there is a sub-system of English used by pre-adolescent and adolescent Negro speakers in Northern ghetto areas which is remarkably uniform over the age range 8–17 years, especially for those who participate fully in the vernacular culture." Labov's position, however, offers no empirical support for this position because none of his studies considered pre-school or early childhood data for empirical verification of his claim.

Apparent-time research that compares AAL features across different ages that usually start at about the age of 10 years, tends to show some support for the hypothesis that adolescence correlates with greater vernacular dialect use (Wolfram 1969; Fasold 1972), though there is not always a straightforward correlation. For example, in North Carolina, Rowe (2005) shows that older, rural speakers as a group may show a higher incidence of some diagnostic vernacular dialect structures while younger speakers show a bimodal distribution in which one subset of younger speakers shows intensified vernacular feature use while another shows reduced vernacular use. Furthermore, the correlation with age may be sensitive to the linguistic variable, so that older speakers may show a high frequency of -s plural absence (Rowe 2005) whereas younger speakers show a much higher use of invariant *be* (Labov et al.1968; Wolfram 1969; Fasold1972; Cukor-Avila 2001). Studies focused on vernacular speech among African American speakers, such as Labov et al. (1968), Baugh (1983), and Rickford (1999), tend to focus on the teenage and early adult age period for their descriptions based on an implicit assumption that this is the primary period for vernacular dialect development.

As indicated in the preceding overview, answers to the question of optimal vernacular use during the lifespan have been elusive for several reasons. First of all, the age distribution in different studies of AAL is complementary rather than comparative. As noted, in the traditional sociolinguistic descriptions of AAL (e.g., Labov et al. 1968; Wolfram 1969; Fasold 1972) the lowest age for participants tends to be in the 10–12 year age range, so that no comparison with speakers at earlier ages can be undertaken. While this minimal-age threshold may be understandable in terms of the goals of particular sociolinguistic studies focused on post-developmental language use, it does not allow these studies to address the early childhood vernacularity hypothesis empirically. By the same token, studies focused on vernacular use in childhood and pre-adolescence typically do not extend their comparisons to later adolescence and the early adult years, so that Craig and Washington's research studies (Craig and Washington 2006) extend from preschool (ages 3–4 years) or Kindergarten (about age 5 years) through Grade 5 (about age 10 years), thereby precluding the possibility of comparison with subjects during later adolescence. Consequentially, there are no long-term, longitudinal sociolinguistic studies of African American speakers from early childhood through the teenage and early adult years, making it difficult to evaluate hypotheses about the development of vernacularity over this period on an empirical basis. In this study, we address some of the fundamental questions about the trajectory of vernacularity during the early lifespan of African American speakers based on the unique, longitudinal set of cohorts we have followed progressively from birth through the first 20 years of their lives.

There are also some longitudinal studies of teenage and older speakers of African American English from late adolescence and early adulthood into adulthood (Cukor-Avila and Bailey 2011). Over a three-decade period, they have interviewed some of the residents of a small receding population in rural Texas repeatedly and followed the lives of some of the adolescents as they have moved to more urban areas and back to the town showing that the diffusion of urban vernacular takes place among older teens who move to urban areas and then move back. Teenagers who moved to urban areas and then back intensified their use of vernacular features. This period in the lifecycle seems especially vulnerable to the intensification of vernacular AAL features, and it is clearly enabled by extended contact with speakers from urban areas.

On the other hand, panel studies of speakers comparing teenage and adult time frames generally show a decline in the use of vernacular features. Baugh (1996), in a case study of four men as teens and again as adults, showed an overall decline in the use of vernacular features. Although each of the participants had taken different career paths, every individual used fewer vernacular AAL morphosyntactic features, including copula absence and non-standard negation, in the adult interview. This is particularly striking considering that one of the adult participants was interviewed during his incarceration, a linguistic marketplace force quite likely to differ from typical young adult settings.

Finally, Rickford and Price (2013) reported on a couple of case studies in which participants in earlier studies were re-interviewed when they were about twenty years older following their first teenage interviews. Both women showed significantly lower usage rates of key vernacular AAL features as adults than as teenagers. Despite the complicating factor of stylistic variability which led them to recommend that studies of change in real time utilize at least three data points rather than two, the authors concluded that the contrasts represented stable age-grading rather than generational change (cf. Sankoff and Blondeau 2007).

The current study of vernacular AAL can offer essential profiles of the type of changes that take place within and across speakers, addressing both similarities and differences in trajectories of change exhibited by a range of speakers.

3.5   Trajectories of Vernacular AAL in the Early Lifespan

In this section, we consider trajectories of change in vernacular AAL based on a set of seven temporal data points. For the sake of our discussion, we consider morphosyntactic/consonantal variation separately from vowels (see Chapter 4), in part because of the nature of the structures and in part because of the different methodologies used to measure the variables.

3.5.1   Morphosyntactic and Consonantal Change

In our profile of change, we rely on the use of the Dialect Density Measure (DDM), the composite metric introduced and justified in Chapter 2. We also consider select individual variables to complement the overall scores offered by the DDM. As noted, the obvious advantage offered by the DDM is that it

Table 3.1 *DDM scores from seven language*
samples of one FPG child over her lifespan.
From Van Hofwegen and Wolfram (2017: 81).

Age (years)	DDM (fpu)
4	0.12
6	0.06
9	0.07
11	0.17
13	0.20
15	0.04
20	0.04

provides a "snapshot" glimpse of the dialect usage of a speaker in a given
speech sample so that we can tabulate how many AAL features per communication unit[1] of speech are produced for any speaker in any sample – regardless
of relative differences in talking time – and get a *features per utterance* (fpu)
score. This method controls for length of the language sample and results in a
continuous measure. Table 3.1 illustrates the DDM scores for one child in the
FPG longitudinal sample at seven temporal points in her life. What is evident in
this particular child's set of scores is that she is a relatively and consistently low
user of vernacular AAL, with only a slight rise at age 11 and 13 years.

For longitudinal studies with a sample of this type, the advantage of the
DDM is that it can reflect language use for many speakers at many points in
their lives. Figure 3.1 depicts the DDM scores for thirty-one FPG longitudinal
children; these speakers were used originally in Van Hofwegen and Wolfram
(2010), but with additional data from the latest temporal point, post-high
school, roughly 20 years old. The figure provides a useful visual display of
the various trajectories of AAL usage in this particular population.

From Figure 3.1, we can see that the low, consistent AAL usage trajectory
exhibited by the speaker from Table 3.1 is an anomaly from the overall
pattern. In fact, many children exhibit wide swings from relatively high
usage at 4 years old to relatively low usage at 6–9 years old, then to
extremely high usage in early adolescence (11–13 years old), and finally
back down again in later adolescence and early adulthood. While it varies in
relative magnitude from child to child, this pattern is the most prevalent in
the FPG sample, dubbed the "roller-coaster" trajectory by Van Hofwegen
and Wolfram (2010). At the same time, it is clear from the figure that there

---

[1] A communication unit is operationalized as an independent clause plus its modifiers (Loban
1976).

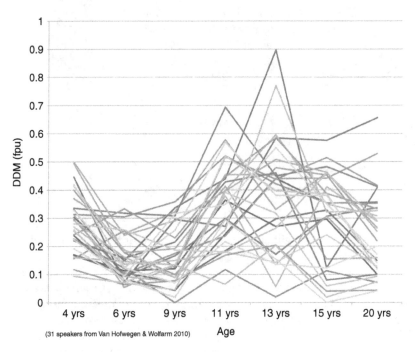

Figure 3.1 DDM scores from seven temporal points for thirty-one FPG
children over their lifespans. Image from Van Hofwegen and Wolfram
(2017:82)

are other patterns in lifespan AAL usage as well, including a curvilinear
pattern, where children start out as high AAL users, reduce their use over the
years of early schooling, and then swing gradually upward without declining
in later adolescence. Other patterns include stable patterns (like the speaker
in Table 3.1), as well as gradual linear increases or decreases in usage across
the lifespan. So there is a predominant pattern in the trajectories, but
restricted, alternative minority trajectories as well.

DDM trajectory analysis allows us to answer the question of when the
minimal and optimal times for vernacular AAL usage are likely to be on an
empirical basis. Statistical smoothing of these trajectory trend lines results
in the overall roller-coaster pattern exhibited in Figure 3.2. Here, we can
see that for the majority of FPG children, the minimal period of vernacular
speech is at ages 6–9 years, while the optimal period is at ages 11–15 years.
In Van Hofwegen and Wolfram (2010), we conclude from this that the early
years of schooling (when most AAL speakers are getting their first institu-
tionally enforced instruction in Standard English) have a dramatic

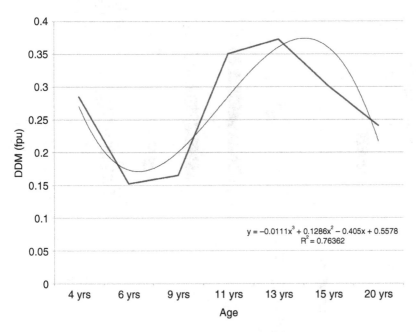

Figure 3.2 Polynomial regression line illustrating the most prominent "roller-coaster" trajectory. Image from Van Hofwegen and Wolfram (2017: 83)

influence on young AAL-speaking children, prompting them to minimize the use of their home dialect. Keeping in mind that the language samples at these ages come from mother–child interactions, it is noteworthy that the children generally use less AAL than their mothers (Van Hofwegen 2015, Chapter 5). In contrast, it is perhaps not surprising that children are most vernacular (i.e., highest DDM scores) at the early adolescent ages. Much research on adolescent speech confirms this period to be particularly innovative and non-standard (cf. Eckert 2004). Then, as speakers enter later adolescence and early adulthood, and begin to feel the influence of the standard language market (Eckert 2011), their DDM scores dip down accordingly.

While the roller-coaster trajectory, in which there is a higher level of AAL use at 48 months, a dip during Grade 1 and 4, a rise in AAL use in Grade 6 and 8, and then a recession in Grade 10, is the dominant pattern, there is also a curvilinear trajectory, in which early AAL use at 48 months recedes in Grade 1 and 4, then accelerates through Grades 6, 8, and 10, dipping in the post-secondary school period (age 20). These two primary trajectories account for twenty-six of the thirty-one speakers included in this subset.

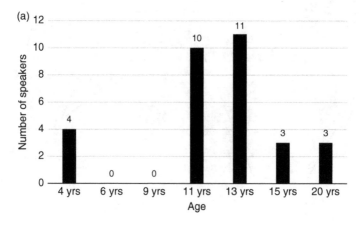

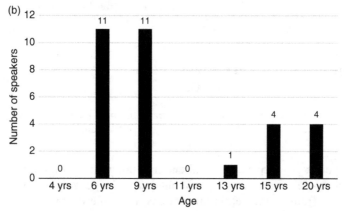

Figure 3.3 Optimal and minimal periods of AAL use by age periods
(a) Number of speakers, optimal AAL use
(b) Number of speakers, minimal AAL use

It is also instructive to examine speakers in terms of their optimal and minimal periods of vernacular dialect usage based on the DDM scores. In Figures 3.3a, b, we indicate the number of speakers in each period with respect to optimal and minimal periods of AAVE use.

While the periods of maximal vernacular AAL use are varied, it is note-worthy that it never occurs during the early schooling period. Conversely, this period is the period where the absence of AAL is paramount for most speakers, indicating a strong correlation in the diminishing use of AAL with early schooling. It is equally noteworthy that this pattern does not last, hence the roller-coaster pattern in AAL use that we noted previously.

3.6   Complementing the Dialect Density Measure

In order to address the DDM's relative lack of nuance for assessing individual feature trajectories over the lifespan, we have also conducted two complementary analyses to support and triangulate the DDM's role as a composite language-use index. First, we have conducted a type-based analysis of AAL that focuses on different types of AAL features represented in a sample as opposed to the frequency of AAL tokens. A speaker may, for example, show a high incidence of AAL tokens per word or communication unit in their token-based DDM, but it is possible that this may be due to a limited number of AAL structures used more frequently, thus potentially skewing the representation of vernacular AAL. It is therefore important to determine how many different AAL structures might be represented in a language sample. Type-based profiles of AAL may operate in tandem with, or independent from, token-based accounts (Oetting and McDonald 2002), but in some current studies type-based tabulations are employed along with token-based metrics (Oetting and McDonald 2002; Van Hofwegen and Wolfram 2010). In our analyses (Van Hofwegen and Wolfram 2010; Van Hofwegen 2015), we have consistently found that higher DDM scores correlate significantly with higher numbers of feature types, supporting the idea that the DDM is an appropriate reflection of general usage of AAL.

In Figure 3.4, we examine the relationship between the token-based frequency analysis and the type-based representation in terms of the different structural AAL features that are included in our analysis. In other words, we are concerned with the number of different AAL structural types that are used as compared with the token analysis given previously. The token score is indicated on the Y-axis and the type score is indicated on the X-axis.

The results of the linear regression analysis ($r^2 = .467, p < .001$) indicate that token-based and type-based analyses of AAL are mutually supportive in terms of indexing AAL speakers. Thus, the most vernacular children will also use the most varied AAL feature types and vice versa. It is also important to determine if children are consistent in utilizing the same structures. In examining the cases of a selected subset of high-vernacular children who scored quite high on the general DDM measure, Van Hofwegen and Wolfram (2010) showed that speakers tend to match features. For example, two speakers who used twenty-one and nineteen different features each, respectively, shared fifteen of those features. Similarly, the low-vernacular children tended to share features; for example, two speakers who used ten and nine different features each, respectively, shared five of the same features. Regardless of the level of vernacularity, the children all tended to use the same features most frequently

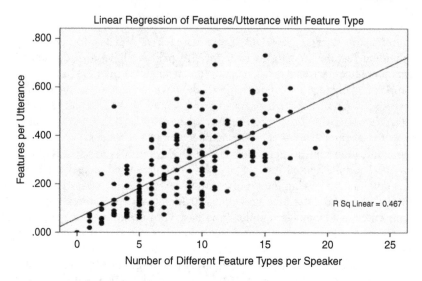

Figure 3.4 Linear regression of AAL token frequency and structural type. Image from Van Hofwegen and Wolfram 2010:443.

(i.e., (ING), copula absence, modal/auxiliary absence, third person singular -*s* absence, and invariant *be*). The type-based tabulation undertaken here expands on the DDM and addresses one of its potential skewing limitations. The analysis shows further that there is a shared, preferred set of structures regardless of vernacular status.

Another complementary analysis considers the relative frequency of selected dialect variants in relation to the potential cases where they might occur, following the traditional variationist paradigm (Cedergren and Sankoff 1974; Tagliamonte 2006, 2011) focused on the variable incidence of individual variants. For three prominent features of the DDM, copula absence, third person singular –*s* absence and (ING) (a feature shared with all varieties of English), we conducted just such an analysis, using multivariate logistic regression via the Goldvarb tool (Sankoff, Tagliamonte, and Smith 2005). Figure 3.5 shows the factor weights for each of these variables plotted over time. This analysis aligns closely with the DDM trajectory analysis, in that each of these variables shows a favoring effect (factor weight greater than 0.5) at 4 years old and 11–15 years old, with disfavoring effects at 6–9 years old and at 20 years old. While there are small individual differences in relative factor weights among these variables, the largely parallel trajectories are striking. Moreover, the similarity for these three variables' trajectories with the

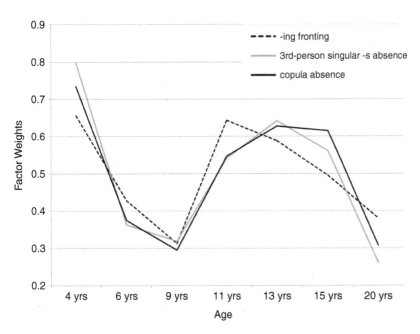

Figure 3.5 Factor weights for three AAL variables, copula absence, third person singular –*s* absence. Image from Van Hofwegen and Wolfram (2017:84)

overall composite index trajectory patterns (Figures 3.1 and 3.2) is also noteworthy.

The similarities between the factor weight trajectories of copula absence, third person singular –*s* absence, and (ING) are telling because they align closely with the overall DDM trajectories. However, in the case of another hallmark AAL feature, invariant *be*, there is a striking difference from the overall DDM trajectory data, specifically at the age of 4. Figure 3.6 illustrates the trajectory of invariant *be* across the same seven life points as before. Note that as traditional variation analysis cannot be conducted on this variable, due to the difficulty of determining potential versus actual cases, raw counts are tabulated here, following Rickford and Price (2013). While we see a higher relative favoring effect at age 4 years for the three variables tabulated in 3.5, for invariant *be* we find that 4-year-olds are hardly using this feature at all. In contrast, in early adolescence its use skyrockets. In Van Hofwegen and Wolfram (2010), we conclude this to be evidence of invariant *be* later acquisition profile (Green 2011). Invariant *be* has complex aspectual properties that indicate "habituality" (Green 2002, 2011; Labov 1998) and may be difficult for younger speakers to use competently.

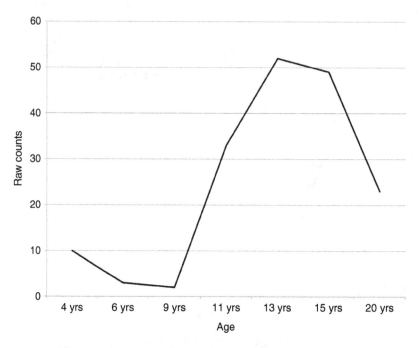

Figure 3.6 Raw counts for invariant *be* tabulated from seven temporal points in their lifespans. Image from Van Hofwegen and Wolfram (2017:86)

The triangulation of different types of analyses of structural features found here provides an important vantage point that combines the complementary perspectives of token-based, type-based, and variationist analytical traditions within linguistics and sociolinguistics to reliably reflect overall patterns of use as well as the use of particular structures in AAL. Triangulation of this type is especially critical when testing the reliability of a new composite index. If a type-based analysis does not align with a token-based (composite) analysis, for example, we might claim that there is an imbalance in the representativeness of the features that comprise the composite index. This suite of findings, however, reveals the complementary utility of both composite and structurally specific analyses in the assessment of longitudinal language development, underscoring the need for analytical and descriptive triangulation in providing an authentic picture of longitudinal language change in the lifespan. While the fact remains that the DDM is a composite of many well-documented AAL features, and not an exhaustive inventory of all features of the language variety or their structural complexity (Green 2011), these analyses have shown that it is valuable as an overall assessment of AAL usage across the lifespan.

3.7   Conclusion

The longitudinal analysis offers insight into the developmental trajectory of AAL in the early lifespan as well as the methodological utility of a composite index in accessing such development. With respect to AAL, the data reveal a dominant trajectory at the same time that it indicates that vernacular AAL use cannot be reduced to a unilateral trajectory over the lifespan. The roller-coaster pattern of vernacular use is dominant, but there are also several authentic trajectory patterns of use based on the sample. With respect to particular linguistic structures, some variables (e.g., copula absence, 3rd sg. –s absence, unstressed (ING)) may align but others, such as invariant *be*, show a different pattern that may involve the intersection of language development, structural complexity, and age-grading.

One of the most consistent aspects of AAL trajectories is the minimization of AAL use, starting in Grade 1 and reaching its lowest point in Grade 4. Though vernacular optimization can vary greatly, none of the speakers shows vernacular optimization peaks at Grade 1 or Grade 4, supporting Craig and Washington's hypothesis (2006) about the decline of the vernacular during the early years of schooling. There may be a variety of factors that contributes to this early decline, but the corrective effect of early school socialization in Mainstream American English would appear to be a primary explanation. This interpretation is supported by the trajectory of the representative individual linguistic variables that we examined. For example, a highly salient, generally stigmatized structure of American English such as (ING) shows that the *-in* variant is sharply reduced at this stage. After almost a half-century of inquiry into the use of AAL over the childhood, adolescent, and early adult lifespan, we have finally come to an empirically based response to the earlier hypotheses about its change and variation during childhood, adolescence, and early adulthood. Not surprisingly, it is much more nuanced than it has been set forth by previous scholars, though there is also a predominant trajectory that had not, in fact, been included in the competing hypotheses about language change from early child through early adulthood.

The investigation also underscores the utility of complementary methods of analysis, since the token-based, type-based, and variation-based analyses provide insight into the different dimensions of vernacular development and change through childhood and adolescence. None of the methods may be sufficient in itself, but together they help provide perspective on the overall development and the development of particular structures in vernacular AAL. The overall profile and the individual variable analyses suggest that it is important to examine both the sociolinguistic forest of variability as well as the individual, variable trees within the forest for an authentic picture of language change in the early lifespan of AAL – or any language variety.

References

Arnett, Jeffery J. 2001. *Adolescence and Emerging Adulthood: A Cultural Approach.* Upper Saddle River, NJ: Prentice Hall.

Baugh, John. 1983. *Black Street Speech: Its History, Structure, and Survival.* Austin, TX: University of Texas Press.

Bigham, Douglas S. 2008. *Dialect Contact and Accommodation among Emerging Adults in a University Setting.* Ph.D. Dissertation. Austin, TX: University of Texas at Austin.

Bigham, Douglas S. 2012. Emerging adulthood in sociolinguistics. *Language and Linguistics Compass* 6(8): 533–544.

Brice Heath, Shirley. 1983. *Ways with Words: Language, Life, and Work in Communities and Classrooms.* Cambridge: Cambridge University Press.

Bucholtz, Mary. 1999. "Why be normal?": Language and identity practices in a community of nerd girls. *Language in Society* 28(2): 203–223.

Callahan-Price, Erin. 2011. Generalized acquisition constraints and dialect-specific norms in child AAE copula development. Paper presented at *New Ways of Analyzing Language Variation* (NWAV) 40, Washington, DC: Georgetown University.

Cameron, Richard. 2005. Aging and gendering. *Language in Society* 34(1): 23–61.

Cedergren, Henrietta and David Sankoff. 1974. Variable rules: Performance as a statistical reflection of competence. *Language* 50(2): 333–355.

Chambers, Jack. 1995. *Sociolinguistic Theory: Linguistic Variation and Its Social Significance.* Oxford: Blackwell.

Chambers, Jack. 2003. *Sociolinguistic Theory: Linguistic Variation and Its Social Significance.* Oxford: Blackwell.

Cheshire, Jenny. 1987. Age and generation-specific use of language. In Ulrich Ammon, Norbert Dittmar, and Klaus Mattheier (eds.), *Sociolinguistics: An Introductory Handbook of the Science of Language and Society*, 760–767 Berlin: Mouton de Gruyter.

Cheshire, Jenny. 2005. Age and generation-specific use of language. In Ulrich Ammon, Norbert Dittmar, Klaus Mattheier, and Peter Trudgill (eds.), *Sociolinguistics: An Introductory Handbook of the Science of Language and Society*, 1552–1563. Berlin: Mouton de Gruyter.

Craig, Holly K., and Julie A. Washington. 2006. *Malik Goes to School: Examining the Language Skills of African American Students from Preschool-5th Grade.* Mahwah, NJ: Lawrence Erlbaum Associates.

Craig, Holly K., Connie Thompson, Julie A. Washington, and Stephanie L. Potter. 2003. Phonological features of child African American English. *Journal of Speech, Hearing, and Language Research* 46(3): 623–635.

Cukor-Avila, Patricia. 2001. Coexisting grammars: The relationship between the evolution of African American and Southern White Vernacular English in the South. In Sonja L. Lanehart (ed.), *A Sociocultural History and Some Phonological Evidence: Sociocultural and Historical Contexts of African American English*, 93–128. Philadelphia, PA/Amsterdam: John Benjamins.

Cukor-Avila, Patricia, and Guy Bailey. 2011. The interaction of transmission and diffusion in the spread of linguistic forms. *University of Pennsylvania Working Papers in Linguistics (Selected papers from NWAV 40)* 17(2): 41–49.

Deser, Toni. 1990. *Dialect Transmission and Variation: An Acoustic Analysis of Vowels in Six Urban Detroit families*. Ph.D. dissertation. Boston, MA: Boston University.

Dillard, J. L. 1972. *Black English: Its History and Usage in the United States*. New York: Random House.

Eckert, Penelope. 1989. *Jocks and Burnouts: Social Categories and Identity in the High School*. New York: Columbia University, Teachers College Press.

Eckert, Penelope. 1997. Age as a sociolinguistic variable. In Florian Coulmas (ed.), *The Handbook of Sociolinguistics*, 151–167. Oxford: Blackwell.

Eckert, Penelope. 2000. *Linguistic Variation as Social Practice*. Oxford: Blackwell.

Eckert, Penelope. 2004. Adolescent language. In Edward Finegan and John Rickford (eds.), *Language in the USA*. New York: Cambridge University Press.

Eckert, Penelope. 2011. Language and power in the preadolescent heterosexual marketplace. *American Speech* 86(1): 85–97.

Eisikovits, Edina. 1998. Girl-talk/Boy-talk: Sex differences in adolescent speech. In Jennifer Coates (ed.), *Language and Gender: A Reader*, 45–58. Sydney: Australian Professional Publications.

Fasold, Ralph W. 1972. *Tense Marking in Black English: A Linguistic and Social Analysis*. Arlington, VA: Center for Applied Linguistics.

Fought, Carmen. 1999. A majority sound change in a minority community: /u/-fronting in Chicano English. *Journal of Sociolinguistics* 3(1): 5–23.

Fought, Carmen. 2003. *Chicano English in Context*. Houndmills, UK/New York, NY: Palgrave Macmillan.

Foulkes, Paul and Gerard Docherty. 2006. The social life of phonetics and phonology. *Journal of Phonetics* 34(4): 409–438.

Foulkes, Paul, Gerard Docherty, and Dominic Watt. 2005. Phonological variation in child directed speech. *Language* 81(1): 177–206.

Giles, Howard, and Nikolas Coupland. 1991. *Contexts of Accommodation: Developments in Applied Sociolinguistics*. Cambridge: Cambridge University Press.

Green, Lisa J. 2002. *African American English: A Linguistic Introduction*. Cambridge: Cambridge University Press.

Green, Lisa J. 2011. *Language and the African American Child*. Cambridge: Cambridge University Press.

Habick, Timothy. 1993. Farmer City, Illinois: Sound systems shifting south. In Timothy Frazer (ed.), *Heartland English*, 97–124. Tuscaloosa, AL: University of Alabama Press.

Hockett, Charles. 1950. Age-grading and linguistic continuity. *Language* 26(4): 449–459.

Kerswill, Paul and Anne Williams. 2000. Creating a new town koine: Children and language in Milton Keynes. *Language in Society* 29(1): 65–115.

Kerswill, Paul and Anne Williams. 2005. New towns and koineisation: Linguistic and social correlates. *Linguistics* 43(5): 1023–1048.

Kohn, Mary. 2013. *Adolescent Ethnolinguistic Stability and Change: A Longitudinal Study*. Ph.D. Dissertation. Chapel Hill, NC: University of North Carolina at Chapel Hill.

Labov, William. 1964. Stages in the acquisition of Standard English. In Roger Shuy, Alva Davis, and Robert Hogan (eds.), *Social Dialects and Language Learning*, 77–104. Champaign: National Council of Teachers of English.

Labov, William. 1966 [2006]. *The Social Stratification of English in New York City*. Cambridge, UK: Cambridge University Press.

Labov, William. 1972. *Sociolinguistic Patterns*. Philadelphia, PA: University of Pennsylvania Press.

Labov, William. 1998. Co-existent systems in African-American Vernacular English. In Salikoko S. Mufwene, John R. Rickford, Guy Bailey and John Baugh (eds.), *African-American English: Structure, History and Use*, 110–153. London and New York: Routledge.

Labov, William. 2001. *Principles of Linguistic Change: Social Factors. Vol. 2*. Oxford, UK: Blackwell.

Labov, William, Paul Cohen, Clarence Robins, and John Lewis. 1968. *A Study of the Non-Standard English of Negro and Puerto Rican Speakers in New York City*. Report on cooperative research project 3288. New York, NY: Columbia University.

Macaulay, Ronald K. S. 1977. *Language, Social Class, and Education: A Glasgow Study*. Edinburgh: Edinburgh University Press.

Mendoza-Denton, Norma. 2008. *Homegirls: Language and Cultural Practice among Latina Youth Gangs*. Cambridge, MA: Blackwell.

Moore, Emma. 2004. Sociolinguistic style: A multidimensional resource for shared identity creation. *Canadian Journal of Linguistics* 49(3/4): 375–396.

Nahkola, Kari and Marja Saanilahti. 2004. Mapping language changes in real time: A panel study on Finnish. *Language Variation and Change* 16(2): 75–92.

Oetting, Janna B. and Janet L. McDonald. 2002. Methods for characterizing participants' nonmainstream dialect use in child language research. *Journal of Speech, Language, and Hearing Research* 45(3): 505–518.

Prichard, Hillary and Meredith Tamminga. 2012. The impact of higher education on Philadelphia vowels. *University of Pennsylvania Working Papers in Linguistics (Selected papers from NWAV 40)* 18(2): 87–95.

Rickford, John R. 1999. *African American Vernacular English*. Malden, MA: Blackwell.

Rickford, John R., and McKenzie Price. 2013. Girlz II women: Age-grading, language change and stylistic variation. *Journal of Sociolinguistics* 17(2): 143–179.

Roberts, Julie. 1994. *Acquisition of Variable Rules: (-t,d) Deletion and (ing) Production in Preschool Children*. Ph.D. Dissertation. Philadelphia, PA: University of Pennsylvania.

Roberts, Julie. 1997. Hitting a moving target: Acquisition of sound change in progress by Philadelphia children. *Language Variation and Change* 9(2): 249–266.

Roberts, Julie. 2002. Child language variation. In J.K. Chambers, Peter Trudgill, and Natalie Schilling-Estes (eds.), *The Handbook of Language Variation and Change*, 333–348. Oxford: Blackwell.

Rowe, Ryan D. 2005. *The Development of African American English in the Oldest Black Town in America: -s Absence in Princeville, North Carolina*. Master's Thesis. Raleigh, NC: North Carolina State University.

Sankoff, Gillian. 2004. Adolescents, young adults and the critical period: Two case studies from "Seven up." In Carmen Fought (ed.), *Sociolinguistic Variation: Critical Reflections*, 121–139. Oxford: Oxford University Press.

Sankoff, Gillian. 2005. Cross-sectional and longitudinal studies in sociolinguistics. In Peter Trudgill (ed.), *Sociolinguistics/soziolinguistik: An International Handbook of the Science of Language and Society*, 1003–1013. Berlin: Mouton de Gruyter.

Sankoff, Gillian and Hélène Blondeau. 2007. Longitudinal change across the lifespan: /r/ in Montreal French. *Language* 83(3): 560–588.

Sankoff, David, Sali A. Tagliamonte, and Eric Smith. 2005. *Goldvarb (Version 3.0b3)* (Computer Program). http://individual.utoronto.ca/tagliamonte/goldvarb.html

Sankoff, David, Sali A. Tagliamonte, and Eric Smith. 2015. Goldvarb Yosemite: A variable rule application for Macintosh. Department of Linguistics, University of Toronto.

Seymour, Harry N., and Thomas Roeper. 1999. Grammatical acquisition of African American English. In Orlando L. Taylor and Lawrence Leonard (eds.), *Language Acquisition across North America: Cross-cultural and Cross-linguistic Perspectives;* 109–153. San Diego, CA: Singular Publishing Co.

Stewart, William A. 1965. Urban Negro speech: Sociolinguistic factors affecting English teaching. In Roger W. Shuy (ed.), *Social Dialects and Language Learning*, 10–18. Champaign, IL: National Council of Teachers of English.

Stewart, William A. 1968. Continuity and change in American Negro dialects. *The Florida F L Reporter* 6: 14–16, 18, 30.

Stockman, Ida. J., and Anna Fay Vaughn-Cooke. 1989. Addressing new questions about black children's language. In Deborah Schiffrin and Ralph W. Fasold (eds.), *Current Issues in Linguistic Theory*, 52, 275–300. Philadelphia, PA: John Benjamins.

Smith, Jennifer, Mercedes Durham, and Liane Fortune. 2007. "Mam, my trousers is fa'in doon!" Community, caregiver, and child in the acquisition of variation in a Scottish dialect. *Language Variation and Change* 19(1): 63–99.

Tagliamonte, Sali A. 2006. *Analysing Sociolinguistic Variation*. New York/Cambridge: Cambridge University Press.

Tagliamonte, Sali A. 2011. *Variationist Sociolinguistics: Change, Observation, Interpretation*. Malden/Oxford: Wiley-Blackwell.

Trudgill, Peter. 1974. *The Social Differentiation of English in Norwich*. Cambridge: Cambridge University Press.

Trudgill, Peter. 1986. *Dialects in Contact*. Oxford: Blackwell.

Van Hofwegen, Janneke. 2015. The development of African American English through childhood and adolescence. In Sonja L. Lanehart (ed.), *Oxford Handbook of African American Language*, 454–474. Oxford: Oxford University Press.

Van Hofwegen, Janneke, and Walt Wolfram. 2010. Coming of age in African American English: A longitudinal study. *Journal of Sociolinguistics* 14: 427–55.

Van Hofwegen, Janneke and Walt Wolfram. 2017. On the utility of composite indices in longitudinal language study. In Suzanne Evans Wagner and Isabelle Buchstaller (eds.), *Panel Studies of Variation and Change*. Routledge Studies in Language Change Series, 71–98. New York: Routledge.

Wagner, Suzanne Evans. 2008. *Language Change and Stabilization in the Transition from Adolescence to Adulthood*. Ph.D. dissertation. Philadelphia, PA: University of Pennsylvania.

Wagner, Suzanne E. 2012a. Real-time evidence for age grad(ing) in late adolescence. *Language Variation and Change* 24(2): 179–202.

Wagner, Suzanne E. 2012b. Age-grading in sociolinguistic theory. *Language and Linguistics Compass* 6(6): 371–82.

Wolfram, Walter A. 1969. *A Sociolinguistic Description of Detroit Negro speech*. Washington, DC: Center for Applied Linguistics.

Wolfram, Walt and Donna Christian. 1976. *Appalachian Speech*. Arlington, VA: Center for Applied Linguistics.

4   Vowel Variation across Time and Space

4.1   Introduction

Chapter 3 traced a wide array of morphosyntactic and a few consonantal variants across the early lifespan, revealing systematic patterns of age-grading and lifespan change. While this analysis provides valuable insight into how children linguistically negotiate their paths to adulthood, it is critical to evaluate multiple kinds of linguistic variation to gain a comprehensive picture of lifespan change (Tagliamonte 2012; Rickford and Price 2013; Kohn 2014; Brook et al. 2018). Such data may reveal which kinds of linguistic variables are most likely to change and why some variables may show little, if any change across the lifespan.

Vowels warrant their own analysis because they are a key component of variation at the phonetic (sound) level of language. Further, several factors would suggest that the vowel system is likely to show trajectories of development distinct from the morphosyntactic variables analyzed in Chapter 3. There is reason to believe that aspects of African American Language (AAL) vowel variation receive different social evaluations when compared to vernacular AAL morphosyntactic variation. Within African American communities, some phonetic variables, such as coda /d/ glottal-ization or PRIZE glide-weakening are common across social classes, unlike some vernacular morphosyntactic variables that show sharp social class divisions, at least in formal speech environments (Wolfram 1969; Nguyen 2006; Farrington 2012, 2019; Britt and Weldon 2015). If AAL vowel variants are not associated with the vernacular, speakers may be less likely to adjust their use of these variables over the lifespan. In contrast to components of the Dialect Density Measure (DDM), vowels within the United States are less likely to receive overt evaluative commentary. Teachers are likely to comment upon variables such as invariant *be,* negative concord, or copula absence on school papers, as morphosyntactic variation is typically transparent in student writing. Differences in vocalic categories, as non-discrete sub-phonemic differences, often fail to gain

orthographic representation.[1] Finally, vowel variation may be a key component of perceptual clues to ethnicity (Purnell et al. 1999), thus underscoring the importance of researching vocalic variants to investigate
critical issues of linguistic discrimination (Rickford and King 2016).
Vowel variation often exists at the phonetic level, so it is hard to characterize for non-linguists due to a lack of a widespread formal representation
system. Accordingly, it may play a different indexical role with regard to
the intersection of class and ethnicity among many African Americans. We
may, in turn, expect that vowel variation will follow a different path across
childhood and adolescence when compared to morphosyntactic variation.

With these considerations in mind, this chapter considers the ways in which
individuals modify their vowel spaces across childhood and adolescence. First,
we identify patterns and trends for childhood and adolescent vocalic variation,
drawing from the limited sociolinguistic studies that have included younger
participants. We set the stage for our current analysis by introducing the
linguistic ecology of the Raleigh-Durham-Chapel Hill metro area, the home
of the FPG participants. We then discuss methodological considerations
for working with child and adolescent acoustic data, which was briefly touched
on in Chapter 2. After establishing appropriate methods, we analyze the vowel
system of twenty FPG participants across four time points at approximately age
10 (4th grade), 14 (8th grade), 16 (10th grade), and 20 (post-high school).

We further consider the relationship between community and school demographics with vowel variation. While all FPG participants grew up in the same
metropolitan area, they attended a wide array of schools that drew from distinct
neighborhoods and communities. The extent to which FPG children grew up in
environments that promoted racial homophily depends upon these community
and institutional structures. Such structures may play a critical role in language
variation as well as lifespan change. Transitions between social institutions
may influence life stage variation as children progress through different institutional structures that can dramatically impact their social networks. As such,
we examine community and school demographics, in addition to age, in order
to investigate social variation in the vowel system.

Our analysis reveals that, in contrast to morphosyntactic variation captured
by the DDM (see Chapter 3), trajectories of change for vocalic variation across
adolescence are much more idiosyncratic. Group-level trends related to

---

[1] Developments in Computer Mediated Communication (CMC) such as texting and Twitter now
offer more informal writing genres to more people. Creative phonetic spellings on these
platforms have been found to encode sociolinguistically meaningful variation (Tatman 2016).
It is possible that such phonetic coding systems will raise the saliency of such variation, similar to
older spelling conventions for velar nasal fronting (-in' for -ing). The extent to which such
vocalic variation will reach similar levels of saliency as easily identified morphosyntactic
variants such as copula absence remains to be seen.

physical and linguistic development from ages 6 through 20 are apparent in the data (Chapter 2), but group patterns of change that might reflect social processes, such as age-grading, are much more limited. Instead of age-related variation, school demographics correlate strongly with participation in the African American Vowel System (AAVS) for many of the variables analyzed in this chapter. Students who come from predominantly African American communities and attend majority-minority schools consistently participate in aspects of the AAVS, while students who attend predominantly European American schools incorporate aspects of the Third Vowel Shift (TVS) identified by Dodsworth and Kohn (2012) among young European Americans in Raleigh, North Carolina. Relative stability may reflect the distinct position many phonetic variables hold in AAL, as variables that potentially index ethnic affiliation, but not class affiliation. Additionally, vowel systems in the region appear to either be stabilizing after a period of change, as Dodsworth and Kohn (2012) document for the TVS, or, in the case of the AAVS, have been relatively stable in the region for some time (Kohn 2014). Intra-speaker lifespan change for vowels may be more common in communities undergoing rapid sound change (Holmes-Elliott 2018).

While group stability predominates, exceptions to this pattern are also revealing. Patterns for PRICE glide-weakening, a variable that is potentially undergoing community-wide change (Fridland 2003), follow a trajectory that appears distinct from other vowels as group patterns of age-grading are apparent (see also Deser 1990). These patterns suggest that vowel variants may be susceptible to lifespan change when such variables reach the status of a stereotype, or when a variable is undergoing community-level change (Labov 2001). The analysis of a range of variables from different linguistic subsystems and with different levels of saliency affords the opportunity to identify whether linguistic variation shows across-the-board predictable patterns of change, or whether change is variant-specific. When read together with results from Chapter 3, it becomes clear that age-grading and adolescent peaks are not pervasive across the entire linguistic system, but instead are constrained to specific components.

4.2   What We Know about Child Vowel Systems

Childhood is a rich and active stage in the acquisition and development of social variation, a pattern that holds true for vocalic variation as well. Yet, childhood receives relatively little attention from sociophoneticians. This is true even though vowels provide an ideal system for longitudinal analysis due to early acquisition and the ability for researchers to consider the entire system together (see Chapter 2). While variation in vowel space size does not stabilize until after puberty when vocal tract anatomy reaches adult-like dimensions, children generally have established phonemic contrast by age three (McGowan et al. 2014) and even produce adult-like vowel formant contours by as young as age five (Assmann et al. 2013).[2] With the phonological system in place, researchers can easily begin examining child vowel systems for social variation. Studies that do include young children confirm that sensitivity to socio-phonetic vocalic variation develops early, even as children may innovate beyond or reanalyze the adult system (Local 1983; Roberts and Labov 1995; Roberts 2002; Kerswill and Williams 2005; Khattab 2007, 2013; Smith, Durham, and Richards 2013; McGowan et al. 2014).

Vowel studies of the very young often focus on how children acquire sociolinguistically meaningful variation. These studies often find that younger children are more likely to align with the speech of their primary caregiver than older children (Kerswill and Williams 2000, 2005; Stanford 2008; Habib 2014), highlighting the importance of caregiver input for early acquisition of the vocalic system. Regional influences in the vowel system are apparent by at least age 4 (Roberts 1997; McGowan et al. 2014).[3] Acquisition of social variation, however, appears dependent on the saliency of the variable, as patterns of style-shifting for the very young seem to be variant-specific (Smith, Durham, and Richards 2013).

Subphonemic variation is less well studied for early childhood, and yet there is reason to believe that the kind of socially conditioned subphonemic variation found in adult populations is also present in the young child's linguistic system (Local 1983). When considering perception, children are capable of perceiving accent differences quite young, and have the ability to identify foreign accents (Girard, Floccia, and Goslin 2008) and US regional distinctions (Jones et al. 2017) by age 4–5, with adult-like levels reached in the adolescent years. As children are exposed early to social variation including broader social categories such as region, gender, and social class, it is no surprise that such variation influences both production and perception for vowel systems in children, even as social categories may be reinterpreted in ways that differ from adult indexical values.

Childhood and preadolescence usher in both physical and social changes that demonstrably impact linguistic performance. This age group uses vocalic variants to actively construct identities that are gendered (Eckert 1996; Habib 2014), regional (Thomas 1996; Jacewicz, Fox, and Salmons

---

[2] Yang and Fox (2013) note that children ages 3 and 5 show some distinctions in subphonemic realizations of phonemes, including formant trajectories, indicating that some fine-tuning of vowel categories is still occurring for young children.

[3] Despite the assumed difficulty of the task, young children appear capable of acquiring complex phonological rules. Famously, preschoolers in Roberts' (1997) study demonstrated the complex Philadelphia phonological conditioning pattern found in adult populations for TRAP, even as they innovate into new environments.

2011; Habib 2014), and, as we demonstrate in this volume, ethnically affiliated. Physical maturational patterns for boys and girls differ so that sex and gender performance interact with age in a complex manner (Khattab and Roberts 2011; Cartei et al. 2014; Habib 2014). During this time, children may begin to sort out the gendered meaning of salient variables, including vocalic variation, leading them to modify their linguistic performances accordingly (Habib 2014). Increased attention to social meaning may (at first) lead to a reduction in stigmatized or regionally marked vocalic variants. So, for example, Deser (1990) found that Detroit pre-adolescents were less likely to use PRIZE glide-weakening, a variant associated with AAL and the southern United States, than their teen counterparts. Research from middle childhood clearly demonstrates that children skillfully employ a range of subphonemic vowel variants depending on social context (see, for example, Khattab 2007). Some evidence also suggests that middle childhood and pre-adolescence may be a key period during which children progress sound change beyond parental models (Eckert 1996; Thomas 1996). As such, this "middle child" of sociolinguistic study deserves much more extensive attention.

As noted in previous chapters, adolescent years have been described as ushering in increased innovation and vernacular use that is occasionally subject to age-grading, or alternatively reshaping the language for future generations. For the vowel system, these hypotheses are largely based on cross-sectional studies that demonstrate an adolescent peak in which teens use more innovative pronunciations for incoming sound changes than children or adults from the same community (Labov 2001). There is some evidence suggesting that individuals do modify vowel production during this time, as two-time point studies reveal modifications to pronunciation between childhood and adolescence (Carter 2007; Holmes-Elliott 2018). This appears particularly true for vowels undergoing change in the broader community. For example, Holmes-Elliott found that adolescents in Hastings, UK, consistently progressed their use of GOOSE fronting, a change below the level of consciousness, between childhood and adolescence (Holmes-Elliott 2018).

Yet, the single longitudinal vowel study of AAL that spans from pre-adolescence to adulthood demonstrates that age-grading may not apply as extensively to components of the vowel system. Rickford and Price's landmark case study of Foxy Boston and Tinky Gates, two African American women from East Palo Alto, California who participated in a twenty-year longitudinal study concluded when the participants were in their 30s, found that even as these two young women "changed their networks and curtailed their use of AAVE grammatical vernacular forms significantly, ... their vowel systems, less subject to stigmatization and conscious control, are essentially unchanged"

(Rickford and Price 2013: 161). This absence of change may also correspond to community stability, as we will discuss in this section.

Changes from middle childhood to adolescence, and from adolescence to adulthood are likely variable-specific and related to saliency (see also Smith et al. 2013). So, while Foxy Boston and Tinky Gates showed little change in their vowel system across childhood and adolescence, Carter's (2007) case study of Maria, an adolescent Latina from North Carolina, found that Maria shifted her use of the BAN vowel when she changed schools from a predominantly white elementary school to a more ethnically diverse middle school. After attending middle school, Maria's BAN production lowered, aligning with her Latinx peers.[4] The contrast between the speech norms in her two schools potentially heightened the saliency of this variable, making it a target for change.

The extent to which an individual can modify subphonemic variation is dependent on linguistic plasticity. As linguistic plasticity is hypothesized to decline with age, emerging adults may be less capable of altering their pronunciations, even if this life stage is characterized by frequent moves and restructuring of social networks, increasing exposure to a range of pronunciations. Yet, some research indicates that has individuals may be able to continue to alter their vocalic system, albeit the resulting changes do not perfectly mirror the assumed target. Sankoff (2004) analyzed two participants from the *Seven Up* documentary series, a series that followed a cohort of British children from the age of seven through adulthood. Upon close examination of two Northern English dialect speakers, Sankoff found evidence for accommodation to Southern English vocalic norms for at least one panel member. Longitudinal studies of adults and adult second dialect acquisition studies similarly indicate that at least some modification to the vocalic system is possible after adolescence (Prince 1987; Munro, Derwing and Flege 1999; Bowie 2000; Harrington et al. 2000; Conn and Horesch 2002; De Decker 2006; Evans and Iverson 2007; Gregerson, Maegaard and Pharaoh 2009; Bigham 2010, 2012; MacKenzie and Sankoff 2010; Nycz 2011).

Previous work on change across childhood and adolescence for vowel systems indicates that individuals can make changes to this linguistic system, even into adulthood, but whether they do so may depend on various factors, including the salience of the variable in question and whether the variable is undergoing change in the broader community. Because pre-adolescents often appear more advanced for vocalic sound change than their parents, while very young children appear to align with parental models, we may hypothesize that children begin the process of incrementing socially relevant changes when

---

[4] A close proximity between the TRAP and BAN classes has been documented in many varieties of Latinx English, while many varieties of Anglx English in the United States, particularly those associated with the TVS, participate in BAN raising (Fought 2003; Thomas 2001).

entering school, perhaps due to new social networks and contacts formed through school attendance (Kerswill and Williams 2000, 2005; Stanford 2008; Habib 2014). As described in Chapter 1, this process likely continues through adolescence, leading to adolescent peaks in innovative vocalic forms (Labov 2001). Alternatively, this system may undergo more idiosyncratic change, or demonstrate stability across childhood and adolescence (Rickford and Price 2013). Without longitudinal data, these trends have yet to be validated empirically. In the following section, we examine changes to the vowel system from approximately age 10 to approximately age 20 for twenty FPG participants to shed light on the extent to which the vocalic system changes over the lifespan.

4.3   The Sociophonetic Context of the Frank Porter Graham Study

Although all FPG participants were recruited from the same census metropolitan area, the linguistic landscape of this area varies extensively across communities and generations – a factor that emerges as central to understanding vocalic variation within the dataset. Figure 4.1 displays three systems historically and currently observed in the region. The African American Vowel System (AAVS); the (European American) Southern Vowel Shift (SVS); and the Third Vowel Shift (TVS). Potentially, FPG participants are exposed to all three systems, and as such, may take up this variation in the construction of style theoretically (Eckert 1996).

The AAVS is a collection of variants that has been identified in a range of predominantly African American communities throughout the United States (Thomas 2007; Kohn 2014), having spread as a result of the Great Migration. The AAVS in North Carolina is characterized by a raised front lax vowel system, but unlike the SVS, the front lax vowels do not undergo diphthongization to the same extent (Kohn 2014; Risdal and Kohn 2014). The AAVS back vowel system retains more backed-high and mid-back vowels (Thomas 2001) that also differ from the fronted variants of the SVS. Further, there is evidence

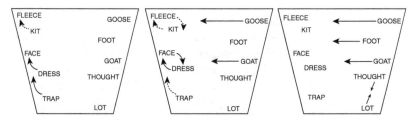

Figure 4.1 Comparison of vowel systems in the Research Triangle region of study participants

to suggest that the AAVS has been remarkably stable among the North Carolina African American communities in focus here, with vowel spaces of octogenarians that are indistinguishable from those of young adults (Kohn 2014: 60).

The European American Southern Vowel Shift can also be found among older speakers in the region (Thomas 2001). This system has much in common with the vowels found in the AAVS, likely due to extensive contact (Thomas 2007). Still, several characteristics set apart the European American SVS, including back vowel fronting, the diphthongization of front lax vowels, and lowering of front tense vowels.

While the SVS historically was widespread throughout the area (Kurath and McDavid 1961; Thomas 2001), an immigration wave of middle-class European Americans connected to the introduction of Research Triangle Park in the 1960s has led to a decline in traditional Southern vowel variants among European Americans (Dodsworth and Kohn 2012). European American communities highly impacted by immigration now show characteristics of the TVS (Labov 1991), including retraction of the front lax vowel system. In contrast, back vowel fronting, a variant found both in traditional European American Southern systems and TVS systems, continues to be widespread, although the exact quality of this fronting likely differs across generations.[5] These sound changes progressed most rapidly between 1950 and 1966, a period of intense middle-class migration into the region. Since that time, many of the sound changes associated with the TVS appear to be slowing or coming to completion (Dodsworth and Benton 2017).

These regional vowel systems are presented in Figure 4.1. Each quadrilateral represents a schema of distinct vowel systems, with the left side of the quadrilateral representing the front of the vowel space and the right side representing the back of the vowel space. The leftmost system is the AAVS (Thomas 2007; Kohn 2014), followed by the SVS (Labov 1991; Thomas 2001; Labov et al. 2006), and the TVS (Labov 1991; Fridland et al. 2016, 2017) is represented by the rightmost quadrilateral.

The extent of ambient variation in the region provides ample opportunity for adolescent identity work. For example, it is possible that incoming supra-local variants associated with the TVS may be associated with overt prestige so that elementary school children might prefer lowered front lax vowels, while adolescents might prefer variants associated with AAL. This pattern would align with Deser's (1990) observations about PRIZE glide-weakening and life stage variation in Detroit and would pattern with many of the morphosyntactic variants described in Chapter 3. It is possible that children increment ongoing

---

[5] Koops (2010), for example, illustrates that traditional Southern GOOSE fronting is more monophthongal, while GOOSE fronting associated with new non-Southern migration tends to be more diphthongal. A similar pattern is likely true for the Research Triangle, as both have been impacted by non-Southern migration.

sound changes as they age, so that the incoming TVS might progress incrementally across time points, leading to monotonic patterns of change. This
pattern would support Labov's (2001) hypothesis that adolescents advance
sound change. Or, as found in Rickford and Price (2013), these variants may
not show predictable patterns at all, indicating that lifespan change targets
specific components of the linguistic system, rather than the full system.

4.4   Methods

To analyze social variation across childhood, it is necessary to understand the
ways in which development impacts speech during this time. Luckily, advances
in acoustic analyses as well as imaging techniques provide insight into how
changes to the vocal tract impact acoustic correlates of speech across childhood
and adolescence (Fitch and Giedd 1999; Vorperian and Kent 2007; Vorperian
et al. 2011; Hodge 2013; Markova et al. 2016), and practical guides to working
with child acoustic data are now more readily available (Khattab and Roberts
2011; Kohn and Farrington 2017). Although the phonological system reaches
adult-like dimension early, different phonetic components of vowel production
reach adult-like levels at distinct times, with most variables matching adult
levels around puberty. As shown in Chapter 2, vowel space areas tend to reach
adult-like values between ages 10 and 14 (see also Lee et al. 1999; Pettinato
et al. 2016; Kohn and Farrington 2017). Vowel duration reaches adult-like
levels roughly in the same time period around age 11 (Lee et al. 1999).

The maturational trajectory for formants is a bit more complex, as different
components of the vowel space display distinct paths of change. Further,
developmental paths vary by gender. Both longitudinal (Kohn and Farrington
2017) and cross-sectional research (Lee et al. 1999; Vorperian and Kent 2007)
confirm independent trajectories of change for F1 and F2 values, with the most
extreme change occurring in the F2 of front vowels and the F1 of low vowels.
These changes are most dramatic between ages 10 and 14, particularly for
males who undergo the descent of the larynx during puberty. In other words, the
vowel space shifts over childhood, with retraction occurring most rapidly for
the bottom and front of the vowel space (see Figure 2.2 from Chapter 2).[6]

While child acoustic data requires that researchers proceed with caution,
most acoustic differences that result from physical development can be
controlled using normalization techniques (Kohn and Farrington 2012). In
studies of adult populations, differences in the overall size and shape of
vowel spaces must be controlled through normalization to facilitate

---

[6] Khattab and Roberts (2011) provide an excellent overview of not only working with child data,
but also approaches to the acoustic analysis of child speech. See Story (2016) for new innovative
approaches for acoustic analysis of very young child speech.

statistical analysis and control of variation attributed to physiological differences across speakers. Longitudinal studies of childhood and adolescence are no different, with distinctions between pre-pubescent and post-pubescent age groups that are reminiscent of size and shape concerns found in adult populations. Specifically, female vowel spaces tend to be more dispersed, particularly for the front and low portion of the vowel space, while male vowel spaces are smaller. Thus, both developmental comparisons and comparisons across gender must account for differences in size and shape of the vowel space. As such, it is unsurprising that normalization techniques which perform well on adult data also perform well in child and adult comparisons (Kohn and Farrington 2012). However, it may be difficult for children under the age of six to be included in acoustic analyses due to a double whammy – increased variance in production and smaller vocabularies (Khattab and Roberts 2011). In addition, Linear Predictive Coding (LPC) analysis, a technique commonly used to estimate formant structure, may be less accurate as the risk of aliasing increases as pitch rises (Rodríguez and Lleida 2009; Rahman and Shimamura 2005).

With these considerations in mind, all data examined in this chapter was normalized using Lobanov (1971) z-score normalization, and the analysis is restricted to four time points from middle childhood to early adulthood: approximately ages 10, 14, 16, and 20. Formant values were semiautomatically extracted using a Praat script that allowed the researchers to hand-adjust vowel boundaries and to alter formant settings. This method is preferred to automatic extraction for child data, as the researcher must use caution to make sure that higher pitches do not lead to aliasing. Further, current automatic extraction programs have not been tested on child speech. To maintain consistency, vowels were extracted using the same methods, regardless of age. Between ten and twenty tokens of stressed vowels between obstruents (unless otherwise specified) were collected for each speaker/time point for each of the vowel classes considered in this chapter.

4.5   Participants

As described in Kohn (2014), speakers and the time points from which the sample derives were selected for recording quality. For example, participants with missing time points or damaged recordings were avoided. Age 6 data were excluded due to speed distortions that would impact acoustic analysis, as well as concerns about the effectiveness of normalization for this group. The participants' sex, age at each time point, and occupation at the last contact are listed in Table 4.1. Additionally, the percentages of African American students in their schools are listed for each time point. These school

Table 4.1 School demographic profile for participants in vowel study

	Sex	4th grade Age 10	%AA	8th grade Age 14	%AA	10th grade Age 16	%AA	Post-high school Age 20	%AA	Occupation as of 2012
K256	M	10.3	**19.8**	14.3	**18**	17.3	**16**	21.7	**16**	Military
K268	F	9.8	18	14.0	19	16.1	14	20.0	14	Community College
K269	M	9.8	21	14.0	26	16.1	17	20.0	17	College
K274	F	9.8	25	14.1	21	16.1	14	20.0	14	HBCU (non-local)
K275	M	9.3	22	13.8	25	15.8	58	20.6	58	Working (non-local)
K280	M	9.8	42	14.1	73	16.2	29	19.7	29	Community College
1001	F	10.1	20	14.0	18	17.1	16	20.9	16	Working (non-local)
1003	M	10.6	87	14.9	77	16.9	84	20.9	84	Employed, Associates Degree
1015	M	11.2	98	15.4	60	17.4	39	20.5	39	Community College
1025	M	9.9	69	14.1	48	16.2	78	20.1	78	HBCU
1035	F	10.1	88	14.3	76	16.5	89	20.4	89	Working
1057	M	10.4	56	14.7	56	16.5	96	20.1	96	Working
1058	F	9.6	54	14.0	55	15.9	78	20.0	78	HBCU
1061	F	10.2	15	14.5	20	16.5	23	19.4	23	College, non-local
1062	F	9.3	26	13.7	25	15.7	14	18.6	14	HBCU, non-local
1070	F	10.4	74	14.7	76	16.8	78	19.7	78	Trade school graduate, working
1072	F	10.6	99	14.6	61	16.6	76	20.1	76	Working
1075	M	10.3	80	14.6	22	17.5	15	19.5	15	Looking for work
1078	F	10.3	34	14.7	56	16.7	89	19.6	89	HBCU
1085	M	9.9	43	15.2	61	17.1	53	19.6	53	Community college, non-local
Mean		10.1		14.4		16.5		20.1		
St. Dev.		0.449844		0.458652		0.553352		0.664727		

demographics vary widely, from 14 percent to 98 percent African American.[7] This variation is partly due to the fact that participants grew up in different communities within the Raleigh-Durham-Chapel Hill metro region. For example, although located only twelve miles apart, Durham and Chapel Hill have very different demographic profiles. Durham is a mid-sized city of 233,252 individuals, of whom 41 percent are African American, 37.9 percent are European American, and 14.2 percent are Hispanic. Chapel Hill is a town of 58,011 individuals, of whom 9.7 percent are African American, 69.5 percent are European American, and 6.4 percent are Hispanic (2011 US Census Bureau). Community and neighborhood demographics are often intimately tied to school demographics in the United States (Benjamin 2012), and these communities are no exception. As such, children who attend majority-minority schools are much more likely to live in majority-minority neighborhoods. Because schools reflect neighborhood demographics, and because social networks are often constrained by such spatial considerations, these numbers likely correlate with social network demographics as well.

While school demographics and community were not considered in participant selection, these variables emerged as highly predictive of variation observed in the data, and thus became a central part of our analysis.

4.6   Vowel Patterns across Childhood

Figure 4.2 displays normalized vowel means for two speakers at approximately age 10, 14, 16, and 20. Speaker K268, on top, attended Chapel Hill schools throughout her public education. Speaker 1078, below, attended public schools in Durham for the entirety of her education, enrolling in and attending an HBCU in Durham. The vowel spaces of these two FPG participants reflect the linguistic context of the communities in which they grew up, with K268 producing lowered DRESS and TRAP classes and fronting GOOSE. These variants all align with the TVS associated with predominantly European American migration as described in Raleigh by Dodsworth and Kohn (2012). 1078, on the other hand, variably raises the TRAP and DRESS class, does not front GOAT, and has minimal GOOSE fronting. As discussed earlier, these variants have been widely attested in many predominantly African American communities (Thomas 2007).

These normalized vowel spaces provide the opportunity to look beyond developmental trends illustrated in Chapter 2 to identify whether patterns of age grading or the progression of language change can be identified within the vowel system. 1078 and K268 illustrate not only regional variation reflecting the demographic makeup of their communities (discussed subsequently), but

---

[7] All school demographic information was retrieved from the "Statistical Profile" available from the Public Schools of North Carolina website, www.ncpublicschools.org/fbs/resources/data/

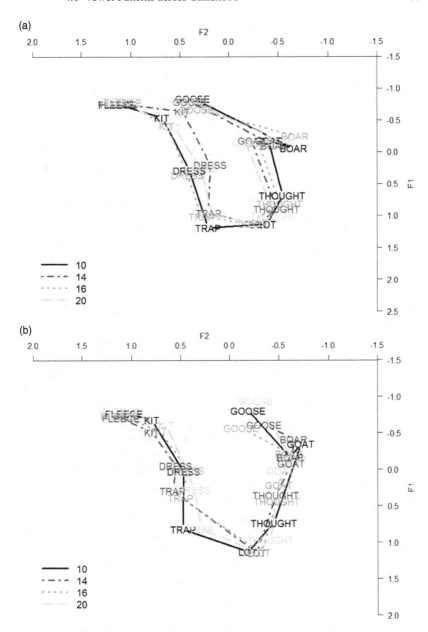

Figure 4.2 Speaker K268 from Chapel Hill and Speaker 1078 from Durham at four age points. Cardinal vowels represent median values for each vowel class

also distinct trajectories of change that vary according to vowel class. For example, speaker K268 displays increased backing of the KIT and DRESS classes at age 14, perhaps representing a peaking pattern for an incoming sound change, but is remarkably stable, overall. Notably, in the post-high school time point, this participant describes her voice as, "[S]o White. Like so articulate," perhaps reflecting her consistent participation in the incoming sound change found among White communities in the area. While K268 discusses noticing family and friends who speak differently from her, and while she describes changing her tone of voice, vocabulary, and articulation in different settings, the vowel system she uses in the context of the Frank Porter Graham Project is remarkably stable across time points.

Speaker 1078, on the other hand, demonstrates a peaking pattern for TRAP, with the vowel class lowered at ages 10 and 20. As retracted TRAP is an incoming middle-class supra-regional variant, this pattern might reflect an alignment towards more overtly prestigious variants during middle childhood and adulthood. A similar pattern can be observed for THOUGHT with a lowered variant at ages 10 and 14, perhaps aligning with the TVS. While speaker 1078 also stayed in the same community throughout her participation in the project, she discusses several life experiences in her post-high school interview that may explain her more dynamic vowel space. She clearly recalls that when she entered high school, her newly adopted role as a volunteer with public speaking responsibilities became a motivating factor for her to code-switch. In her high school interviews, she discusses actively restructuring her friendship groups at this stage in her life. This participant recalls teachers expressing surprise over her linguistic aptitude at switching, illustrating that 1078 might not just have the motivation to modify her speech over time, but also the skill to make larger changes to her system. Overall, 1078 appears more dynamic across time periods, when compared with K268.

Like morphosyntactic patterns identified in Chapter 3, these examples illustrate that there is more than one trajectory across childhood for FPG children. Yet, as shown here, the vowel system stands out as no one dominant trend emerges for the group. Instead, stability and patterns of idiosyncratic fluctuation dominate. For example, Figure 4.3 displays normalized mean values for the TRAP class from age 10 to age 20, for our twenty longitudinal speakers. Some trajectories appear quite flat. Many show change from at least one time point to another, but these patterns do not reveal group trends.

4.6.1   Systemwide patterns

To consider group patterns of change, we constructed Loess curves with 95 percent confidence intervals for normalized F1 and F2 midpoints, across the four age points considered here, and plotted them over individual vowel tokens used to construct the Loess curves (Figures 4.4 through 4.6). These

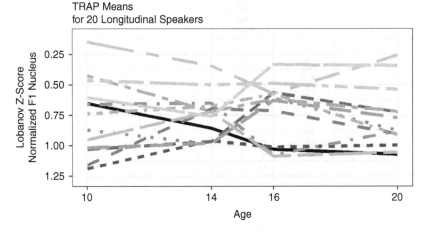

Figure 4.3 Mean values for normalized F1 midpoints of TRAP across four
time points for twenty longitudinal speakers

figures are striking when compared to similar figures for the DDM in
Chapter 3. Specifically, these Loess curves demonstrate remarkable group
stability across the four time points under consideration, even as individual
vowel tokens presented in the scatter plots demonstrate wide pockets of
variation. As we will show later in this chapter, these wide pockets of
variation correlate with school and community demographics rather than
group change. While some participants clearly do modify their vowels as
they age, as demonstrated in Figure 4.3, these modifications appear idiosyncratic, producing few meaningful group-level effects, and often only affecting a handful of vowel classes per speaker. Similar to findings from Rickford
and Price (2013), the vowel systems for these FPG participants simply do
not show predictable patterns of age grading.

Statistical analysis confirms most of these initial results. To consider group
patterns of change, we constructed mixed model hierarchical regressions with
normalized F1 and F2 values as the dependent variable for each vowel class. As
discussed in previous chapters, we took care to model the nonindependent
nature of between-speaker measures by including a random slope for time and
a random intercept for speaker, essentially modeling growth curves for each
speaker (Singer and Willett 2003). Independent variables considered in model
construction included duration, phonetic environment, formality of the interview task, sex, community, and age. Interactions between sex, age, and community were also considered in model selection. Simpler models were

(a)   F1 Front Monophthongal Midpoints
       for 20 Longitudinal Speakers

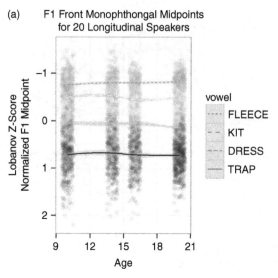

(b)   F2 Front Monophthongal Midpoints
       for 20 Longitudinal Speakers

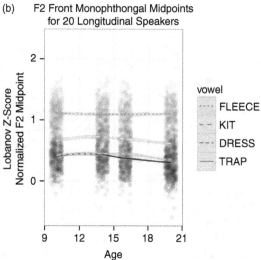

Figure 4.4 Midpoint values for front monophthongs with Loess curves fitted across four time points.

compared to more complex models using likelihood ratio tests that use the analysis of variance function in R to arrive at the best model for each vowel class/formant dimension. Surprisingly, the sex variable only improved the model considered for GOAT F1. The community variable improved the

Table 4.2 *Estimates and t-values for the front monophthongs*

Vowel F1	8th	10th	PHS	Vowel F2	8th	10th	PHS	n
KIT	−.02	.04	.05	KIT	.05	.00	−.04	1490
t	*−.45*	*1.10*	*1.12*	*t*	*1.47*	*.18*	*−1.08*	
DRESS	.01	.01	.09	DRESS	.06	.02	−.01	1207
t	*.29*	*.24*	*2.78*	*t*	*1.57*	*.44*	*−.34*	
TRAP	−.05	−.06	.04	TRAP	.03	−.01	−.09	1401
t	*−.92*	*−.83*	*.86*	*t*	*1.04*	*−.36*	*2.69*	

model for over half the vowel dimensions considered, but an interaction between community and age only improved the model for GOOSE F2. As such, the inclusion of community explains variance in the data, but does not reveal community-internal group patterns of change across time (Kohn 2014). In order to test for adolescent peaks, age was considered as a factor in all models, with the comparison level set at age 10. This allowed us to test whether any subsequent age groups differed from age 10, without assuming linear change. Full details for model selection are available in Kohn (2014).

After adjusting for multiple tests using Bonferroni correction,[8] the only changes that reached the threshold for significance were a pattern of lowering for the nucleus of the FACE class (age 14: t-value = 3.10, age 16: t-value = 3.31, age 20: t-value = 3.58) and an age-graded pattern of fronting for the LOT class (age 14: t-value = 3.6, age 16: t-value 3.4, age 20: t-value = 1.2), though with notably smaller effects sizes. The pattern for FACE would be consistent with incremental sound change from pre-adolescence and across adolescence. However, such a sound change is currently unattested in the region. It is entirely possible that FACE lowering may be a novel sound change, but more evidence would be needed to confirm this hypothesis. Fronted LOT, on the other hand, has been associated with the AAVS (Thomas 2007). This pattern could be interpreted as an age-graded pattern, similar to the vernacular AAL

---

[8] Ten vowel classes were considered on two dimensions, resulting in twenty tests. Bonferroni correction limits the chance of type 1 errors for multiple tests by dividing the p-value threshold by the number of analyses. In this case, assuming an original *p*-value threshold of .05, the new adjusted threshold is .0025. Age dimensions that reached significance before correction include DRESS F1 PHS estimate = 0.09**, t =2.78, FACE F1 8th estimate = .11** t=3.10, 10th estimate = .14** t=3.31, PHS estimate =.15***, t = 3.58, FOOT F1 PHS estimate = .12** t =2.88, GOAT F1 PHS estimate .10*, t =2.11. TRAP F2 estimate PHS -.09**, t = −2.69, FOOT F2 8th grade estimate = .10*, t = 2.27, and LOT F2 8th estimates = .08, t = 3.6*** and 10th grade estimates = .08***, t =3.4. Full models are reported in Kohn (2014). It is notable that PHS was most likely to differ from the age 10 time point, while only FOOT and LOT F2 show a pattern consistent with age-grading.

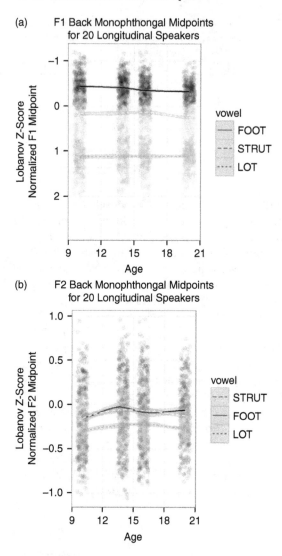

Figure 4.5 Midpoint values for the mid and back monophthongs

morphosyntactic features discussed in Chapter 3. It is striking, though, that only one vowel implicated in the AAVS shows this pattern.

With the exception of FACE and LOT, the remaining results are consistent with findings from Rickford and Price's (2013) case study in which two African

Table 4.3 *Estimates and t-values for the mid and back monophthongs*

Vowel F1	8th	10th	PHS	Vowel F2	8th	10th	PHS	n
FOOT	.03	.07	.12	FOOT	.10	.04	.01	1104
t	*.08*	*1.83*	*2.88*	*t*	*2.27*	*1.12*	*−.15*	
STRUT	−.01	−.02	.10	STRUT	.05	.00	−.04	1074
t	*−.23*	*−.32*	*1.67*	*t*	*1.47*	*.18*	*−1.08*	
LOT	.03	.00	.03	LOT	.08	.08	.03	989
t	*.74*	*.03*	*.78*	*t*	*3.6*	*3.4*	*1.2*	

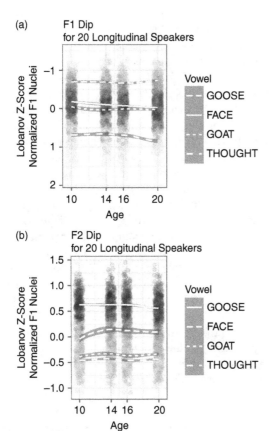

Figure 4.6 Nucleus values for the diphthongs

Table 4.4 *Estimates and t-values for the diphthongs*

Vowel F1	8th	10th	PHS	Vowel F2	8th	10th	PHS	n
FACE	.11	.14	.15	FACE	−.02	−.04	−.04	1480
t	*3.10*	*3.31*	*3.58*	*t*	*−.54*	*−1.43*	*1.42*	
GOOSE	.03	.04	−.01	GOOSE	−.02	.11	.03	857
t	*.66*	*.82*	*−.91*	*t*	*−.19*	*1.32*	*.27*	
GOAT	.08	.05	.10	GOAT	.05	.03	.03	973
t	*1.75*	*.88*	*2.11*	*t*	*1.55*	*.72*	*1.01*	
THOUGHT	−.1	−.08	.08	THOUGHT	.02	−.02	−.01	972
t	*−1.33*	*−1.11*	*1.29*	*t*	*1.1*	*−1.04*	*−.53*	

American youth underwent massive change for morphosyntactic variables but showed little change for the vowel system from the teen years through their mid-30s. It would also, upon first glance, appear to undermine Labov's (2001) hypothesis that adolescents advance sound change as few of these adolescents appear to advance the incoming TVS found among European American populations in Raleigh (Dodsworth and Kohn 2012). Yet, we argue that our data does not refute this hypothesis. Rather, the linguistic context of the Research Triangle is not appropriate for studying the advancement of sound change. Specifically, the vowel systems present in the region appear to be stable or stabilizing. The AAVS appears remarkably stable across generations in this region (Kohn 2014), and the TVS appears to be stabilizing among European Americans, with its largest increment occurring in the early 1960s (Dodsworth and Kohn 2012). As of the 1980s, this system was already quite advanced, with the youngest generations showing a "leveling off of linguistic change" (Dodsworth and Benton 2017: 398). Given that most of our participants were born in 1990, this particular set of sound changes was likely to be slowing or coming to completion during their adolescent years. If this change is slowing, then incremental change among adolescents is expected to slow, if not halt (Labov 2001; Tagliamonte and D'Arcy 2009; Brook et al. 2018). Effectively, there are no ongoing sound changes related to the three vowel systems (AAVS, SVS, and TVS), that we are currently aware of, for these adolescents to advance in the Research Triangle where this study took place.

While this linguistic context makes it challenging to study the ways in which adolescents increment sound change, it provides a unique opportunity to study how children and adolescents modify their vowel spaces in a stable linguistic environment. From this we can learn what kinds of variation may be anticipated across childhood and adolescence, when sound change is not a complicating factor. In other words, do adolescents restructure their vowel system as part of the ongoing identity work associated with this life stage, in the absence of community change? Our research indicates that adolescent peaks are not a de facto aspect of youth language, reflective of potentially age-graded adolescent linguistic identity construction. Unlike the socially salient morphosyntactic variables discussed in Chapter 3, adolescents, as a group, are not modifying their vowel classes in predictable ways as they transition toward adulthood. Some individuals, such as speaker K268, remain remarkably stable, while others show idiosyncratic shifts and ticks that may speak more of individual style or other factors that lend to intra-speaker variation. Broader group processes for the vowel system, however, are not apparent in the community under analysis. As discussed subsequently, this observation holds important implications for the interpretation of adolescent peaks, when such peaks do appear for vowel data.

4.6.2 A Salient Exception: The PRIZE Class

Quite a different pattern emerges for the diphthong found in the PRIZE class, an iconic variable that differs from the previous vowel classes due to its salience (Anderson 2002; Plichta and Preston 2005; Reed 2016), and because it may currently be a target for community-wide change within some African American communities (Anderson 2002; Wolfram and Thomas 2002; Fridland 2003). The PRIZE class is canonically diphthongal in many varieties of American English, meaning that the vowel consists of two targets, with substantial tongue movement during the course of the vowel. In many varieties of English, this vowel starts in a low position at the nucleus, around /a/, and transitions to a high front position, around /ɪ/ or /i/, producing a front-raised glide from the nucleus. AAL and European American Southern English are known for reducing the glide of this vowel class in open syllables and before voiced consonants (Thomas 2001). These varieties thus show less overall tongue movement for the PRIZE class, producing a full monophthong such as /aː/ or a weaker offglide such as /aᵋ/. However, a change in progress has been observed in some African American communities in which glide-weakening is spreading into pre-voiceless conditions (i.e., PRICE) (Anderson 2002; Wolfram and Thomas 2002; Fridland 2003). The PRIZE class thus provides an opportunity to examine a variable that is both salient and potentially undergoing a change in progress.

Because we are interested in the extent to which glide-weakening occurs, the relevant variable for analysis is the amount of formant movement between the nucleus and the glide of the vowel, a measure that can be described by calculating Vector Lengths (VL) for tokens of PRIZE/PRICE. We calculated VL by finding the Euclidian Distance between the normalized F1 and F2 measures at the 25 percent time point from the beginning of the vowel and 75 percent from the beginning of the vowel, following the methods of Fox and

Table 4.5 *Mean and standard deviation for VL in the* PRICE *set for ages 10–20 for 1,157 tokens*

Age	10 (4th grade)	14 (8th grade)	16 (10th grade)	20 (post-high school)
Mean PRIZE	**.63**	**.62**	**.59**	**.46**
St. Dev.	*.53*	*.49*	*.40*	*.40*
Mean PRICE	**1.19**	**0.97**	**0.89**	**.99**
St. Dev.	*.58*	*.53*	*.44*	*.52*

Jacewicz (2009) and Farrington, Kendall, and Fridland (2018). Table 4.5 presents means and standard deviations separately for the PRICE and PRIZE class (also plotted in Figure 4.7). Larger VL rates correspond to longer, more diphthongal vowels. Notably, the PRICE class is almost twice as long as the PRIZE class at the age 10 and 20 time points, following traditional allophonic patterns observed for AAL. The PRIZE class is remarkably stable across ages 10, 14, and 16, with a slight decline, indicative of shorter glides, in the post-high school interview.

In contrast, there appears to be substantial change in the VL for pre-voiceless conditions – the conditions that traditionally favor glide retention. To examine change over time, we constructed hierarchical models for PRICE and PRIZE vowels at ages 10, 14, 16, and 20, including duration and preceding place of articulation, and with speaker as a random intercept and age as a random slope. Four hundred and nineteen tokens were included in the PRICE model, and 738 tokens were included in the PRIZE model. Age 10 was set as the reference point for statistical analysis. Age significantly improved the model for both vowel classes. For PRIZE, the age effect is primarily driven by the shorter glides at the age 20 time point (age 14 estimate: -.01, t = -.14; age 16 estimate: -.05, t=-.71, age 20 estimate: -.18, t=-2.68): FPG participants are more likely to use the traditional weakly glided AAL variant at the post-high school time point, despite its salience, even as participants are simultaneously curtailing their use of AAL morphosyntactic variants (see Chapter 3). This pattern may speak to a general trend in which AAL phonetic variants – specifically vowels – are less subject to stigma or hold different indexical values compared with morphosyntactic AAL variants (Wolfram 1969; Nguyen 2006; Farrington 2012; Britt and Weldon 2015). These variables may be associated with ethnicity, without the class associations that many morphosyntactic AAL variants hold (Jones and Preston 2011; Spears 2015). As such, participants may feel little need to curtail their use of these variables as they enter the workplace, or may even intensify use of such variables to index an upwardly mobile African American identity. Indeed, the slight uptick in glide reduction could represent a trade-off in which participants turn to this vowel variable for stylistic purposes as they turn away from morphosyntactic variables.

In contrast to PRIZE, results for PRICE are consistent with age-grading. Longer glides are present both at age 10 and age 20, while the innovative shorter variant is more apparent during the teen years (age 14 estimate: -.19, t = −2.11; 16 estimate: -.32, t = −3.37; 20 estimate: -.05, t = −0.47). This pattern is intriguing, as it appears to align more closely with patterns observed in morphosyntactic variables than those observed among the vowel classes considered in this chapter. Morphosyntactic variants observed in Chapter 3 also tended to progress in a u-shape, with more vernacular forms becoming more widespread during the adolescent years. In other words, similar to the LOT class, PRICE glide-weakening is behaving more like a vernacular AAL morphosyntactic variant than an AAL vocalic variant.

To explore these patterns further, we expanded the time span for analysis. Figure 4.7 displays VL separately for the phonological conditions that favor glide-weakening (PRIZE class representing pre-voiced and open syllable positions) and those that do not (PRICE class representing pre-voiceless conditions). This figure includes some supplemental data for ten speakers from when they were four years old. Results should be taken with caution due to the smaller subsample and potential issues with normalization. As such, we limit ourselves to a qualitative analysis of these data. Still, this expanded age range allows for some speculation about the role that middle childhood may play in advancing sound change. Changes to the PRIZE class appear small, despite the significant drop at the post-high school time point. Additional data from age 4 suggests that younger children conform most strongly to the more traditional phonological patterns observed in AAL.

In Figure 4.7, notched boxplots present VL values for twenty speakers at ages 10, 14, 16, and 20. The VL for an additional ten speakers at age 4 is included as a supplemental comparison. This figure provides additional insight into trends for PRICE over time. Instead of appearing as a purely age-graded phenomenon, the pattern now suggests a change over the lifespan, with a slight retraction at the post-high school time point. While the youngest age group conforms to the traditional allophonic patterning, teens appear to be doing something different, advancing the less-glided variant of the PRICE class. The ten-year-olds fall in between, perhaps suggesting that they are in the process of incrementing the new sound change, moving towards more teenlike production levels as they age.

Why would the PRIZE class stand out in this analysis? We consider two possible explanations: salience and language change. PRIZE glide-weakening is iconically salient in Southern English; although, as we describe later, saliency alone may be insufficient to explain patterns observed here. PRIZE glide-weakening has iconic associations and is often

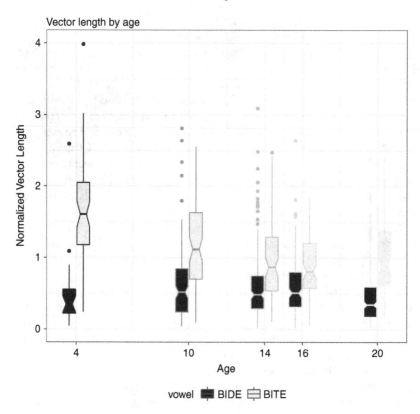

Figure 4.7 Extended age comparison for PRIZE and PRICE vowel glide weakening

imitated, marking it as a stereotype of Southern speech (Plichta and Preston 2005; Reed 2016). Perhaps as a result, this variable does have an orthographic representation, appearing in Southern dictionaries and often portrayed as <ah> for <i> or <y>, as in <North Carolahna> for *North Carolina*, thus further raising the saliency of this variable (Reed 2016). Yet, saliency fails to explain why change is most dramatic for the pre-voiceless condition – the condition least likely to be reduced in Southern dialects for both African Americans and European Americans. Why would change be most dramatic precisely in the position where monophthongization is least likely to occur?

Traditionally, AAL has been described as a variety that preserves glides in pre-voiceless conditions, even as some varieties of White Southern English, including Appalachian English and some European American varieties in

Texas, show a relatively recent advancement of glide-weakening into this condition (Thomas 2001, 2007). However, this pattern may be changing (Anderson 2002; Wolfram and Thomas 2002; Fridland 2003). Fridland (2003) observed that glide-weakening in pre-voiceless conditions was more common among African Americans than European Americans, in her study of Memphis Southern English, around the turn of the century. As glide-weakening in this environment was not reported in the Linguistic Atlas of the Gulf States (LAGS) (Pederson et al. 1981), Fridland concluded that this sound change likely represents a recent development. Similar patterns have been observed in Detroit, where Anderson (2002) found substantial glide-weakening before voiceless obstruents among younger speakers, in stark contrast to data collected by Wolfram (1969) more than thirty years earlier.[9] Finally, Wolfram and Thomas (2002) found a lowering trend for PRICE glides in Hyde County, North Carolina, over apparent time. While more work needs to be done, these results suggest that PRICE glide-weakening may be a change in progress that is occurring among some regional varieties of AAL.

When the results reported on PRICE are put in conversation with a real-time study in which a change in progress is well-documented, we find support for cross-sectional studies that interpret adolescent peaks as evidence that adolescents progress sound change (Labov 2001). In the United Kingdom, Holmes-Elliott (2018) conducted a two-time point panel study of thirteen young speakers of Hastings English. This variety shows a documented change in progress that GOOSE is progressively fronting, across generations. An apparent-time study of this community reveals the familiar adolescent peak for this sound change. Importantly, the panel study demonstrates that twelve of thirteen adolescents in the study had a more fronted GOOSE class at the second time point, collected around age thirteen to fifteen years, when compared to the first time point collected between ages nine and eleven. These results indicate that the youth each incremented the sound change within their idiolect. Further, this change only occurred in environments favoring the change, so the GHOUL class remained unaffected (Holmes-Elliott 2018). Notably, this variable showed little to no style-shifting, and was below the level of consciousness.

The comparison between Hastings's GOOSE fronting and FPG PRICE glide-weakening offers support for the hypothesis that children and adolescents modify vowel pronunciations that are undergoing change in their communities. Further, when a sound change is present, researchers may need to look beyond the teens to identify the source of this change. FPG youth show a dramatic

---

[9] Deser's (1990) reanalysis of Wolfram's (1969) Detroit data found that pre-adolescent children had less glide-weakening for PRIZE than the teenaged cohort in the study. However, it is difficult to draw conclusions based on these data, as the study did not control for phonological environment.

decrease in their PRICE glide between ages 4 and 10. This pattern may suggest that children get the ball rolling on sound change. Their adolescent peers may show a lead, but the actual process of change may initiate earlier than previously suggested. Clearly, these earlier age groups deserve more attention.

However, the FPG data reveals that this process is not a default adolescent behavior. If vowels in the community are stable or stabilizing, adolescents may have little reason to modify this aspect of their speech. Even as the PRIZE/PRICE class underwent longitudinal change, other potentially salient vowels in the community did not. For example, variation in back vowels within the region offer the opportunity for adolescent identity work; and such identity work may be occurring for some individuals in this study. Yet, if this identity work is occurring, it is not widespread enough to develop into group patterns. The same is true for the front lax vowel system that so recently underwent change in the community. Idiosyncratic changes may occur, but widespread group level patterns are not common. This observation is key in defending Labov's (2001) assertion that adolescent peaks in apparent-time data reflect individuals progress a sound change. Stylistic variation and age-grading may be associated with adolescence, but such patterns are not widespread in the data analyzed here.

4.7   Vowel Variation and School Segregation

Group stability masks extensive variation as seen earlier. In this section, we consider the connection between this variability and school demographics. Given the sheer amount of time students spend in school, it is unsurprising that this institution has a large impact on social networks. One student in the study commented about his classmates, "you're around school people like seven hours a day, so you get to know them very well" (K256, Grade 8, Chapel Hill). Indeed, schools are the most common source of friendship for school-aged youth in the United States (Thomas 2019). Beyond friendships, schools are also likely to foster the kinds of weak ties frequently hypothesized to influence linguistic behavior (Milroy 1980; Milroy and Milroy 1985, 1992; Dodsworth and Benton 2017). As Dodsworth and Benton note, "[s]hared school attendance does not, of course, guarantee that two people talked to one another, but it does suggest repeated exposure to many of the same people and sociolinguistic norms during childhood and adolescence" (2017: 382). For speaker K256, a student who attended predominantly European American schools his entire life, it would be reasonable to assume that part of those seven hours a day included exposure to European American varieties of English. The sheer amount of contact afforded in the school environment is thus likely to influence child and adolescent language. While schools were not a variable included in initial participant selection, we quickly came to realize that many of the patterns emerging in our data showed at least some correlation with this institution.

The social ecology of US schools reflects broader social structures within the context of the United States. US school districts are often based on neighborhoods, so social contacts within neighborhoods frequently attend the same schools, as well.[10] As discussed earlier, since segregation, due to historical and contemporary social structures, continues to shape the face of American neighborhoods, US schools, to variable degrees, also reflect embedded segregation in our society. In Durham, roughly 60 percent of students attend schools assigned by geographic considerations, and those who opt out of assigned schools typically attend schools that intensify ethnic homophily, when compared to their district neighborhood (Bifulco et al. 2008). As such, despite the influences of Brown versus Board of Education, schools in the United States remain sites of segregation, in many districts. So, for example, speaker 1035 attended majority-African American schools her entire life, with African American students ranging from 76 to 89 percent of her school population. Speaker 1072 attended an elementary school that was almost entirely composed of African American students, at 99 percent of the school population. For these Durham participants, school environments recapitulate or intensify racial segregation found in their neighborhoods, exposing them to a linguistic ecology that would necessarily be quite distinct from the one experienced by speaker K256, twelve miles away in Chapel Hill. It is thus unsurprising that childhood friendships formed within school contexts tend to show greater racial homophily than those formed in workplaces later in life, as workplaces in the United States tend to be less racially segregated than our educational system (Thomas 2019). While friendship interactions characteristic of childhood and adolescent peer groups are often thought of as agentive, these broader institutional contexts place constraints on both friendship choices and casual interactions. Such constraints may influence or shape patterns of life stage and/or ethnic variation.

Given the importance of school contexts on child and adolescent friendships, network structures, and linguistic exposure, we ask what the relationship is between school demographics and vowel variation across the lifespan. Figure 4.8 displays normalized values for the F1 of the front lax vowels for twenty speakers at ages 10, 14, and 16, or roughly grades 4, 8, and 10. These values are plotted against the proportion of African American students in the schools that each speaker attended in the school year preceding the date when the utterance was collected. A clear pattern emerges. Students who attended predominantly

---

[10] Indeed, Dodsworth and Benton (2017) use school as a proxy for neighborhood, when examining the influence of network ties on the loss of the SVS in Raleigh, North Carolina.

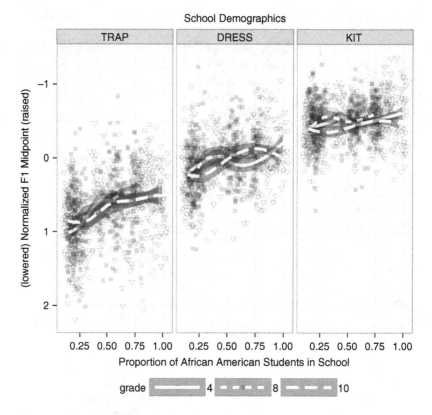

Figure 4.8 Pronunciation of front lax vowels for each speaker arranged in order of school demographics at the elementary (age 10); middle school (age 14); and high school (age 16) time point. Image from Kohn (2014: 96)

European American schools tend to produce lowered front lax vowels, while those who attended predominantly African American schools tend to produce more raised front lax vowels. This pattern is so strong that the TRAP class produced by participants in majority-African American schools is almost indistinguishable from the DRESS class produced by students in majority-European American schools. In other words, the students who are most likely to be exposed to the retracted variants found among European Americans in the region also produce more retracted front lax vowels, while those who attend majority-African American schools produce more raised variants that have been documented in a range of majority-African American communities throughout the South (Yaeger-Dror and Thomas 2009). Regression results confirm these observations for both the TRAP ($-.59$, $t = -5.6$***) and DRESS classes ($-.39$, $t = -5.22$***).[11]

Loess curves with 95 percent confidence intervals plotted for each grade illustrate that this correlation is consistent across grades, so the pattern holds true in elementary school, middle school, and high school. An interaction between grade and the proportion of African Americans in the school does not improve the goodness of fit for any of the regression models discussed previously, illustrating that the relationship between school demographics and vowel height is similar at each time point. This pattern can be at least partially explained by the fact that the majority of students in this sample attend schools with similar demographics at each time point. Given that cross-district segregation is frequently greater than within-district segregation, this pattern is likely to be common for many students in the United States (Fiel 2013).

Because school assignment is intertwined with neighborhood characteristics in the United States, it is difficult to assess the extent to which this pattern reflects the impact of communities or schools on speech. However, this pattern does provide clear evidence that segregation correlates with speech patterns across childhood and adolescence. Anecdotally, several of the FPG participants acknowledge the effect social contact at school has on their language. So, for example, speaker 1072, a female participant who grew up in Durham attending predominantly African American schools, reflected that her informal speech may be hard to understand for some, but "most people I hang around . . . would understand what I'm saying. Most of the people that I went to school with would. That's how I learned most of the talk – from school, you know."

While individual schools restrict friendship networks, school systems further reproduce geographic segregation (Fiel 2013). We examined the impact of district segregation by considering school district as a factor variable with three levels: Durham (participant n = 9), Chapel Hill (participant n = 5), and Other (participant n = 6). The majority of the students in this subsample spent the majority of their schooling within a school district, either Durham or Chapel Hill. The *Other* category captures students who were in primarily rural school district in the county as well as students who moved between multiple districts. This variable improved the goodness of fit for nine of the sixteen regression models considered in Kohn (2014). Notably, Durham participants had more raised and fronted front lax vowels, a more backed GOOSE class, and a more

---

[11] Models were constructed with speaker as a random intercept and grade as a random slope to account for the non-independent relationship of tokens produced by the same speaker over time (Singer and Willett 2003). Phonetic factors including vowel duration, preceding place of articulation, and formality of the elicitation task were included in each base model considered in the analysis. Grade, sex, and school demographics were also considered in model construction, with more complete models compared to less complete models with likelihood ratio tests, using the analysis of variance function in R. Full descriptions of models are available in Kohn (2014).

raised FOOT class when compared with Chapel Hill. So, students in the Durham Public School District, a predominantly African American district, produce vowels that are more consistent with observed patterns of the AAVS, when compared with students from Chapel Hill, a predominantly European American district. School districts capture a snapshot of community and school segregation. Such patterns of segregation become relevant for language use, even when comparing districts within the same metro area.

One critique of examining school segregation at the district or school level is that it may not represent the experience of individual students within classrooms. A major study of within-school segregation in North Carolina found that classroom segregation is not as relevant for primary schools as it is for secondary schools, while transitions from middle school to high school lead to increases in classroom segregation (Clotfelter, Ladd, and Vigdor 2003). These patterns suggest that, if anything, broader school demographics in more advanced grades underestimate racial homophily experienced by students, so research using these broader metrics offers conservative estimates of the impact of segregation on language use in the middle school and high school years.

More broadly, these kinds of structural patterns may influence linguistic behavior over the lifespan. For example, increased classroom segregation in middle school and high school may relate to increases in the use of AAL morphosyntactic forms observed in Chapter 3. Workplace segregation is less intense than segregation within schools. As such, friendship networks in adulthood are often more diverse than those experienced in childhood (Thomas 2019) and may similarly encourage changes in linguistic behavior. These observations further illustrate the importance of considering emerging adulthood as a critical life stage in linguistic development. Yet, as Section 4.4.1 illustrates, these structural changes may not equally impact all types of linguistic behavior as group-level patterns of change associated with transitions into and out of school institutions are not as apparent for vowel variation, when compared to socially salient morphosyntactic variation. In other words, differences between districts, previewed in our comparison of speakers K268 and 1078, explain quite a bit of variance in our vowel data, while age does not.

The extensive variation observed in Section 4.4, at least, partially, is explained by the distinct school experiences of each child, whether due to demographics of the school district, or due to the demographics of the individual schools attended by each child. These patterns provide critical evidence that in the United States, school demographics contribute to participation in regional and/or ethnic vowel systems. These patterns speak to broader concerns regarding the influence of segregation, in this case represented as an intertwining of school and neighborhood segregation, on intra-regional variation. This finding holds important implications as the impact of linguistic prejudice is well-known (Rickford and King 2016). Children who attend majority-minority schools, or schools in which the majority of the population are considered ethnic minorities within the United States, are more likely to have vowel systems that reflect the demographic makeup of their school. It also appears that adolescents are less likely to modify their vowel systems as they transition toward adulthood, when compared to socially salient morphosyntactic variants. Given evidence that suggests that listeners are savvy at identifying ethnicity using vowel information (Purnell et al. 1999), students who attend majority-minority schools in the United States are at high risk for becoming targets of linguistic discrimination. As efforts to desegregate schools have increasingly been dismantled (Reardon and Yun 2003), linguists should take calls to action to combat linguistic subordination and discrimination as the most urgent issue in the field to date.

4.8 Conclusion

Our analysis of the full vowel space allows us to conclude that the adolescents in the FPG study do not modify vowel pronunciations across the lifespan in the way that they do morphosyntactic variation. While group patterns were evident in Chapter 3 across both aggregate variables such as the DDM, as well as individual variables such as our consideration of copula absence and third-person singular -s absence, the same could not be said for the majority of the vowels analyzed here. Pockets of change, such as that identified for the PRICE class, suggest that vowel variants potentially implicated in community change are more likely to be modified by children and adolescents. This finding holds important implications for the interpretation of adolescent peaks, suggesting that children and adolescents do play a critical role in sound change (Labov 2001). If group-level patterns of stylization are not common for vowel variation, then researchers can feel more confident about interpreting adolescent peaks as evidence for individuals progressing community-wide change. This may be particularly true for less salient or less stigmatized variables, as such variables may play a smaller role in adolescent stylization.

Longitudinal studies benefit from the examination of a range of variables, as such analyses guard against the kinds of overly broad conclusions that may emerge when selective and/or highly salient variables are included in the analyses. Many of the components of the DDM include highly salient well-researched AAL morphosyntactic variants that showed group-level patterns of age-grading over time. Clearly, such patterns do not extend to the full linguistic system, as illustrated by our analysis of vowel variables. Whether due to issues such as linguistic plasticity or saliency, different linguistic subsystems may have vastly different patterns of development and change across the lifespan. When researchers include variables from a range of linguistic subsystems and with different levels of saliency, we can begin to tease apart the extent to which different components of the linguistic system undergo lifespan change and why.

We additionally found that variation in the vowel space correlated strongly with school demographics, once again illustrating the formative role schools play in child and adolescent language. When considering lifespan change, different institutions impact the social experience of each age group. Adults in the workforce, for example, experience more diversity than children in school as workplaces within the United States are less segregated than school systems (Thomas 2019). The intensification of segregation that children experience within the school system likely impacts their linguistic performance. And yet, at least for our students considered here, moving beyond these segregated institutions does not result in systematic patterns of change to the vowel system. Indeed, Kohn (2018) illustrates that at age 20, previous experience of school segregation still predicts participation in the AAVS. Entrance into a more diverse workplace is likely to be accompanied by changing levels of exposure to distinct speech varieties. It would only make sense that the combined forces of exposure and changing social identity would lead to changing linguistic behavior. Yet, whether due to issues of linguistic plasticity or to differences in indexical features, it appears that such changes do not impact vowels in the same way they do variables analyzed in the DDM.

While vowels illustrate a picture of group stability in the FPG Project, this stability provides a critical baseline for studies that examine language change across the lifespan in communities undergoing change. These results bolster the call to further examine youth and adolescent language in communities undergoing rapid sound change. Additionally, this work highlights the importance of considering emerging adulthood and middle childhood as life stages that are potentially critical to the advancement of sound change and the development of style. When considering the question of incremental change we must look beyond adolescent peaks to the uphill climb in childhood linguistic development.

References

Anderson, Bridget. 2002. Dialect leveling and /ai/ monophthongization among African American Detroiters. *Journal of Sociolinguistics* 6(1): 86–98.

Assmann, Peter, Santiago Barreda, and Terrance Nearey. 2013. Perception of speaker age in children's voices. *Proceedings of Meetings on Acoustics 19*(1): 060059.

Benjamin, Karen. 2012. Suburbanizing Jim Crow: The impact of school policy on residential segregation in Raleigh. *Journal of Urban History* 38(2): 225–246.

Bigham, Douglas S. 2010. Mechanisms of accommodation among emerging adults in a university setting. *Journal of English Linguistics.* 38(3): 193–210.

Bigham, Douglas S. 2012. Emerging adulthood in sociolinguistics. *Language and Linguistics Compass* 6(8): 533–544.

Bifulco, Robert, Helen F. Ladd, and Stephen L. Ross. 2009. Public school choice and integration evidence from Durham, North Carolina. *Social Science Research* 38(1): 71–85.

Bowie, David. 2000. *The Effect of Geographic Mobility on the Retention of a Local Dialect*. Ph.D. Dissertation. Philadelphia, PA: University of Pennsylvania.

Britt, Erica and Tracey Weldon. 2015. African American English in the middle class. In Sonja L. Lanehart (ed.), *The Oxford Handbook of African American Language*, 800–816. Oxford: Oxford University Press.

Brook, Marisa, Bridget L. Jankowski, Lex Konnelly, and Sali A. Tagliamonte. 2018. "I don't come off as timid anymore": Real-time change in early adulthood against the backdrop of the community. *Journal of Sociolinguistics* 22(4): 351–374.

Cartei, Valentina, Wind Cowles, Robin Banerjee, and David Reby. 2014. Control of voice gender in pre-pubertal children. *British Journal of Developmental Psychology* 32(1): 100–106.

Carter, Phillip. 2007. Phonetic variation and speaker agency: Mexicana identity in a North Carolina middle school. *University of Pennsylvania Working Papers in Linguistics* 13(2): 1–14.

Clotfelter, Charles T., Helen F. Ladd, and Jacob L. Vigdor. 2003. Segregation and resegregation in North Carolina's public school classrooms. *North Carolina Law Review* 81(4): 1463–1512.

Conn, Jeff and Uri Horesh. 2002. Assessing the acquisition of dialect variables by migrant adults in Philadelphia: A case study. *University of Pennsylvania Working Papers in Linguistics* 8(2): 47–57.

De Decker, Paul. 2006. A real-time investigation of social and phonetic changes in post-adolescence. *University of Pennsylvania Working Papers in Linguistics* 12(2): 65–76.

Deser, Toni. 1990. *Dialect Transmission and Variation: An Acoustic Analysis of Vowels in Six Urban Detroit Families*. Ph.D. dissertation. Boston, MA: Boston University.

Dodsworth, Robin and Richard, Benton. 2017. Social network cohesion and the retreat from Southern vowels in Raleigh. *Language in Society* 46(3): 371–405.

Dodsworth, Robin and Mary Kohn. 2012. Urban rejection of the vernacular: The SVS undone. *Language Variation and Change* 24(2): 221–245.

Eckert, Penelope. 1996. Vowels and nail polish: The emergence of linguistic style in the preadolescent heterosexual marketplace. In Natasha Warner (ed.), *Gender and Belief Systems: Proceedings of the Fourth Berkeley Women and Language Conference*, 183–190. Berkeley, CA: Berkeley Women and Language Group.

Evans, Bronwen and Paul Iverson. 2007. Plasticity in vowel perception and production: A study of accent change in young adults. *Journal of the Acoustical Society of America* 121(6): 3814–3826.

Farrington, Charlie. 2012. The social distribution of devoicing in urban southern African American English. Paper presented at *New Ways of Analyzing Variation* 41. Bloomington, IN, October.

Farrington, Charlie. 2019. *Language Variation and the Great Migration: Regionality and African American Language*. Ph.D. Dissertation. Eugene, OR: University of Oregon.

Farrington, Charlie, Tyler Kendall, and Valerie Fridland. 2018. Vowel dynamics in the Southern Vowel Shift. *American Speech* 93(2): 186–222.

Fiel, Jeremy E. 2013. Decomposing school resegregation: Social closure, racial imbalance, and racial isolation. *American Sociological Review* 78(5): 828–848.

Fitch, W. Tecumseh and Jay Giedd. 1999. Morphology and development of the human vocal tract: A study using magnetic resonance imaging. *Journal of the Acoustical Society of America* 106(3 Pt 1): 1511–1522.

Fought, Carmen. 2003. *Chicano English in Context*. New York, NY: Palgrave-Macmillan.

Fox, Robert Allen and Ewa Jacewicz. 2009. Cross-dialectal variation in formant dynamics of American English vowels. *The Journal of the Acoustical Society of America* 126(5): 2603–2618.

Fridland, Valerie. 2003. "Tie, tied and tight": The expansion of /ai/ monophthongization in African-American and European-American speech in Memphis, Tennessee. *Journal of Sociolinguistics* 7(3): 279–298.

Fridland, Valerie, Tyler Kendall, Betsy Evans, and Alicia Beckford Wassink (eds.). 2016. *Speech in the Western States, Volume 1: The Coastal States*. Durham, NC: Duke University Press.

Fridland, Valerie, Tyler Kendall, Betsy Evans, and Alicia Beckford Wassink (eds.), 2017. *Speech in the Western States, Volume 2: The Mountain West*. Durham, NC: Duke University Press.

Girard, Frédérique, Caroline Floccia, and Jeremy Goslin. 2008. Perception and awareness of accents in young children. *British Journal of Developmental Psychology* 26 (3): 409–433.

Gregersen, Frans, Marie Maegaard, and Nicolai Pharao. 2009. The long and short of (æ)-variation in Danish - A panel study of short (æ)-variants in Danish in real time. *Acta Linguistica Hafniensia: International Journal of Linguistics Publica* 41: 64–82.

Habib, Rania. 2011. Meaningful variation and bidirectional change in rural child and adolescent Speech. *University of Pennsylvania Working Papers in Linguistics* 17(2): 81–90.

Habib, Rania. 2014. Vowel variation and reverse acquisition in rural Syrian child and adolescent language. *Language Variation and Change* 26(1): 45–75.

Harrington, Johnathan, Sallyanne Palethorpe, and Catherine I. Watson. 2000. Does the Queen speak the Queen's English?. *Nature*, 408(6815): 927–928.

Hodge, Megan. 2013. Development of the vowel space in children: Anatomical and acoustic aspects. In Martin Ball and Fiona Gibbon (eds.), *Handbook of Vowels and Vowel Disorders*, 1–25. New York; London: Psychology Press.

Holmes-Elliott, Sophie. 2018. Do birds of a feather flock together? Real time incrementation and type of sound change. Paper presented at *New Ways of Analyzing Variation* 47. New York: New York University.

Jones, Zack, Qingyang Yan, Laura Wagner, and Cynthia G. Clopper. 2017. The development of dialect classification across the lifespan. *Journal of Phonetics* 60: 20–37.

Jacewicz, Ewa, Robert Allen Fox and Joseph Salmons. 2011. Regional dialect variation in the vowel systems of typically developing children. *Journal of Speech, Language, and Hearing Research* 54(2): 448–470.

Jones, Jamila and Dennis R. Preston. 2011. AAE and identity: Constructing and deploying linguistic resources. In David Dwyer (ed.), *The Joy of Language:*

Proceedings of a Symposium Honoring the Colleagues of David Dwyer on the Occasion of his Retirement, 65–87. East Lansing, MI: Michigan State University.

Kerswill, Paul. 1996. Children, adolescents, and language change: The state of the art. *Language Variation and Change* 8(2): 177–202.

Kerswill, Paul and Ann Williams. 2000. Creating a new town koine: Children and language change in Milton Keynes. *Language in Society* 29(1): 65–115.

Kerswill, Paul and Ann Williams. 2005. New towns and koineisation: Linguistic and social correlates. *Linguistics* 43(5): 1023–1048.

Khattab, Ghada. 2007. Variation in vowel production by English-Arabic bilinguals. *Laboratory Phonology* 9: 383–410.

Khattab, Ghada. 2013. Phonetic convergence and divergence strategies in English-Arabic bilingual children. *Linguistics* 51(2): 439–472.

Khattab, Ghada and Julie Roberts. 2011. Working with children. In Marianna Di Paolo and Malcah Yaeger-Dror (eds.), *Sociophonetics: A Student's Guide*, 163–177. London: Routledge.

Kohn, Mary Elizabeth. 2014. *"The Way I Communicate Changes but How I Speak Don't": A Longitudinal Perspective on Adolescent Language Variation and Change.* Durham, NC: Duke University Press.

Kohn, Mary Elizabeth. 2018. (De)Segregation: The impact of de-facto and de-jure segregation on African American English in the New South. In Jeffery Reaser, Eric Wilbanks, Karissa Wojcik, and Walt Wolfram (eds.), *Language Variety in the New South: Contemporary Perspectives on Change and Variation*, 223–240. Chapel Hill, NC: UNC Press.

Kohn, Mary Elizabeth and Charlie Farrington. 2012. Evaluating acoustic speaker normalization algorithms: Evidence from longitudinal child data. *The Journal of the Acoustical Society of America* 131(3): 2237–2248.

Kohn, Mary Elizabeth and Charlie Farrington. 2017. Longitudinal sociophonetic analysis: What to expect when working with child and adolescent data. In Suzanne Evans Wagner and Isabelle Buchstaller (eds.), *Using Panel Data in the Sociolinguistic Study of Variation and Change*, 122–152. New York/London: Routledge.

Koops, Christian. 2010. /u/-Fronting is not monolithic: Two types of fronted /u/ in Houston Anglos. *University of Pennsylvania Working Papers in Linguistics* 16(2): Article 14.

Kurath, Hans and Raven I. McDavid. 1961. *The Pronunciation of English in the Atlantic States*. Ann Arbor, MI: University of Michigan Press.

Labov, William. 1991. The three dialects of English. In Penelope Eckert (ed.), *New Ways of Analyzing Sound Change*, 1–44. San Diego, CA: Academic Press.

Labov, William. 2001. *Principles of Linguistic Change. Vol.2, Social Factors*. Malden, MA: Blackwell.

Labov, William, Sharon Ash, and Charles Boberg. 2006. *The Atlas of North American English: Phonetics, Phonology and Sound Change: A Multimedia Reference Tool*. Berlin, Germany: Mouton/ de Gruyter.

Lee, Sungbok, Alexandros Potamianos, and Shrikanth S. Narayanan. 1999. Acoustics of children's speech: developmental changes of temporal and spectral parameters. *The Journal of the Acoustical Society of America* 105(3): 1455–1468.

Lobanov, Boris M. 1971. Classification of Russian vowels spoken by different speakers. *The Journal of the Acoustical Society of America* 49(2B): 606.

Local, John. 1983. How many vowels in a vowel? *Journal of Child Language* 10(2): 449–453.

Mackenzie, Laurel and Gillian Sankoff. 2010. A quantitative analysis of diphthongization in Montreal French. *University of Pennsylvania Working Papers in Linguistics* 15(2): 92–100.

Markova, Diana, Louis Richer, Melissa Pangelinan, Deborah Schwartz, Gabriel Leonard, Michel Perron, Bruce Pike, et al. 2016. Age- and sex-related variations in vocal-tract morphology and voice acoustics during adolescence. *Hormones and Behavior* 81: 84–96.

McGowen, Rebecca, Richard McGowen, Margaret Denny, and Susan Nittrouer. 2014. A longitudinal study of very young children's vowel production. *Journal of Speech, Language, and Hearing Research* 57(1): 1–15.

Milroy, James and Lesley Milroy. 1985. Linguistic change, social network and speaker innovation. *Journal of Linguistics* 21(2): 339–384.

Milroy, Lesley. 1980. *Language and Social Networks*. Baltimore, MD: University Park Press.

Milroy, Lesley and James Milroy. 1992. Social network and social class: Toward an integrated sociolinguistic model. *Language in Society* 21(1): 1–26.

Munro, Murray J, Tracey M Derwing, and James E Flege. 1999. Canadians in Alabama: A perceptual study of dialect acquisition in adults. *Journal of Phonetics* 27(4): 385–403.

Nguyen, Jennifer. 2006. *The Changing Social and Linguistic Orientation of the African American Middle Class*. Ph.D. dissertation. Ann Arbor, MI: University of Michigan.

Nycz, Jennifer. 2011. *Second Dialect Acquisition: Implications for Theories in Dialect Representation*. Ph.D. dissertation. New York: New York University.

Pederson, Lee, Susan Leas McDaniel, Guy Bailey, Marvin Bassett, Carol Adams, Caisheng Liao, and Michael Montgomery. 1981. *The Linguistic Atlas of the Gulf States*. Athens, GA: University of Georgia Press.

Pettinato, Michele, Outi Toumainen, Sonia Granlund and Valerie Hazan. 2016. Vowel space area in later childhood and adolescence: Effects of age, sex, and ease of communication. *Journal of Phonetics* 54: 1–14.

Plichta, Bartłmiej and Dennis R Preston. 2005. The /ay/s have it: Perception of /ay/ as a North-South stereotype in United States English. *Acta Linguistica Hafniensia* 37(1): 107–130.

Prince, Ellen. 1987. Sarah Gorby, Yiddish Folksinger: A case study of dialect shift. *International Journal of the Sociology of Language* 67: 83–116.

Purnell, Thomas, William Idsardi and John Baugh. 1999. Perceptual and phonetic experiments on American English dialect identification. *Journal of Language and Social Psychology* 18(1): 10–30.

Rahman, M. Shahidur and Tetsuya Shimamura. 2005. Formant frequency estimation of high-pitched speech by homomorphic prediction. *Acoustical Science and Technology* 26(6): 502–510.

Reardon, Sean and John Yun. 2003. *Integrating Neighborhoods, Segregating Schools: The Retreat from School Desegregation in the South, 1990–2000*. Chapel Hill, NC: University of North Carolina Press.

Reed, Paul E. 2016. *Sounding Appalachian: / ai / Monophthongization, Rising Pitch Accents, and Rootedness*. Ph.D. dissertation. Columbia, SC: University of South Carolina.

Rickford, John R. and Sharese King. 2016. Language and linguistics on trial: Hearing Rachel Jeantel (and other vernacular speakers) in the courtroom and beyond. *Language* 92(4): 948–988.

Rickford, John R. and Mackenzie Price. 2013. Girlz II women: Age-grading, language change, and stylistic variation. *Journal of Sociolinguistics* 17(2): 143–179.

Risdal, Megan L. and Mary Elizabeth Kohn. 2014. Ethnolectal and generational differences in vowel trajectories: Evidence from African American English and the Southern Vowel System. *University of Pennsylvania Working Papers in Linguistics* 20(2): Article 16.

Roberts, Julie. 1997. Hitting a moving target: Acquisition of sound change in progress by Philadelphia children. *Language Variation and Change* 9(2): 249–266.

Roberts, Julie. 2002. Child language variation. In J.K. Chambers, Peter Trudgill, and Natalie Schilling-Estes (eds.), *The Handbook of Language Variation and Change*, 333–348. Oxford, UK: Blackwell.

Roberts, Julie and William Labov. 1995. Learning to talk Philadelphian: Acquisition of short *a* by preschool children. *Language Variation and Change* 7(1): 101–112.

Rodríguez, William R. and Eduardo Lleida. 2009. Formant estimation in children's speech and its application for a Spanish speech therapy tool. In *Proceedings of the 2009 Workshop on Speech and Language Technologies in Education (SLaTE)*, 81–84. Wroxall Abbey Estates, United Kingtom. www.isca-speech.org/archive/slate_2009/sla9_081.html

Sankoff, Gillian. 2004. Adolescents, young adults and the critical period: Two case studies from "Seven up." In Carmen Fought (ed.), *Sociolinguistic Variation: Critical Reflections*, 121–139. Oxford: Oxford University Press.

Schilling, Natalie and Jermay Jamsu 2010. Real-time Data and Communal Change in Washington, D.C., African American Vernacular English. Paper presented at *New Ways of Analyzing Variation* 39, San Antonio, TX, November.

Singer, Judith and John Willett. 2003. *Applied Longitudinal Data Analysis: Modeling Change and Event Occurrence*. Oxford: Oxford University Press.

Smith, Jennifer, Mercedes Durham, and Hazel Richards. 2013. The social and linguistic in the acquisition of sociolinguistic variation. *Linguistics* 51(2): 258–324.

Spears, Arthur K. 2015. African American Standard English. In Sonja L. Lanehart (ed.), *The Oxford Handbook of African American Language*, 786–799. Oxford: Oxford University Press.

Stanford, James N. 2008. Child dialect acquisition New perspectives on parent peer influence. *Journal of Sociolinguistics* 12(5): 567–596.

Story, Brad H. and Kate Bunton. 2016. Formant measurements in children's speech based on spectral filtering. *Speech Communication* 76: 93–111.

Tagliamonte, Sali A. 2012. *Variationist Sociolinguistics: Change, Observation, Interpretation*. Malden, MA and Oxford: Wiley-Blackwell.

Tatman, Rachael. 2016. "I'm a spawts guay": Comparing the use of sociophonetic variables in speech and Twitter. *University of Pennsylvania Working Papers in Linguistics* 22(2): Article 18.

Thomas, Erik R. 1996. A comparison of variation patterns of variables among sixth-graders in an Ohio community. In Edgar W. Schneider (ed.), *Focus on the U.S.A.*, 149–68. Amsterdam: John Benjamins.

Thomas, Erik R. 2001. *An Acoustic Analysis of Vowel Variation in New World English*. Durham, NC: Duke University Press.

Thomas, Erik R. 2007. Phonological and phonetic characteristics of African American Vernacular English. *Language and Linguistics Compass* 1(5): 450–475.

Thomas, Reuben J. 2019. Sources of friendship and structurally induced homophily across the life course. *Sociological Perspectives* 62(6): 822–843.

Vorperian, Houri K, and Ray D. Kent. 2007. Vowel acoustic space development in children: a synthesis of acoustic and anatomic data. *Journal of Speech, Language, and Hearing Research* 50(6): 1510–1545.

Vorperian, Houri K., Shubing Wang, E. Michael Schimek, Reid Durtschi, Ray D. Kent, Lindell R. Gentry, and Moo K. Chung. 2011. Developmental sexual dimorphism of the oral and pharyngeal portions of the vocal tract: An imaging study. *Journal of Speech, Language, and Hearing Research* 54(4): 995–1010.

Wolfram, Walter A. 1969. *A Sociolinguistic Description of Detroit Negro Speech. Urban Language Series*. Washington, DC: Center for Applied Linguistics.

Wolfram, Walt and Erik R. Thomas. 2002. *The Development of African American English*. Malden, MA: Blackwell.

Yaeger-Dror, Malcah and Erik R. Thomas (eds.), 2010. *African American English Speakers and their Participation in Local Sound Changes: A Comparative Study*. Durham, NC: Duke University Press.

5   Caretaker's Influence on Vernacularity

5.1   Introduction

Speaker K280 grew up in an exurb of Raleigh, North Carolina, but his mom volunteered to drive him to school in Durham, North Carolina, every single day until his sophomore year in high school so that he could be with the friendship group that he chose. This participant highly identifies with Durham and with his peer group, is very social, and fashion-forward with plans to study fashion design in college. As researchers, we expect that he will adeptly fit in with his peers, perhaps pushing trends forward as he crafts his persona. From previous analyses, we also can watch as K280 modifies his speech, following the prototypical curvilinear pattern of vernacularity identified in Chapter 3. But will all those long car conversations have no impact on his language? In his post-high school interview, K280 reported that "Of course I would talk differently to my mom than I would to anybody else." Might he consider his parents as role models as he moves into professional spheres? Could the language he uses with his mom become a language which he finds useful in the new situations he confronts as an adult?

In the previous chapters, we focused on the trajectory of change in AAL development and how to assess a system using different measures. We considered a composite index for morphosyntactic and segmental consonants as well as the stability and change in one of the phonological subsystems, the developing vowel systems of maturing African American speakers. The primary focus was temporal, showing trajectories of change from four years through twenty years of age. Naturally, there is much more to consider than temporal progression; in fact, our study included the examination of a vast array of social, sociopsychological, demographic, and interactional factors for our sample of speakers. In this chapter, we consider the relationship between one of those variables – the relationship between caretaker speech and the speech of the children.

The primary caregiver serves as the earliest model for language acquisition. As the child grows and develops, however, models for language acquisition increase in number and compete with the caregiver for influence in language accommodation. What other factors vie for influence and at what points in time? To what extent does the primary caregiver's linguistic influence wax and wane across the lifespan? Can a child's relative use of AAL change across the lifespan according to predictive caregiver and family factors?

Over the past several decades, sociolinguists (e.g., Kerswill 1996; Roberts 1997; Labov 1989; Foulkes, Docherty and Watt 1999; 2005; Smith, Durham and Richards 2013) have attempted to answer these sorts of questions but have been limited by the cross-sectional nature of their data as well as the relatively narrow time frame in which their speakers were analyzed. These limitations are understandable given the logistical challenges of long-term longitudinal studies. Furthermore, a narrowed temporal frame often leads to a focus on specific features, factors, and practices relevant to the age span under examination. Notwithstanding the functional validity of the *apparent time* construct (cf. Bailey 2002), a longitudinal study that follows children from a vernacular speech community through their early and later childhood years, coupled with language data from their caregivers and social data from their everyday contexts, would greatly augment and help explain the influence of caretaker speech on early and later dialectal development.

5.2   Caregiver Influence on Language Acquisition and Sociolinguistic Competence

As Snow (1995) argues, speech directed toward young children (called *child-directed speech,* CDS) is qualitatively different from speech among peers. It is syntactically simpler, lexically limited, and exaggerated intonationally. It also tends to be "more correct, and more fluent" (Snow 1995:180). The usual source for CDS is the child's primary caregiver, which in most (but not all) cases is the mother. Naturally, CDS becomes less and less essential as the child ages. Snow (1972) shows how mothers use shorter utterances with fewer subordinate clauses and compound verbs and increased repetition with two-year-old children compared with 10-year-olds. Bellinger (1980) looks with detail at the earliest years, documenting the increasing sentence complexity and mean length of utterance (MLU) used by mothers to their children between the ages of one and five. Bellinger finds that the greatest rate of change (in complexity and MLU) occurred at the earliest ages (between one and two), tapering off at five years of age. During this time period, caregivers also incorporate more salient vernacular variants into their speech so that parents of older children incorporate more salient vernacular variants than those of very young children (Smith et al. 2013). The need for CDS, it appears, is virtually non-existent beyond the age of five, and comprehension and production begin to mirror adult values by this time (Snow 1985). Thus, the child uses the caregiver's speech as a model for their own acquisition and it can be, therefore, assumed that the child and caregiver would closely correlate in terms of the more basic morphosyntactic and phonetic structures of their language variety.

While the direct, mechanistic language-teaching function of caregivers' speech tapers off in early childhood, the social and pragmatic functions (as well as the more nuanced and complex syntactical functions) of language are by no means fully acquired by this time. *Sociolinguistic competence* (Hymes 1974:75) is a life-long endeavor, and the acquisition of the "system of its [language's] use, regarding persons, places, purposes other modes of communication, etc ... [is] develop[ing] patterns of the sequential use of language in conversation, address, standard routines, and the like." In addition to the pragmatic realm, sociolinguistic competence can also incorporate traditional sociolinguistic variation, in the use/non-use of specific features and the knowledge of "what variants are generally (though subconsciously) recognized as being appropriate" (Meyerhoff 2006:96). As an authority figure and a frequent interlocutor in the child's life, the caregiver plays a prominent role in the development of sociolinguistic competence as well.

As Smith, Durham and Fortune (2007:64) explain, variation in child's speech has been often been viewed as little more than a developmental stage. At first glance, variation in the use/non-use of standard morphosyntactic and phonetic features in child speech may seem to be the result of incompletely learned linguistic principles or learner errors, and language acquisition scholars such as Snow (1972, 1986, 1995) have treated it that way. However, this assumes that caregivers themselves utilize little variation in speech and that the primary language input of the caregiver leans toward the standard variety. In reality, as sociolinguists have broadly found, adult caregiver speech varies widely along the standard/vernacular continuum, even within the same speaker. A child growing up in a vernacular household may rarely hear instances of many standard features. Thus, if their speech lacks such features, it cannot be concluded that they are deficient in language acquisition; rather, the child is simply acquiring a vernacular variety and *systematic patterns* of variation appropriate to the variety to which they are most frequently exposed (Díaz-Campos 2005; Chevrot, Nardy and Barbu 2011).

Roberts (2002) has noted that variation is an "integral part" of the language acquisition process and therefore should not be discounted or overlooked in the study of child language development. And, given that caregiver input is likewise an integral part of the language acquisition process, the detailed scrutiny of the relationship between caregiver variation and the emerging variation of the child is essential. In an early study of this relationship, Labov (1989) found that, through mirroring their parents, children seem to acquire the patterns of social variation before they had fully grasped the syntactic and phonological patterns of variables. Kerswill (1996) explains that it may not be quite as simple as that, and provides a hierarchy of features and forms and a timeline for acquisition based on feature complexity and exposure. Essentially, phonological forms and constraints are acquired first, followed by morphologically conditioned ones, most of the patterns for which are set in place before the age of six. Even after these features are established in the child's linguistic repertoire, children still show more heterogeneous variation than do their caregivers, which he attributes to the disparity between the parents' more comprehensive awareness of style and social factors and the child's lack thereof (Smith et al. 2013).

Meanwhile, others have shown that children can be quite sociolinguistically savvy even at early ages. Roberts (1997) and Roberts and Labov (1995) found that children in their Philadelphia sample had acquired patterns of stable variation by the age of 3–4, as well as fully completed sound changes and even changes in progress. They attribute this phenomenon, especially the changes in progress, to the influence of a child's prominent linguistic input from their primary caregiver. The likelihood of that caregiver being female coupled with the fact that females tend to be language innovators (Labov 1990) offer a plausible explanation for why young children acquired such new language features.

The primary caregiver remains, in no small part, the model for the child's sociolinguistic competence, though beyond the age of four it is practically impossible to control for caregiver effects (Foulkes et al. 2005). As the child enters schooling and approaches adolescence, peer influence becomes another prominent input source. In the incipient days of the study of language variation, Labov (1965:95) concluded that it was in "roughly ages five to twelve [that] the child learns the use of the local dialect in a form consistent with that of his [sic] immediate group of friends and associates."[1] Not only do the child's peers serve as prominent linguistic influences during this time, but their influence is also strongly in the direction of the vernacular (Labov 1965). Eckert (2000) showed in great detail through the *community of practice* construct how indelibly the peer group influences an adolescent's vernacular usage, almost to the exclusion of home and other factors. For children from vernacular speech communities, the question remains unanswered as to which influence is more important in dictating their everyday speech.

5.3   AAL Development across the Early Lifespan

Little is known about the relationship between caregiver speech and child's vernacularity in African American speech communities. After a flurry of

---

[1] There is some evidence that peer influence can have an impact as early as preschool. For example, Nardy, Chevrot and Barbu (2014) found that children of ages 4–5 converged with peers after one year of frequent contact, while other factors such as teacher speech and child awareness of social norms had little impact.

studies in the 1970s and 1980s (e.g., Steffenson 1974; Kovac 1980; Kovac and Adamson 1981; Stockman and Vaughn-Cooke 1982, 1989), sociolinguistic research on early childhood development of AAL subsided until the last decade (Craig and Washington 2002, 2006; Van Hofwegen and Wolfram 2010; Green 2011). At the time of the earlier studies, the research was geared toward affirming the *difference* (not *deficit*) perspective in vernacular dialect acquisition and paid little attention to sociolinguistic variation. One notable exception: Kovak (1980) was able to confirm that AAL-speaking children utilized the same constraints and frequencies for copula and auxiliary forms as did their parents by the age of seven, but not consistently before that.

Two decades later, Washington and Craig (2002) examined AAL-speaking caregivers and their children (age range four through seven) in terms of the usage of specific morphosyntactic forms prominent in AAL. Language data from these speakers were analyzed in terms of the DDM discussed in Chapter 2, total feature counts, and specific counts of the most frequent AAL features. What they found was that there was no significant difference in the DDM between the children and their caregivers. When counting specific features from the DDM inventory, they found the most frequent features for both groups to be copula deletion, auxiliary deletion, and subject-verb variation. However, beyond these forms, it was found that the caregivers used a much broader range of features than did their children. Some features, such as completive *done* and preterit *had*, were not found in the child data at all, while they were found (albeit sparingly) in the adult data.

It also has been found that AAL-speaking children do not necessarily resemble older speakers in relative vernacularity and can often diverge quite starkly from them. One notable example shows pre-adolescent African American children utilizing preterit *had* before that feature had been widely noted in adult AAL speech (Rickford and Théberge Rafal 1996). Another shows a teenage girl using less copula deletion as she transitions out of adolescence, approaching her mother's frequency for the feature (Rickford et al. 1991), suggesting that copula deletion may be age-graded. When taken together, these studies plus those of childhood AAL depict a picture of a caregiver-child alignment and then divergence across the lifespan. But none of these studies are able to follow the same children (and their parents) across both early and later childhood. In this respect, only a longitudinal study that follows the development of AAL across the early lifespan can reliably reveal the relationship to caretaker speech vis-à-vis other emerging social and educational factors.

Chapter 3 measured the DDM at seven time points, from age four through post-secondary school at about age 20, finding that the children exhibited a range of trajectories for vernacular change across the lifespan, generally characterized by a dip in early childhood (Grades 1 and 4, approximate ages six through nine) and a peak in early adolescence (Grades 6 and 8, approximate ages 11–13). In later adolescence (Grade 10, about age 15) the majority of children decreased in vernacularity (a "roller coaster" pattern) while some children increased (a curvilinear pattern).

With regard to specific features, it was found that both the high-vernacular and the low-vernacular children shared the same core and most frequent features (e.g., nasal fronting, copula absence, auxiliary absence, third-person singular –s absence) but that the highly vernacular speakers had a wider repertoire of features. Of the social factors considered, mother's education (in terms of years of formal schooling) was found to significantly predict a child's vernacularity across the lifespan, in that mothers with more education tended to have less-vernacular children.

Beyond this, much remains to be done with the FPG longitudinal dataset to answer questions heretofore unanswerable: 1) What relationship (and likely influence) does a primary caregiver's relative AAL vernacularity have with a child's vernacular life trajectory? 2) What core AAL features are shared by the two groups? 3) What social and family factors also impact the caregiver-child linguistic influence? In the FPG study, the language samples included mother-child interactions, peer interactions, and contrasting formal/informal settings as well as data chronicling each child's language development and change during childhood and adolescence, data describing family, peer, and school environment, and data measuring metalanguage, literacy, and academic achievement measures. These data afford us the opportunity to examine the questions outlined earlier.

5.4   The Study of Mother-Child Speech

Out of all of the available data, this study selects a subsample of 34 children, 19 females and 15 males (32 of these children have been previously reported on in Chapter 3 at seven temporal data points: 48 months, Grade 1 (about age 5–6), Grade 4 (about age 9–10), Grade 6 (about age 10–11), Grade 8 (about age 12–13), Grade 10 (about age 14–15), and post-secondary school (about age 20–21). All of these 34 children had primary caregivers who were their mothers.

The mothers' language samples were taken from the mother-child inter-actions recorded at the Grade 1 and Grade 4 age points of their children, which were the same interactions from which the child data from those age points were extracted. While these interactions were assumed to exhibit comfortable and fluent language for examination, several questions about the reliability of the mothers' speech had to be considered. (1) Due to the near-universal use of CDS at earlier ages, to what extent can it be assumed that the mother's speech with her child at these ages would be indicative of her more general speech patterns? (2) If CDS is a factor in mothers' speech, might her speech change over time as her child gets older? (3) Might it also be that a mother's speech would change over time as a result of other factors (e.g., her age, education, demographic data, etc.)? The first question can be addressed through previous research; for example, Bellinger (1980) and Snow (1986) conclude that little, if any, CDS lingering would be maintained in the mother speech data by Grade 1. The other two questions can be answered empirically using these data. Each mother's speech transcript was tabulated using the same DDM as was used for the child data, resulting in a *features per utterance* score for each mother at each age point. Linear regression analysis of the Grade 1 mother scores against the Grade 4 scores established that there was a significant correlation between the two time points ($p < 0.01$; $R^2 = 0.194$). Paired-sample t-tests also confirmed that there was no significant difference between the two ages ($p = 0.387$). Figure 5.1 illustrates the linear regression results.

After it was confirmed that the mothers' speech data did not change significantly over time, the data from Grade 1 and Grade 4 were combined to create one vernacularity score for each mother. It was this singular score against which the child vernacularity and other factors could be compared. Altogether, the

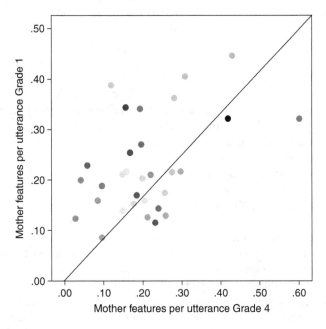

Figure 5.1 Linear regression analysis of mothers' vernacularity at Grade 1 against mothers' vernacularity at Grade 4

language data for this study comprised just fewer than 9,000 utterances for the mothers, within which approximately 2,000 total AAL features from the DDM were tagged (or coded) for analysis. For the children, analysis resulted in around 5,500 AAL features in about 20,000 total utterances.

5.4.1 Social and Family Factors

The monumental nature of the longitudinal dataset is underscored not only by the language data itself, but also by the battery of standardized tests and psychosocial and academic measures administered to the children and their families across the lifespan. In addition to analyzing the language data in terms of what, if any, relationship exists between the mothers' and the childrens vernacularity and feature types used, we also examined relevant family and psychosocial factors that might have played a role in this relationship. These factors were considered independently and also in terms of their potential interactive effects with mothers' vernacularity.

Language and gender studies have shown females to be simultaneously more conservative (i.e., more standard) and more innovative than males in their language variation (Labov 2001). Thus, one hypothesis could be that girls in this study would be less vernacular than boys. However, the analysis reported in Chapter 3 found this not to be the case. But, perhaps gender and mothers' vernacularity will reveal significant patterns related to gender. Studies (e.g., Foulkes et al. 2005) have shown that mothers from nonmainstream language backgrounds will tend to use more standard language with daughters than with sons. This study specifically tests the interaction between mothers' vernacularity and child's gender (categorized in terms of female = 1 and male = 0) across the lifespan of the child.

Another social factor considered is the relative poverty level of the family. Demographic data collected for the children showed that a majority of them (31 out of 34) had lived all or some of their lives under the federally determined poverty line. Other studies of the acquisition of language variation in children of non-standard-speaking speech communities has shown that AAL-speaking children can show socioeconomic differentiation in their variation as early as age 4 (Reveron 1978; Kovac 1980). The dataset here incorporates poverty information (1 = poverty; 0 = no poverty) for each child at each of the six temporal time points under study. Perhaps, poverty would have a significant predictive effect on a child's vernacularity trajectory over the lifespan, or perhaps at one or another point in time over others.

It is also possible that the presence of another significant adult in the household (in addition to or instead of the mother) such as a partner, grand-parent, aunt/uncle, etc. might have an impact on the child's linguistic development. The mere presence of such a person adds another model for the child in their linguistic development, and in some cases could mitigate or even usurp the mother in terms of being the most prominent impact. Demographic data collected with the FPG children included a value for whether or not another adult lived in the household in addition to the primary caregiver at any of the six temporal points used in this longitudinal analysis. The presence of this significant other adult was considered (1 = other adult present; 0 = no other adult present) as an important social factor in the statistical analysis conducted here.

Two psychosocial measures were also included in this analysis as they could perhaps themselves either predict child vernacularity or interact with mothers' vernacularity in terms of its relative impact on the child. Each of these measures was used with the aim of quantifying some aspect of the quality of the mother-child relationship, the sociolinguistic assumption being that children with closer emotional relationships with their mothers would be closer to them in terms of relative vernacularity. The first psychosocial factor considered is the impact of stressful life events, measured in terms of the Holmes-Rahe Social Readjustment Scale (Holmes and Rahe 1967). This scale has been widely used in a variety of fields, but was originally utilized to connect stressful life events, such as the death of a spouse, change in residence, change in job, illness, and so forth (Holmes and Rahe 1967). Garbarino, Sebes and Schellenbach (1984) used it to assess the risk of destructive parent-child relationships in families of adolescents, in that higher relative stress indices were correlated with destructive relationships and other at-risk measures for adolescents. In this study, the Holmes-Rahe scale was not scored in the traditional fashion but rather each stressful event in the child's life was given one point (out of a 43 total), so that a score of 43 would be the maximum number of stressful events possible, and a 0 would be no stressful events. For this sample, the children's scores ranged from 0 to 11.

The other psychosocial measure, the Child-Parent Relationship Scale (CPRS) (Pianta 1992), is a measure for rating the closeness, conflict, interdependency, and inter-involvement in a parent-child relationship, asking the respondents (the parents) to address emotional and interactional realities in the home. Research has shown this measure to be a reliable predictor of the child's early success in school and other cognitive and development measures (e.g., Pianta, Nimetz and Bennett 1997). For this study, only the closeness and conflict components of this measure were utilized and their scores (Likert scale out of 5 possible) were averaged (the conflict score was reversed first) to get a score for each child at each point in time. Scores approaching 5 were those indicating relationships that exhibited the most closeness and the least amount of conflict.

5.4.2   Regression Analyses of Social Factors

The aforementioned social factors were incorporated into a series of regression analyses with the aim of understanding which of them influenced the relative vernacularity of the children at six temporal points (48 months, Grade 1, Grade 4, Grade 6, Grade 8, and Grade 10) of the lifespan. The children's vernacularity scores (in terms of DDM features per utterance) were the dependent variable (hereafter: $cfpu^2$), because the goal of the analysis was to trace the development of the child's vernacularity across the lifespan, and the predictive impact of family and social factors upon that development.

As it was for the analysis in Chapter 3, the factor of time (*age/grade*) was the principal factor upon which *cfpu* is considered because the potential impact of each of the maternal and social factors considered here is primarily in terms of their impact upon the childrens vernacular trajectories. Thus, for a longitudinal study such as this one, time is a special factor, one which exists as both a fixed and random factor in the regression analysis (Singer and Willett 2003). A discussion of how to properly incorporate time into the regression model is found in Van Hofwegen (2015) and in Singer and Willet (2003), but it is important to note that for this portion of the analysis, regression models were created on a cross-sectional basis.[3]

The primary independent variable in terms of the goals of this study was the mothers' vernacularity score (*mfpu*). As with the children, this was operation-alized in terms of DDM features per utterance, which came from the combined Grade 1 and Grade 4 mother-child interaction data. While assessing the pre-dictive relationship of the mothers' vernacularity upon the children's' vernacu-larity, which was the primary investigative aim of this study, the potential impact of other social factors – the gender of the child (*gender*), the experience of poverty (*poverty*), the presence of another adult in the household (*other adult*), the impact of stressful life events (*life events*), and the child-parent relationship (*relationship*) – was also considered, as well as their potential interactions with the mothers' vernacularity scores.

5.5   Results

The complementary nature of the linguistic and statistical analyses conducted here allows for a complex picture to emerge about the impact of mothers' AAL vernacularity upon their children's dialect development across the early life-span. That picture is described here, first in terms of the descriptive

---

[2] An effort was made in this analysis to utilize the terms *cfpu* and *mfpu* strictly when referring to them as operationalized variables in a regression schema. Elsewhere, the full term: features per utterance is used for the sake of clarity.

[3] Because trajectories of change for the children in this study are predominantly curvilinear, it would be necessary to include a cubic polynomial function into any growth curve analysis for the data considered here (Singer and Willett 2003). This would greatly complicate the interpretation of regression results.

comparisons between the two groups, then in terms of the variation analyses, and finally in terms of the regression analyses.

5.5.1   Descriptive Statistics: Features per Utterance and Feature Type Count Comparisons

As mentioned earlier, the language data here comprise approximately 9,000 utterances for the mothers and 20,000 utterances for the children. Within these, the mothers averaged 0.22 features per utterance, meaning that on average, one AAL feature from the DDM list was found in every five utterances of the mothers' speech. The children, however, varied widely in their average features per utterance across the lifespan – ranging from 0.14 features per utterance at Grade 1 (the lowest vernacular age, only marginally lower than Grade 4) to 0.38 features per utterance at Grade 8. This means that the children were on average using one AAL feature in seven utterances at Grade 1, but at Grade 8 were using one feature in three utterances. Table 5.1 shows the means and standard deviations in features per utterance, for the children at each grade point, compared to the mothers' means.

The mean values alone present the picture of the children fluctuating around the mothers' mean – at times higher (48 months, Grade 6, Grade 8, and Grade 10) and at times lower (Grade 1 and Grade 4). Figure 5.2 presents this relationship graphically (note that for ease of comparison, the figure presents the mothers' mean as though it were longitudinal across the child's lifespan; in reality, the mothers' mean comes from the combination of the mother data at the children's Grade 1 and Grade 4). However, the mean values themselves do not present a complete picture of the variation amongst the children at their various life stages. That is, the standard deviations at five out of the six age points are higher than that for the mothers, with the widest variation exhibited at Grade 8.

Table 5.1 *Mean and standard deviations for AAL features per utterance for children and mothers*

Speakers	Mean	Standard deviation
Children (48 months)	0.287	0.111
Children (Grade 1)	0.148	0.085
Children (Grade 4)	0.170	0.103
Children (Grade 6)	0.348	0.156
Children (Grade 8)	0.384	0.205
Children (Grade 10)	0.299	0.158
Mothers (Grade 1 + Grade 4)	0.219	0.086

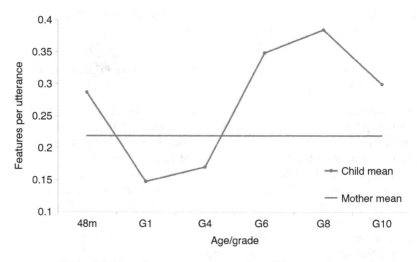

Figure 5.2 Mean features per utterance for children over time; mothers' features per utterance included as a reference

Figure 5.3 presents a box plot diagram showing the children's means and standard deviations compared to the mothers from Van Hofwegen (2015:467).

In his report of dialect acquisition, Kerswill (1996:190) notes that even as children acquire the linguistic constraints necessary for different dialect variables, they show great variation in terms of how they acquire the "social evaluation" for how those variables should be used. That is, children are much more heterogeneous in terms of how and when they use dialect variants, illustrating that they are operating from different measures of social evaluation than are their parents. While our sample does not quite replicate Kerswill's contention because the children in this study show similar hetero-geneity to their mothers at many points in the lifespan, the children do vary their use of vernacular language widely (much more than their mothers) in early adolescence. This is consistent with a picture of children using similar degrees of social evaluation or sociolinguistic competence compared to those of their caregivers through most of the lifespan, save for the adolescent years.

In terms of the types of features used by each of the groups, beyond the top three features (copula, (ING), third sg. –s) the most prominent features varied. For the child data, the analysis in Chapter 3 identified the most prominent features used by 32 speakers of the longitudinal dataset, seven of which comprised over 75 percent of the total AAL features of the DDM. Expansion of the child sample to 34 speakers exhibited similar feature frequencies.

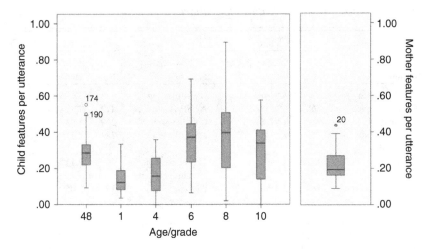

Figure 5.3 Box plot diagram of DDM scores for children across the early lifespan and mothers

Table 5.2 shows the most prominent features for each group in the order of most- to least-occurring. The seven prominent features – nasal fronting, copula absence, modal auxiliary absence, third-person singular *–s* absence, invariant *be*, negative concord, and *ain't* for *is + not* – are perfectly consistent with the six features identified by Renn (2007) as a reliable subset of features from the DDM to be used with similar validity to the DDM in full. However, when compared with the mothers' list of most prominent features, striking disparities are revealed. Beyond the first three features (which for both groups was the same, though not in the same order) of prominence, the features varied. One notable difference was the relative paucity of third-person singular *–s* absence in the mother language data. For the children, it constituted 5.51 percent of the total AAL features found in their sample, while for the mothers, only 2.11 percent. Mothers did more *is/was* leveling (4.11 percent of the total AAL tokens) while their children only did it 1.54 percent of the time. Another striking disparity is the relative lack of invariant *be* tokens in the mother data: only two tokens of invariant *be* were found in all 9,000 utterances. Out of all of the AAL tokens, invariant *be* amounted to less than 1 percent (0.11 percent) of the total for the mothers. For the children, on the other hand, invariant *be* was one of the top seven more prominent features, comprising almost 7 percent of the total AAL features used.

The three features that constituted the bulk of all of the AAL features used by both groups were nasal fronting, copula absence, and modal auxiliary absence. However, the groups used them at different frequencies. For the mothers, these

Table 5.2 *Most prominent features for children and mothers*

		Children			Mothers	
Feature	N	% of total AAL features	Feature	N	% of total AAL features	
Nasal fronting	1794	32.20%	Nasal fronting	726	38.25%	
Copula absence	868	15.58%	Auxiliary absence	412	21.71%	
Auxiliary absence	709	12.72%	Copula absence	269	14.17%	
Third-pers. sing. *–s* absence	363	5.51%	*Is/was* leveling	78	4.11%	
Invariant *be*	177	3.18%	Third-pers. sing. *– s* absence	40	2.11%	
Negative concord	163	2.93%	Past tense *–ed* absence	39	2.05%	
Ain't (*to be*)	138	2.48%				
Total	4212	75.59%		1564	82.40%	
Total AAL features in sample	5572	100.00%		1898	100.00%	

three features constituted 74 percent of all of the total AAL feature count, while for the children, these features made up comparatively less: 61 percent. Perhaps most notable was the relative favoring by the mothers of auxiliary absence by a margin of 22 percent to 16 percent. Mothers also did more nasal fronting than their children – a 6 percent difference which chi square analyses determined to be significant ($p < 0.01$). Copula absence, on the other hand, was comparatively similar in frequency of use. Given the prominence of these three features above all of the others, it is possible that a relative score of AAL vernacularity could be computed with a simple subset of three features (as opposed to Renn's [2007] subset of six): nasal fronting, copula absence, and auxiliary absence. Statistical calculations of the validity of such an approach would be necessary to ascertain this and are beyond the scope of this paper.

5.5.2   *Variation Analysis*

This study sought to analyze three of the most prominent features (nasal fronting, copula absence, and third-person singular *–s* absence) in terms of their potential versus actual occurrences, a method which has become the hallmark in variation analysis tradition. These features were also considered independently for the sample of speakers considered over time in Chapter 3. Using Goldvarb software (Sankoff, Tagliamonte, and Smith 2005), a logistic regression analysis was carried out to determine what family and social constraints might be at play with regard to these features. The family/social factors considered with this analysis were: *speaker, gender, age/grade, mfpu,* and *poverty.* One shortcoming of this particular analysis is the requirement that all variables be categorical. For the dependent variable (any of the three features in question), this is not difficult, for that feature is "present" or "not present" at any given time. Also, for *gender* and *poverty,* categorization is relatively easy. The *mfpu* variable, on the other hand, had to be artificially stratified into three categories: low vernacular (*mfpu* below 0.10), mid-vernacular (*mfpu* between 0.10 and 0.33), and high vernacular (*mfpu* above 0.33). The three other variables considered in the further regression analyses reported subsequently (i.e., *other adult, life events* and *relationship*) were omitted from this portion of the analysis for two reasons: 1) there is little in the way of theoretical hypotheses that could account for their effect on the features in question; and 2) *life events* and *relationship* are particularly difficult to demarcate into categories.

The Goldvarb analysis for these three features revealed nothing new from the results reported in Chapter 3, where the only consistently significant factors in all three features were *speaker* and *age.* Because none of the other factors emerged as significant, it underscores the *lack* of impact that mother's vernacularity had on these particular features, which seemed to be operating independently as a function of the speaker's age and unique circumstances.

5.5.3   Cross-sectional Regression Analyses

Using STATA/IC 10.1 software, linear regression analyses were conducted for each of the six age/grade points in question, which regressed the DDM scores for children (*cfpu*) against mothers (*mfpu*), *gender, poverty, other adult, life events*, and *relationship*. Additionally, interaction effects were also tested between *mfpu* and each of the other variables in question. The potential correlation of greatest interest in this study was that between *cfpu* and *mfpu*, and once that correlation could be determined, additional factors were included and excluded in order to find the best model (Measures of Deviance, Akaike Information Criterion (AIC), and Bayesian Information Criterion (BIC) goodness-of-fit tests were used to determine the strongest models for the data).

Several findings are notable. First, *cfpu* correlated significantly with *mfpu* at every age *except* Grade 6 and Grade 8 (significant correlations were all $p < 0.05$). Low R-squared values for each of these correlations mean that this relationship accounts for relatively little of the variation exhibited in the data, but the relationship was significant. Table 5.3 illustrates the linear regression findings for these two variables.

The significant correlation between the child vernacularity scores and the mother vernacularity scores is noteworthy, considering the lack of significant correlation for most of the other social variables at any of the points in time. For

Table 5.3 *Cross-sectional regression results for children's features per utterance against mothers' features per utterance at each point in the lifespan*

Age/grade	Coefficient	Standard Error	R^2	P value
48 m	0.494	0.212	0.145	$p < 0.05$*
Grade 1	0.363	0.163	0.134	$p < 0.05$*
Grade 4	0.429	0.199	0.127	$p < 0.05$*
Grade 6	0.599	0.304	0.108	$p = 0.058$
Grade 8	0.278	0.419	0.014	$p = 0.512$
Grade 10	0.699	0.300	0.145	$p < 0.05$*

* Denotes significant correlation

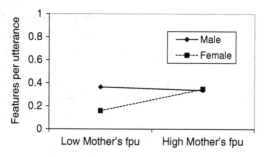

Figure 5.4 Illustration of the interaction effect between mothers' features per utterance and gender at Grade 10

example, neither *poverty, other adult, life events,* nor *relationship* emerged as significant predictors for child vernacularity. And none of these variables interacted in any significant way with *mfpu*. Thus, the theoretical hypotheses relating to the effect of these factors on child speech cannot be confirmed.

The only social factor that was significant was *gender,* which interacted with mother's vernacularity. Gender was a significant predictor of child vernacularity at 48 months ($p < 0.05$) and at Grade 10 ($p < 0.05$). Additionally, at Grade 10, the interaction between *mfpu* and *gender* was significant as well ($p < 0.05$). For Grade 10 children with low-vernacular mothers, there was a significant difference between boys and girls (boys were more vernacular than girls). However, for high-vernacular mothers, there was no significant difference between males and females. Thus, it would appear as though the mother's vernacularity at Grade 10 impacts the extent to which a girl is more vernacular or less vernacular, but has little impact on a boy's relative vernacularity. The strength of this significant interaction and the significance of gender in this Grade 10 model actually reduced the significance of *mfpu* as an independent factor ($p = 0.742$), meaning that at Grade 10, the effect of gender was stronger than the effect of mothers' vernacularity on the child vernacularity scores. Figure 5.4 illustrates the interaction effect between *mfpu* and *gender* at Grade 10.

5.6   Discussion

The complementary analyses presented here contribute to three general conclusions about the relationship between mothers' and children's AAL vernacularity across the lifespan: (1) mothers' vernacularity scores and their children's vernacularity scores are statistically similar at every point in the lifespan except the early adolescent years; (2) this similarity can likely be attributed to the mothers' linguistic influence in the earlier years, but perhaps not in the later years; and (3) the role of social and family factors (save for gender) in this relationship are minimal compared to the linguistic and age factors at play.

5.6.1   Mother-child Vernacularity Relationship over the Lifespan

Children show a fluctuating relationship with their mothers over the lifespan. On average, children begin the lifespan at a more vernacular point than their mothers are, but switch during early schooling. The early school grades (Grade 1 and Grade 4) exhibit mean values for the children that are lower than their mothers, but by the time the children reach early adolescence (Grades 6 and Grade 8), they have flip-flopped. At these ages, they are much more vernacular than are their mothers. Finally, at Grade 10, on average, the children are less vernacular and begin to approach their mothers' mean. Cross-sectional regression analyses correlating features per utterance for these two populations confirm that there is a significant relationship between mothers and children at the grades at which their mean vernacularity scores are closest to each other: 48 months, Grade 1, and Grade 4. There is no significant relationship between the two populations at Grades 6 and 8.

Given the literature on both language acquisition and the development of sociolinguistic variation (Snow 1986; Labov 1989; Kerswill 1996; Smith et al. 2007), it is not surprising that the children closely reflect their mothers' speech in the early years. Further, it is not surprising that mothers are situated on the more standard side of the vernacularity continuum of this population, especially as the mother data come from mother-child interactions (Roberts 2002; Smith et al. 2007). There is no statistical difference between the mothers' and the children's overall vernacularity scores at any of the early ages. And, aside from the statistical similarities, the differences in means could be accounted for by acquisitional variables and/or social realities. For example, the higher relative vernacularity of the children over their mothers at 48 months could be attributed to increased instances of highly salient acquisitional and dialect-specific features like copula absence and third-person singular –*s* absence. Copula deletion is a difficult AAL feature to study in small children as it conflates both acquisitional and dialect-specific constraints (Kovac 1980; Stockman and Vaughn-Cooke 1982). Further, the lower relative vernacularity (the "dip") in early schooling noted in Chapter 3 can be attributed to the influence of formal education (biased toward the standard dialect) on the children's language choices.

It is not surprising that children diverge from their parents in adolescence. The divergence in our study did not happen as early as age seven, as Kerswill (1996) found in some cases, but it did happen as early as age eleven, a finding consistent with the literature on adolescent language variation (Labov 2001). Also, that this divergence occurs in the direction of the vernacular is consistent with what has been discussed elsewhere in studies of adolescent speech (cf. Eckert 2000). However, while the predominant trend is toward the vernacular, it should also be noted that the Grade 6 and Grade 8 ages are the most varied in terms of the features per utterances scores for the children (cf. Kerswill 1996). At these ages, especially at Grade 8, the standard deviations from the mean are very wide, illustrating extreme heterogeneity in the children at this age. While many of the children are becoming more vernacular at this age, there is certainly a subset of children who are experimenting with more standard speech. This dataset underscores the fact that heterogeneity and experimenta-tion are, without question, a feature of the adolescent period of linguistic development.

What is perhaps surprising is the fact that after this period of prominent divergence, the children converge again with their mothers at the Grade 10 (about age 15) time point. Their mean value is above the mother value (that is, they are about twice more vernacular at this point), but they are still significantly correlated at this age. What accounts for this correlation? When *gender* as a factor was added to the Grade 10 regression model and interacted with *mfpu*, it becomes apparent that the mothers' language has bearing on only one segment of the child population – the females. In fact, with the interaction factor in the regression model, *mfpu* loses its signifi-cance altogether, while both *gender* and the interaction factor are signifi-cant. Regression coefficients and standard errors for these terms illustrate the relationship depicted in Figure 5.4, which helps to explain the signifi-cant correlation with this data despite the twice-higher vernacularity scores for the children overall. At Grade 10, it is the *daughters of low-vernacular mothers* who show extremely low vernacular scores. Daughters of high-vernacular mothers do not show significant correlation with their mothers, and sons show no effect of their mothers' vernacularity at all on their levels.

5.6.2   *Family and Social Factors*

What happens at Grade 10 that would create the realignment with mother's speech? Before addressing that question in greater detail, we need to consider a few items about the social and family factors that were regressed in the analysis. First of all, the relatively low R-squared values for the regression models overall (none higher than 0.15) indicate that there is quite a bit of variation in the data that is not accounted for by the mother's language data in particular. However, except for *gender*, none of the social and family factors tested emerged as significant predictors of child vernacularity at any point in the lifespan, including those factors (*life events* and *relationship*) that were aimed at representing the strength of the relationship between the mother and the child. Thus, while perhaps other measures of the quality of the relationship would be more effective, it can be concluded at this point that the convergence between the mothers and their children in the early and later childhood are not related to emotional closeness, but other factors heretofore not examined.

If the correlation between *cfpu* and *mfpu* is not an element of the closeness of the mother-child relationship, the presence of another adult, or the poverty level of the family, what factors could contribute to their linguistic similarities? This is consistent with the literature. In early schooling, social pressures toward conformity with adults (i.e., teachers) could be a factor in the lowered vernacularity at the early grades. Mothers themselves might be relatively low in their vernacularity scores because they are accommodating with their children (keeping in mind that the mother-language data come from mother-child interactions at the "dip" points in vernacularity in the child lifespan) or affected by the recording situation, which invokes a degree of formality. Models of accommodation (Giles and Powesland 1975), including the mechanism behind CDS, would dictate that parents would seek to be similar to their children in an effort to be accommodative to them linguistically. Hazen (2002: 503) describes how it is not unusual for parents to accommodate to their children's linguistic patterns in an effort to "win back the affections of their children." While it is not clear that there are any affections to be won back at the Grade 1 and Grade 4 age points with this data, given that these children do not yet seem to be as peer-oriented as they are at Grades 6 and 8, it may that at the Grade 1 and Grade 4 ages, the children would be influencing the mothers' comparatively standard speech, not the other way around.

At Grade 10, however, the picture of contributing factors is clearer than it is at the other ages, because here two factors are significant – *gender* and the interaction between *gender* and *mfpu*. With *gender* in the picture, mothers' vernacularity is no longer a significant predictor (independently) of child vernacularity – that is, unless the child is a low-vernacular daughter of a low-vernacular mother. Then, the two are highly correlated. And, because *mfpu* is not significant independently, it would appear that the situation is a bit more complicated than a simple explanation of mothers speaking more standardly with their female children (as with Foulkes et al. 2005). Rather, it seems more likely that low-vernacular mothers and low-vernacular daughters are both simultaneously influenced by the same external pressures toward being standard and are participating in an age-graded and gender-specific speech community in which their more vernacular male and female counterparts do not participate. These results are reminiscent of Eckert's jocks and burnouts dichotomy (Eckert 2000) where there existed a "super-standard" category of jock girls, while the comparatively more vernacular burnout boys and girls did not show such standard/vernacular differentiation. Except here, we see not only the low-vernacular girls (the "super-standard jock girls" as it were) but also their mothers doing the same thing, while the boys remain vernacular regardless of what their mothers are doing. Sons of low-vernacular mothers are comparatively high-vernacular themselves, and (though not statistically significant) are even slightly more vernacular than are sons of high-vernacular mothers, in a trend suggestive of Eisikovits (1987, cited in Eckert and McConnell-Ginet 2003), where girls became more standard with a standard-speaking interviewer, while boys became less standard. Regardless of motives or circumstances, these data suggest an age-grading effect in the development of AAL that prompts the daughters of low-vernacular mothers to become significantly more standard themselves at Grade 10 (about age 15), an effect that leaves the rest of the child population untouched. A closer analysis of the specific communities of both these daughters and these mothers could perhaps illuminate the reasons behind this phenomenon.

5.7   Conclusion

Several conclusions emerge from the analysis conducted in the previous sections. First, it has established that there is a significant relationship between the relative vernacularity of AAL-speaking mothers and their children across most of the early lifespan. Second, the analysis of the impact of relevant social and family factors on the development of AAL vernacularity uncovered gender as a significant determiner at only the earliest and the latest points in the early lifespan. Third, the analysis revealed some of the nuanced picture of the relationship between mothers' and children's vernacularity – that adolescent females from low-vernacular families are likely to become low-vernacular speakers (like their mothers) in older adolescence. Finally, we see the departure of the children from the parents in the early stages of schooling, following the roller-coaster trajectory we described in Chapter 3. These observations constitute noteworthy insights as we seek to understand the complex relationship of caretakers' speech to their children, not only in the early stages of childhood, but as they progress through the lifespan into adulthood.

References

Agresti, Alan. 2007. *An Introduction to Categorical Data Analysis*, 2nd ed. Hoboken, NJ: John Wiley & Sons.

Baayen, R. Harald. 2008. *Analyzing Linguistic Data: A Practical Introduction to Statistics using R*. Cambridge: Cambridge University Press.

Bailey, Guy. 2002. Real and apparent time. In J.K. Chambers, Peter Trudgill, and Natalie Schilling-Estes (eds.), *The Handbook of Language Variation and Change*, 312–331. Oxford: Blackwell.

Bellinger, David. 1980. Consistency in the pattern of change in mothers' speech: Some discriminant analyses. *Journal of Child Language* 7(3): 469–487.

Brugman, Henni and Peter Wittenburg. 2005. Eudico Linguistic Annotator (ELAN) (Version 3.3.0) [Computer Program]. Retrieved February 24, 2008, from www.lat-mpi.eu/tools/elan/

Chevrot, Jean-Pierre, Aurélie Nardy, and Stéphanie Barbu. 2011. Developmental dynamics of SES-related differences in children's production of obligatory and variable phonological alternations. *Language Sciences* 33(1): 180–191.

Craig, Holly K. and Julie A. Washington. 2006. *Malik Goes to School: Examining the Language Skills of African American Students from Preschool-5th Grade*. Mahwah, NJ: Lawrence Erlbaum Associates.

Díaz-Campos, Manual. 2005. The emergence of adult-like command of sociolinguistic variables: A study of consonant weakening in Spanish-speaking children. In David Eddington (ed.), *Selected Proceedings of the 6th Conference on the Acquisition of Spanish and Portuguese as First and Second Languages*, 56–65. Somerville, MA: Cascadilla Proceedings Project.

Eckert, Penelope. 2000. *Linguistic Variation as Social Practice: The Linguistic Construction of Social Meaning in Belten High*. Oxford: Blackwell.

Eckert, Penelope and Sally McConnell-Ginet. 2003. *Language and Gender.* Cambridge: Cambridge University Press.

Eisikovits, Edina. 1997. Sex differences in inter- and intra-group interactions among adolescents. In Anne Pawels (ed.), *Women and Language in Australia and New Zealand Society*, 45–58. Sydney: Australian Professional Publications.

Foulkes, Paul, Gerard Docherty, and Dominic Watt. 1999. Tracking the emergence of structured variation realizations of (t) by Newcastle children. *Leeds Working Papers in Linguistics and Phonetics* 7: 1–23.

Foulkes, Paul, Gerard Docherty, and Dominic Watt. 2005. Phonological variation in child-directed speech. *Language* 81(1): 177–205.

Garbarino, James, Janet Sebes, and Cynthia Schellenbach. 1984. Families at risk for destructive parent-child relations in adolescence. *Child Development* 55(1): 174–183.

Giles, Howard and Peter F. Powesland. 1975. *Speech Style and Social Evaluation*. London/New York: Academic Press, Inc.

Green, Lisa J. 2011. *Language and the African American Child*. Cambridge: Cambridge University Press.

Hazen, Kirk. 2002. The family. In J.K. Chambers, Peter Trudgill and Natalie Schilling-Estes (eds.), *The Handbook of Language Variation and Change*, 500–525. Oxford: Blackwell.

Holmes, Thomas H. and Richard H. Rahe. 1967. The social readjustment rating scale. *Journal of Psychosomatic Research* 11(2): 213–218.

Hymes, Dell. 1974. *Foundations in Sociolinguistics: An Ethnographic Approach*. Philadelphia, PA: University of Pennsylvania Press.

Johnson, Daniel Ezra. 2009. Getting off the Goldvarb standard: Introducing Rbrul for mixed-effects variable rule analysis. *Language and Linguistics Compass* 3(1): 359–383.

Kerswill, Paul. 1996. Children, adolescents, and language change. *Language Variation and Change* 8(2): 177–202.

Kovac [Lucas], Ceil. 1980. *Children's Acquisition of Variable Features*. Ph.D. Dissertation. Washington, D.C.: Georgetown University.

Kovac, Ceil and H. Douglas Adamson. 1981. Variation theory and first language acquisition. In David Sankoff and Henrietta Cedergren (eds.), *Variation Omnibus: Current Inquiry into Language and Linguistics*, 403–410. Edmonton, AB: Linguistics Research, Inc.

Labov, William. 1965. Stages in the acquisition of Standard English. In Roger W. Shuy (ed.), *Social Dialects and Language Learning*, 77–103. Champaign, IL: National Council of Teachers of English.

Labov, William. 1989. The child as linguistic historian. *Language Variation and Change* 1(1): 85–97.

Labov, William. 1990. The intersection of sex and social class in the course of linguistic change. *Language Variation and Change* 2(2): 205–254.

Labov, William. 2001. *Principles of Linguistic Change, Vol. 2: Social Factors*. Malden, MA: Blackwell.

Loban, Walter. 1975. *Language Development: Kindergarten Through Grade Twelve*. Urbana, IL: National Council of Teachers.

Meyerhoff, Miriam. 2006. *Introducing Sociolinguistics*. New York: Routledge.

Miller, Jon and Aquiles Iglesias. 2008. Systematic Analysis of Language Transcripts (SALT) (Version 2008.0.1) [Computer Software]. SALT Software, LLC.

Nardy, Aurélie, Jean-Pierre Chevrot, and Stéphanie Barbu. 2014. Sociolinguistic convergence and social interactions within a group of preschoolers: A longitudinal study. *Language Variation and Change* 26(3): 273–301.

Oetting, Janna B. and Janet L. McDonald. 2002. Methods for characterizing participants' nonmainstream dialect use in child language research. *Journal of Speech, Language, and Hearing Research* 45(3): 505–518.

Pianta, Robert C. 1992. *Child-parent Relationship Scale*. Unpublished measure, University of Virginia. https://curry.virginia.edu/faculty-research/centers-labs-projects/castl/measures-developed-robert-c-pianta-phd

Pianta, Robert C., Sheri L. Nimetz, and Elizabeth Bennett. 1997. Mother-child relationships, teacher-child relationships, and school outcomes in preschool and kindergarten. *Early Childhood Research Quarterly* 12(3): 263–280.

Renn, Jennifer E. 2007. *Measuring Style Shift: A Quantitative Analysis of African American English*. Master's thesis. Chapel Hill, NC: University of North Carolina at Chapel Hill.

Renn, Jennifer E. 2010. *Acquiring Style: The Development of Dialect Shifting among African American Children*. Ph.D. Dissertation. Chapel Hill, NC: University of North Carolina at Chapel Hill.

Renn, Jennifer E. and J. Michael Terry. 2009. Operationalizing style: Quantifying style shift in the speech of African American adolescents. *American Speech* 84(4): 367–390.

Reveron, Wilhelmina Wright. 1978. *The Acquisition of Four Black English Morphological Rules by Black Preschool Children*. Ph.D. dissertation. Columbus, OH: The Ohio State University.

Rickford, John R., Arnetha Ball, Renée Blake, Raina Jackson, and Naomi Martin. 1991. Rappin on the copula coffin: Theoretical and methodological issues in the analysis of copula variation in African American Vernacular English. *Language Variation and Change* 3(1): 103–132.

Rickford, John R. and Christine Théberge Rafal. 1995. Preterite *had* + v-*ed* in the narratives of African-American preadolescents. *American Speech* 71(3): 227–254.

Roberts, Julie. 1997. Hitting a moving target: Acquisition of sound change in progress by Philadelphia children. *Language Variation and Change* 9(2): 249–265.

Roberts, Julie. 2002. Child language variation. In J.K. Chambers, Peter Trudgill, and Natalie Schilling-Estes (eds.), *The Handbook of Language Variation and Change*, 333–348. Oxford: Blackwell.

Roberts, Julie and William Labov. 1995. Learning to talk Philadelphian: Acquisition of short *a* by preschool children. *Language Variation and Change* 7(1): 101–12.

Scherre, Maria Marta Pereira and Anthony J. Naro. 1992. The serial effect on internal and external variables. *Language Variation and Change* 4(1): 1–13.

Sankoff, David, Sali A. Tagliamonte, and Eric Smith. 2005. GoldVarb (Version 3.0b3) [Computer Program]. Retrieved March 31, 2008, from http://individual.utoronto.ca/tagliamonte/goldvarb.html.

Shonkoff, Jack and Deborah Phillips (eds.), 2000. *From Neurons to Neighborhoods: The Science of Early Childhood Development*. Washington, DC: National Academy Press.

Singer, Judith and John Willett. 2003. *Applied Longitudinal Data Analysis: Modeling Change and Even Occurrence*. Oxford: Oxford University Press.

Sirkin, R. Mark. 2005. *Statistics for the Social Sciences*, 3rd ed. Thousand Oaks, CA: Sage Publications.

Smith, Jennifer, Mercedes Durham, and Liane Fortune. 2007. "Mam, my trousers is fa'in doon!": Community, caregiver, and child in the acquisition of variation in a Scottish dialect. *Language Variation and Change* 19(1): 63–99.

Smith, Jennifer, Mercedes Durham, and Hazel M. Richards 2013. The social and linguistic in the acquisition of sociolinguistic norms: Caregivers, children, and variation. *Linguistics* 51(2): 285–324.

Snow, Catherine E. 1972. Mothers' speech to children learning language. *Child Development* 43(2): 549–565.

Snow, Catherine E. 1985. Conversations with children. In Paul Fletcher and Michael Garman (eds.), *Language Acquisition*, 2nd ed., 69–89. Cambridge: Cambridge University Press.

Snow, Catherine E. 1995. Issues in the study of input: Fine tuning, universality, individual and developmental differences, and necessary causes. In Paul Fletcher and Brian MacWhinney (eds.), *The Handbook of Child Language*, 180–193. Oxford: Blackwell.

Steffenson, Margaret S. 1974. *The Acquisition of Black English*. Ph.D. Dissertation. Urbana, IL: University of Illinois, Urbana-Champaign.

Stockman, Ida J. and Fay Boyd Vaughn-Cooke. 1982. A re-examination of research on the language of Black children: The need for a new framework. *Journal of Education* 164(2): 157–172.

Stockman, Ida. J. and Anna Fay Vaughn-Cooke. 1989. Addressing new questions about black children's language. In Deborah Schiffrin and Ralph W. Fasold (eds.), *Current Issues in Linguistic Theory* 52, 275–300. Philadelphia, PA: John Benjamins.

Van Hofwegen, Janneke. 2011. A Caregiver's Influence on AAE Vernacularity across the Early Lifespan. Paper presented at *the Linguistic Society of America* 2011 Annual Meeting. Pittsburgh, Pennsylvania, January.

Van Hofwegen, Janneke. 2015. The development of African American English through childhood and adolescence. In Sonja L. Lanehart (ed.), *The Oxford Handbook of African American Language*, 454–474. Oxford: Oxford University Press.

Van Hofwegen, Janneke and Walt Wolfram. 2010. Coming of age in African American English: A longitudinal study. *Journal of Sociolinguistics* 14(4): 427–455.

Washington, Julie A. and Holly K. Craig. 2002. Morphosyntactic forms of African American English used by young children and their caretakers. *Journal of Applied Psycholinguistics* 23(2): 209–231.

6 The Influence of Peers on the Use of African American Language

Speaker 1072 lived in Durham all her life and is keenly aware that her speech reflects her community. During her post-high school interview, she relates traveling to New York City, only to find that people found the way she spoke to be "country," in comparison to their speech patterns. An adept style-shifter, she said she speaks differently to those closest to her: "I really just talk slang to like my friends." As 1072 reports, "Most of the people that I went to school with . . . that's how I learned most of the talk – from school." Yet, this way of communicating, as she relates, may have been generation-specific: "Trying to talk to my mom . . . I have tried to talk to her in slang and she just like 'what?' or 'what that mean?'" The effect of peers has been a primary focus of analysis for sociolinguistics; yet, while cumulative outcomes for peer effects have been well-documented, we know little about how moment-to-moment might produce this effect. Further, the effect of more casual and less-sustained interactions demands further attention. To what extent do informal interactions with acquaintances impact language variation? Does the closeness of a friendship matter as children develop their sense of style?

6.1 Introduction

It is well-established that adolescents use the language of peers as models for dialect acquisition in ways that sometimes diverge from their family or home variety (Kerswill 1996; Bucholtz 2000; Chambers 2003; Eckert 2004), often leading to broad heterogeneity and unpredictability during this period. Communication Accommodation Theory (CAT) (Giles 1973, 2008; Giles and Gasiorek 2013) predicts that speakers in an interaction will either *converge* to, *diverge* from, or *maintain their distance* from others' communication styles (including dialect), based on the social and psychological characteristics of the speakers and/or the community with which they identify. Given the relative prominence of identity practices and peer relationships, peer interactions have the potential to show rather dramatic similarities or differences based on these factors.

This chapter examines dimensions of peer accommodation in AAL based on the examination of dyadic speech. As described in Chapter 2, the collection of data in this study added a peer subject in Grade 6 for each of the primary subjects, and the analyses of students in secondary school included dyad interviews as a regular part of collecting language data subsequent to Grade 6 (Grade 8, 10), thus providing longitudinal data for dyads as well as other language samples.

To examine relative linguistic accommodation within peer dyads, the study explores two novel analytical tools that have not previously been applied to the CAT framework (Giles 1973; Giles and Ogay 2007). First, we use the composite index of linguistic features – specifically, a DDM of AAL that we use elsewhere in this study (see Chapter 3). As noted throughout this book, the DDM allows us to assess overall usage of a particular linguistic variety in comparison to another variety with which it shares most of its linguistic system. Given its applicability as a tool for assessing ethnic dialect usage, the DDM is appropriate for CAT-related studies, particularly those that take *ethnolinguistic vitality* (Giles and Johnson 1987) into consideration. As many CAT studies have found, accommodative behavior can be predicted by the degree to which interactants relate to the predominant social categories to which they and their interlocutors belong (Giles and Ogay 2007). In this framework, ethnicity is one major social category. As Giles and Ogay (2007) explain, in the American context, the subjective ethnolinguistic vitality experienced by an African American may lead them to actively maintain their ethnic identity via the use of uniquely AAL patterns and other African American sociocultural markers. Depending on the subjective ethnolinguistic reality of speakers, the ethnic language and cultural features they use in interactions will vary by their perceptions of the ethnic identity of both themselves and their interlocutors. Thus, a holistic quantitative measure of the linguistic features of African American ethnic identity can index accommodation based on the use of ethnolinguistically indexed variants.

Another analytical advantage to using a DDM is that it allows for post hoc, feature-specific, or feature-subset analyses. As an index composed of many individual linguistic features, it is relatively easy to isolate a feature or a subset of features for a more in-depth analysis. As explained in Chapter 2, the DDM used in this analysis is composed of forty-one morphosyntactic and three phonological features of AAL, but not all of these features carry the same kind of sociolinguistic salience. For example, some of the features are salient markers of AAL identity. Other features, while utilized in AAL, are also prevalent in other varieties of English to mark relative formality/informality. If we divide the DDM into feature subsets based on these different types of sociolinguistic salience, we can assess the extent to which different types of AAL features may accommodate differently and for whom.

The second novel analytical tool used in this peer accommodation study is *dyadic analysis* through multilevel mixed effects regression (Kenny et al. 2006). This statistical methodology allows an analyst to test whether *within-dyad* similarity is greater or less than *between-dyad* similarity in a very large dyadic dataset. Coupled with a DDM, this analysis can be used to draw broad-scale conclusions about linguistic behavior within many dyads in a large speech sample. Moreover, this sort of regression analysis also allows for the incorporation of external factors, aimed at testing whether they may significantly affect relative accommodation within peer dyads. Using these two powerful analytical tools, we offer a comprehensive analysis of accommodation in a speech community of high interest for sociolinguists and social scientists alike.

In the following section, we offer a basic overview of CAT and its applications in the study of linguistic variation. We then offer a general summary of accommodation and variationist work on adolescent language, particularly in the communicative practices of African American adolescents. Following that, we explore how different inter-group and contextual saliences corresponding to different linguistic feature sets may exhibit different accommodation patterns. Finally, we consider the potential impact of psychosocial factors on linguistic accommodation.

6.2   Communication Accommodation Theory and Linguistic Variation

CAT provides a framework through which analysts have been able to understand dynamics between two or more interactional participants. For scholars of language variation in particular, accommodation theory has done much to explain why the use of some linguistic features of the same speaker can vary so much in different contexts with different interlocutors. Observations of this situation-based linguistic variation have informed sociolinguistic theories of style (e.g., Labov 1972b; Bell 1984; Eckert 2001; Coupland 2007), and the tenets of CAT are either directly incorporated in or indirectly parallel to these theories. Stylistic and linguistic variations are indelible markers of interactional moves toward or against individuals, social groups, and institutions. Thus, CAT offers an important theoretical resource for understanding the social and psychological influences on linguistic variation.

CAT's primary thrust involves gauging the extent to which *accommodation* occurs in an interaction, whether speakers *converge*, *diverge*, or *maintain* their distance in terms of relevant features of communication. Upon close consideration, we can see that this framework is quite complex to implement in analytical practice. What does accommodation actually look like in real interactions? What are the measurable units involved? How can we gauge whether a particular group in interaction has in fact accommodated to a sufficient or significant degree? Finally, how might we be able to measure accommodation across many interactions?

A review of the variationist literature shows many instances in which analysts have addressed the first three questions in meaningful ways (e.g., Coupland 1980, 1984; Rickford and McNair-Knox 1994; Hazen 2000; Schilling-Estes 2004). To be sure, there is much to be learned from an in-depth analysis of one or a small number of linguistic variables in the speech of just one person as they interact with more than one interlocutor. However, in this new era of "big data," with publicly available large-scale corpora comprising millions of words – with data from many, many speakers of all stripes – we now have the ability to answer larger, population-level questions about accommodation. Macroscale analysis can shed brighter light on the dynamics of linguistic change and sociological phenomena that a microscale study might only dimly illuminate.

6.2.1   Accommodation in Adolescent Speech

What is known about peer influence on adolescent speech, particularly African American adolescent speech? As discussed in Chapter 5, we know that a child's earliest models for language acquisition come from their caregivers; we also know that beyond the age of four, it is virtually impossible to control for caregiver effects (Foulkes et al. 2005) on a child's speech. In reality, once a child enters school all bets are off as to which are her most profound linguistic influences. Especially during adolescence, peer influence becomes perhaps the most prominent input source. Labov (1965: 91) observed that "roughly ages five to twelve the child learns the use of the local dialect in a form consistent with that of his [sic] immediate group of friends and associates." In fact, not only do the child's peers serve as prominent linguistic influences during this time, but their influence is also strongly in the direction of the vernacular (Labov 1972b).

Many studies of adolescent speech reveal adolescent speakers to be marching to the beat of their own multifarious drums. As Eckert (1997) says, "Adolescents lead the entire age spectrum in sound change and in the general use of vernacular variables, and this lead is attributed to adolescents' engagement in constructing identities in opposition to – or at least independently of – their elders" (p. 163). This observation has played out repeatedly in the variationist literature, from Cheshire's (1982) study of adolescent "vernacular culture" in Reading, England, to Labov's (1972a) landmark study of African American youths in New York.

Variationists are not the only ones to notice this trend. Theorists in Intergroup Communication have analyzed the intergenerational communicative divide in great detail, recognizing that interpersonal communication is more than just one person talking to another. Rather, "communication with one another provides information about groups in society, and the ways in which information about groups and group memberships shape communication" (Giles et al. 2010:2). Representatives of different generations are, in many ways, representatives of different social groups; hence, communication across generations is a type of intergroup communication.

Those who study inter-generational communication between adolescents and their parents or grandparents have observed two phenomena important for the discussion here. First, adolescents' need for autonomy and attachment with peers contributes to divergent communicative patterns in interactions with parents and teachers (Garrett and Williams 2005). In language variation, these patterns play out in the use of drastically different or contrastive features between adolescent speakers and their elders, that is, they show divergence.

Adolescents may not just oppose elders; they may also oppose other peer groups, institutions, or entire social categories, an opposition that also plays out linguistically. For example, Bucholtz (1996) observed this in her study of "geek" girls in Northern California, who persisted in using super-standard and even supra-regional (i.e., British English) features, to set themselves off (*divergence* in CAT terms) from the "cool California" personae that their peers in school embodied. In another study, Mendoza-Denton (1996, 2008) illustrated how language choice (between Spanish and English) or even different styles of English were utilized by adolescent Latinas as means of opposing some groups and affiliating with others in contextually differing ways; again, all salient examples of intergroup communication with important ramifications for relative accommodation. Moore (2003, 2004) also looks at this with Sheffield school girls in a two-time-point study, illustrating that trajectories of change were dependent on peer group identity.

An important observation about adolescent communication is that it tends to the informal (oftentimes vulgar) (de Klerk 2005) and functions toward peer-relational and leisurely ends (Hendry and Kloep 2005). Again, in language variation terms, this would predict a preference for non-mainstream, vernacular speech. Particularly, as Eckert (2004) describes it, it is an orientation towards a *locally defined vernacular*. Eckert describes the vernacular as existing in opposition to the *standard*, or the language used by parents, teachers, institutions, etc. Whether they are characterized by "toughness," as with Cheshire's adolescents in Reading, England, or super-standard speech like Bucholtz's geeks in California, there is good reason to suspect that, linguistically speaking, adolescents who share the same locally defined contexts will be more similar to each other than they will be to individuals from different contexts.

For those who speak an ethnic variety, a large part of what "local" means may be ethnic identity. For African American adolescents, however, studies of linguistic accommodation are very limited, and we might look to the intergroup communication literature for some insight on what patterns to expect in interactions between these kinds of individuals. Additionally, ethnolinguistic vitality theory sheds light on why individuals reflect or promote their ethnic identity in interactions with others in myriad ways. Studies have shown that African Americans, as a group, are generally very sensitive to these dynamics. For example, Hecht et al. (1992) found that in interethnic encounters between African and European Americans, racial group membership was the most salient factor in determining communicative satisfaction, as "interethnic communication may be mainly an enactment of larger group identity" (Hecht et al. 1992:226). In their study of African American identity, Hecht and Ribeau (1991) found that participants were extremely aware of the differences in communication behaviors (including dialect) between ethnic groups, and indeed these factors were important contributors to cultural identity and experience. Not only are they sensitive to these interethnic dynamics, but many African Americans also actively pursue avenues for presenting their ethnic identities through everyday practices (Abrams and Giles 2007). Ethnolinguistic communication is one important practice for exhibiting ethnic identity.

The most notable variationist study conducted on data gathered from interactions with African American interlocutors (Rickford and McNair-Knox 1994) demonstrated that a female African American adolescent named Foxy Boston in the study used more AAL features (i.e., possessive -s absence, plural -s absence, third-singular -s absence, copula absence, invariant be) with another adolescent female African American interlocutor than she did with an adult African American female interlocutor. Moreover, in a separate setting with a white female interlocutor, she used even less vernacular AAL than with the adult African American female. From this study, we see a pattern emerging where both age (adolescence) and ethnicity (African American) predict vernacularity and accommodation together, a pattern consistent with accommodation, intergroup, and ethnolinguistic vitality theories.

Another intergroup framework in adolescent interactions is that of intergender communication. CAT studies have found women to be generally more accommodating than men (Giles and Ogay 2007), especially in mixed-gender interactions, but still the results are varied. Oftentimes it is not gender, but communicative style that determines men's or women's communicative patterns (Hannah and Murachver 1999). Indeed, when gender is not a salient factor in an interaction, men and women are often indistinguishable in their communicative styles (Palomares 2004; Kalbfleisch 2010). For adolescents in particular, constructing gender identities and participating in the heterosexual marketplace are paramount pursuits (Eckert 2005). Thus, for most adolescents, gender and sexuality are very salient sociocultural determiners of communicative practices and are thus extremely important factors to consider in any study of accommodation.

Gender is important not just from an accommodation perspective, but also a sociolinguistic one. Linguists have long noted gender to be a major social factor predicting language variation. Indeed, Labov (1990) proposes in his three principles regarding gender and language variation that females are (paradoxically) more standard and also more innovative in their use of linguistic variables. Work on AAL (e.g., Wolfram 1969) has found that female speakers use fewer AAL features than male speakers do. Thus, a study like this one – that controls for ethnicity, age, and social class – must also consider gender in the analysis of accommodation of linguistic features. Accordingly, we consider not only relative accommodation for the whole dyadic sample, but also for male and female dyad subsamples.

6.2.2   Psychosocial Factors and Accommodation

As Giles, Coupland, and Coupland (1991) explain, the application of accommodation theory has expanded beyond the domains of speech/language alone and has taken on more interdisciplinary perspectives. Indeed, accommodation is a *communicative* practice, encompassing not just language variables, but also other discursive components of social interaction. Moreover, the underpinnings of accommodation/non-accommodation derive from social/psychological impulses. Soliz and Giles (2014:115) report that 76 out of 104 quantitative studies of CAT to date include psycho-social correlates such as *compliance, group/individual evaluation, group salience, power, well-being, relational solidarity*, etc. We know from work on adolescent development that the effects of self-esteem as well as social engagement and environment are profound (Thurlow 2005). Thus, it is prudent to include psychosocial information in the consideration/analysis of accommodation, where such information is available.

6.2.3   Large-scale Studies on Adolescent African American Peer Dyads

There are no large-scale variationist accommodation studies on adolescent dyadic speech, much less African American adolescent speech. There are, however, some nonvariationist studies on African American adolescent dyads that look at discourse features and interactional characteristics for larger sample sets. These studies have found mixed results regarding the effect of ethnicity on dyadic similarity. For example, Ciccia and Turkstra (2002) and Turkstra et al. (2003) analyzed twenty-five same- and mixed-race dyads and found no ethnicity effect on the similarity in use of various discourse features, but they did find age and, to a lesser extent, gender to be significant predictors. Filardo (1996), analyzing twenty-two White and twenty African American mixed-gender adolescent dyads, found that African American dyads illustrated greater equality of activity and level of influence than did the White dyads, suggesting that ethnicity plays an important role in predicting interactional similarity (i.e., accommodation), even when other important identity markers (gender) are different.

Further, issues of replicability and generalizability demand that we go beyond the case-study format typical of peer dyad studies such as Rickford and McNair-Knox (1994) – as insightful as they are for our understanding and formulating further hypotheses. We need studies with more features and more dyads, and our dataset of dyad interviews affords us this opportunity.

6.3   The Dataset

This study analyzes the extent of accommodation in terms of both overall AAL usage and feature-subset usage, as well as the effects on accommodation of relevant psychosocial variables, in 201 African American adolescent dyads, composed of 119 female and 82 male pairs. The dyads were derived from the original cohort of seventy participants. We focus on three temporal points for the peers: Grade 6 (about 11 years old), Grade 8 (about 13 years old), and Grade 10 (about 15 years old). At Grades 6 and 8, the longitudinal children interacted with peers of their own choice (i.e., friends); a subset of the kids chose the same friends for both interactions. At Grade 10, the longitudinal children were given a nonfamiliar peer to interact with, who shared their age, gender, and ethnic characteristics. Overall AAL usage was assessed through a DDM as described in Chapter 2, and dyadic analysis was used to assess accommodation. Table 6.1 summarizes the composition of the sample.

As the first study of this kind to incorporate the tenets of CAT, the goals are ambitious, but the richness of the data enables us to address a number of questions. First, the analysis asks whether same-age and -gender African American adolescent dyads exhibit any significant degree of accommodation in terms of overall AAL usage. Given the literature on adolescent communication, we would expect that all adolescent dyads might accommodate to a significant degree and that girls might be more accommodative than boys. Thus, we can offer the following hypotheses:

Hypothesis 1a: Within-dyad similarity will be high and significant (i.e., accommodation) for all dyads across all age points.

Hypothesis 1b: Within-dyad similarity (i.e., accommodation) will generally be higher for girls than for boys.

The analysis also asks whether accommodation differs across time or according to specific sampling characteristics of the dyads (whether dyad members know each other or not, or whether they have consistently chosen each other or not). As summarized in Table 6.1, this longitudinal dyadic sample

Table 6.1 *Summary of dyadic types for each set of dyadic analyses (overall AAL usage). From Van Hofwegen 2015a: 32.*

	N (Dyads)	Grade 6	Grade 8	Grade 10
Age/Grade	N (Total)	65	82	54
	N (Girls)	39	50	30
	N (Boys)	26	32	24

	N (Dyads)	Same friend Grades 6, 8	Different friend Grade 6	Different friend Grade 8
Peer Consistency	N (Total)	21	44	61
	N (Girls)	12	27	38
	N (Boys)	9	17	23

	N (Dyads)	Peer chosen Grades 6, 8	Random Grade 10
Peer Selection	N (Total)	126	54
	N (Girls)	89	30
	N (Boys)	58	24

is composed of several different dyadic types. The main distinctions between these types are *how long/well the peers know each other* (peer consistency) and *whether they know each other at all* (peer selection). In both cases, we would predict that dyads whose members have longstanding friendships would show greater accommodation, and that dyads composed of strangers would show comparatively less accommodation, leading to the following hypotheses:

Hypothesis 2a: All children (boys and girls) will show greater accommodation with someone they know than with a stranger.

Hypothesis 2b: All children (boys and girls) will show greater accommodation with a friend they have chosen twice over two years than with different friends.

Next, the study explores the question of sociolinguistic salience in accommodation. That is, are formality-based or ethnicity-based linguistic features more likely to be accommodated in adolescent peer interactions? In this exploratory analysis, a portion of the DDM was excised to create two feature subsets with different sociolinguistic saliences: formality/informality and ethnicity. Given what we know about the adolescent tendency toward the vernacular, including casual/informal styles, we might expect that these features would figure prominently in accommodative practices. The same would be expected for ethnically salient features, given the importance of ethnolinguistic identity in interaction. Thus, both feature subsets should show significant accommodation; the question remains as to whether their accommodative patterns would differ based on peer characteristics. Accordingly, this leads to the next hypotheses:

Hypothesis 3a: Ethnicity-salient linguistic features will be accommodated significantly by both boys and girls across all ages. These features will show less accommodation with peers who do not know each other.

Hypothesis 3b: Formality-salient linguistic features will be accommodated significantly by both boys and girls across all ages. These features will show less accommodation with peers who do not know each other.

Finally, we address the question of whether accommodative patterns are impacted by psychosocial factors, since CAT and its sister theories are grounded thoroughly in the social and psychological domains. To address this question specifically, several measures pertaining to dyadic friendship quality, speaker self-esteem, ethnic identity, social skills, number of African American or White contacts, and percentage of African Americans in speakers' schools were incorporated in the dyadic analysis. We can therefore hypothesize the following:

Hypothesis 4: Psychosocial factors related to the quality of the dyadic relationship, the personal and ethnolinguistic identities of the speakers, and the social skills and contexts of the speakers will affect the degree to which dyads accommodate.

Dyadic analysis is a way of assessing the *within-dyad* similarity vis-à-vis the *between-dyad* (i.e., population) similarity in a particular dyadic sample. As Kenny et al. (2006:1) explain, "The dyad is arguably the fundamental unit of interpersonal interaction and interpersonal relations." In fact, much of human experience is dyadic in nature: interpersonal relationships (e.g., marriage, friendship), professional relationships (e.g., manager-employee), and even the carrying out of daily tasks (e.g., store clerk-customer, doctor-patient, teacher-student, etc.). As a consequence of this basic fact of human experience, much of the academic study of these experiences is necessarily dyadic. However, as Kenny et al. point out, a common error in research is one of *pseudo-unilaterality*: that is, thinking that a dyadic measure refers to only one of the interaction partners. Researchers guilty of committing this error often carry out analyses in which one member of the dyad is the dependent variable and the other member is included as a predicting factor, not a necessary component of the unit under analysis.

In dyadic analysis, it is the *dyad* that is the unit under analysis, with some other quantity (for example, a DDM score) being the unit of measure. The members of a dyad are *nonindependent* by the very nature of sharing in the same enterprise (i.e., the interaction or transaction in question). Thus, it is the degree of nonindependence between them that needs to be operationalized in dyadic analysis. The degree of non-independence across a sample of dyads can be quantified (for *indistinguishable* dyads[1]) by means of an *intraclass correlation coefficient* (ICC), based on the quantity of measure. A significant ICC reflects the significant effect of within-dyad variance. That is, the variance in the unit of measure is accounted for by the *dyad*, as opposed to random chance.

ICC scores between two different dyad samples can be statistically compared (Haggard 1958; Donner and Bull 1983) to see if one sample's ICC reflects significantly more within-dyad similarity (accommodation) than the other does. Other predictors can be incorporated into a model as well, thus calculating a *partial* ICC in order to assess the effect of those predictors on the overall within-dyad variation. Altogether, dyadic analysis is a useful tool for accommodation theorists, because it enables them to calculate relative similarities (for some measure) within dyads for a large sample and to determine which other factors might affect relative accommodation.

6.4   Parameters of Analysis

In order to address the questions and hypotheses outlined earlier, this dyadic analysis consisted of numerous sub-analyses, depending on the dyadic characteristics and the measures in question (overall AAL usage, feature subset usage, psychosocial factors, etc.). The following sections first provide detailed information about the dyadic types and then about the analytical process.

6.4.1   Dyad Distinguishing Characteristics

Given the way in which peers were selected for the longitudinal children at each time point, the samples of peer dyads in the analysis have several distinguishing characteristics. The first, most obvious difference within the dyad set is age/grade – there are three different ages at which the peer interactions were recorded. Thus, three different dyad samples can be

---

[1] *Distinguishability* is an important factor to consider in any dyadic analysis. As Kenny et al. (2006:6) define it, "Dyad members are considered distinguishable if there is a meaningful factor that can be used to order the two persons." If dyad members are *indistinguishable*, then there is no factor by which their two scores can be ordered. Examples of indistinguishable dyads include same-sex friendship pairs, identical twins, etc. By definition, then, the dyads in this study are indistinguishable. *Distinguishable* dyads, in contrast, are composed of members that are dissimilar in some crucial way (e.g., husband and wife, parent and child, waiter and customer). Thus, distinguishable dyad scores must be ordered based on this variable, and instead of an *intra-class correlation coefficient*, a *Pearson correlation coefficient* is calculated to assess their relative accommodation.

compared based on potential change over time. Because the types of dyads were different at each age group, however, any age-related results must be taken as merely suggestive, rather than definitive, of overall patterns.

Another distinguishing factor for the dyad samples was peer choice, primarily whether there was consistency between the peers chosen at Grades 6 and 8, and the fact that the Grade 10 peers were strangers. As mentioned earlier, at Grades 6 and 8, the children chose their peer interlocutor, which, in most cases, was a close friend from school or the community. In fact, as shown in Table 6.1, a subset of twenty-one children chose to bring the same friend to both the Grade 6 and Grade 8 peer interactions. Hence, in the Grade 6 and 8 dyad samples, twenty-one dyads contain exactly the same participants. These dyads are called *same-friend*, for the purposes of this study. The rest of the dyad samples are *different-friend*, meaning they selected different friends between Grade 6 and Grade 8.

Finally, at Grade 10, the peer interlocutor was randomly chosen, and thus not known by the child, though they still shared age, gender, and ethnicity characteristics. Altogether, these distinguishing features enabled three types of (albeit intersecting) analyses, testing: (1) whether age differences are reflected in relative peer accommodation; (2) whether accommodation between two same-friend interlocutors is greater than two different-friend interlocutors; and (3) whether prior relationship with the peer increases relative accommodation. Each of these analyses was conducted in two phases: first with all of the dyads, then according to gender.

6.4.2   The Application of Dyadic Analysis to the Data

For each of the dyadic samples indicated in Table 6.1, an ICC score was calculated for total dyads and by gender. For each dyad, a DDM score was calculated for each interlocutor, resulting in a *features-per-utterance* score (*fpu*) for every speaker. Then, multi-level mixed effects regression modeling was conducted for each dyadic sample, using the *xtmixed* function in STATA/IC 10.1. For these models, *fpu* was regressed as the sole outcome variable, with the dyad (*pair*) included as a random intercept. The key result to take note of in dyadic analysis is the *variance*, both for the constant and the residual. The variance of the constant in these models indicates the proportion of the variation that is predicted by the random effect of the dyad. Thus, in order to calculate the ICC for each analysis, the variance of the constant is divided by the total variance (constant plus residual) in the entire model. The ICC value, then, is essentially a percentage. For example, an ICC of 0.266 means that 26 percent of the overall variance in the DDM scores for the whole sample is accounted for by the dyadic character of the data. If the ICC is low, it means that the dyadic character of the data is not contributing much to the patterning of the outcome variable, and that the individual units (i.e., speakers) in the dyads are behaving independently. In terms of CAT, we can say that high ICCs indicate high accommodation and that low ICCs indicate very little accommodation (maintenance) or even divergence within dyads.[2] Relevant comparisons between ICCs for different dyadic samples were then conducted, as described in Kenny et al. (2006), using procedures developed by Haggard (1958) and Donner and Bull (1983). Next, z for each sample comparison was computed as the difference between the two transformed ICCs divided by the standard error of the difference. Finally, the (two-tailed) p- value corresponding to the z- score was recorded. The null hypothesis for this comparison is that there is no difference between the ICCs of the two samples. Thus, a significant p- value (alpha level = 0.05) at the end of the process reveals two ICCs that are significantly different from each other. This means that two dyadic samples are significantly different in the extent to which they accommodate. The calculation/identification of significant ICCs, as well as the comparison of ICCs across the dyadic types identified in Table 6.1, enables us to address the posed questions leading to Hypotheses 1a, 1b, 2a, and 2b.

6.4.3   Feature-subset Analysis

As mentioned earlier, a DDM can be divided into feature subsets based on different sociolinguistic saliences, and then dyadic analysis can be conducted using feature-subset scores, instead of overall DDM scores. Two feature subsets were identified in order to address Hypothesis 3a and 3b of whether or not they would exhibit different accommodative patterns. These subsets were determined based on their relative prevalence in the data and according to two different saliences: *ethnicity* and *formality*. The *ethnicity* features were *copula absence* and *third-person singular –s absence;* these are features specific to AAL and are not found in mainstream American English. Moreover, they are very salient identifiers of AAL (cf. Wolfram and Schilling 2016). The *formality* feature selected was an apical articulation of the nasal consonant in *–ing* (e.g., *walkin'* for *walking*), referred to, in this book, as *nasal fronting*. This feature is very prevalent in AAL, but is also found in most all varieties of English worldwide, and has been widely found to be sensitive to contextual formality (cf. Fischer 1958; Labov 1966; Wolfram et al. 2016). For each of these feature subsets,

---

[2] In order to do this, first, the ICC of each sample needed to be transformed via *Fisher's z-transformation*. Then the standard error of the difference between the two transformed ICCs being compared was calculated as the square root of: $1/(n_1-2) + 1/(n_2-2)$, where n_1 and n_2 refer to the number of dyads in each of the two samples. Next, z for each sample comparison was computed as the difference between the two transformed ICCs divided by the standard error of the difference. Finally, the (two-tailed) p-value corresponding to the z-score was recorded.

a *features-per-utterance* score (*subset-fpu*) was calculated for each speaker in each dyadic interaction, and dyadic analysis was subsequently conducted.

6.4.4   The Incorporation of Psychosocial Factors

The last stage in the analysis incorporates additional psychosocial factors, to address Hypothesis 4. When these are added into the multilevel mixed effects regressions utilized in dyadic analysis, they may or may not affect within-dyad similarity (ICC), and so a *partial intraclass correlation coefficient* (pICC) can be calculated in lieu of an ICC. The formula for calculating the pICC is identical to that for the ICC; the only difference being that for the ICC, the model is controlling for only the random effect of *pair*, while for pICC, the model includes additional controls in the form of relevant independent variables. If the pICC is higher than the original ICC (i.e., closer to 1.0), the analyst can conclude that the addition of factors has improved the within-dyad similarity (i.e., accommodation).

As mentioned earlier, the FPG database contains very rich and diverse data for each longitudinal child. In addition to the language samples, data available at any of the Grade 6, 8, and 10 points include all of the psychosocial and demographic factors shown in Table 6.2. These factors can be classified into dyad-specific (i.e., they pertain to the dyadic relationship), intrapersonal (i.e., they measure individual psychological characteristics of speakers), and interpersonal (i.e., they measure individual social characteristics of speakers) factors. These controls were incorporated into the dyadic analysis because each of them was hypothesized to affect the degree of within-dyad similarity (accommodation) in overall AAL use between peers in an interaction. The specific psychosocial factors included in the analysis, and at which age points, are summarized in Table 6.2.

The factors can be classified into three separate categories. The first category, *dyad-specific factors*, includes just one factor, the *Friendship Quality Questionnaire* (Parker and Asher 1993). This 40-item questionnaire asked each child to rate on a 5-point scale various truths about their friendship with their dyad partner. Even though the questionnaire produces individual scores for each member in the dyad, it is called a *dyad-specific* here, because the scores reflect the quality of each of the dyadic relationships in the sample from the perspectives of the dyad members. Data were gathered for this factor only in Grades 6 and 8, when the longitudinal children were asked to bring a friend of their choice. Questions comprised six different subscales, including validation and caring, conflict, help and guidance, companionship, and communication. A main principle of CAT is that communicators in interaction will be more motivated to accommodate if they are pleasantly inclined toward their interlocutor (Dragojevic et al. 2016). Thus,

Table 6.2 *Summary of dyad-specific, intrapersonal, and interpersonal psychosocial factors, and the grades for which these data were available. From Van Hofwegen 2015a: 36.*

	Grade 6	Grade 8	Grade 10
Dyad-specific factors			
Friendship Quality Questionnaire	✓	✓	
Intrapersonal factors			
HARE General and Area-specific Self-Esteem Scale (PEER Self-Esteem)	✓		✓
Multidimensional Inventory of Black Identity (MIBI; Centrality Scale)	✓		✓
Interpersonal factors			
Social Skills Rating System (Standard Student Score)	✓		✓
African American Social Contacts	✓		✓
White Social Contacts	✓		✓
Percentage of African Americans in school	✓		✓

we would expect dyad friendship quality to have an effect on relative accommodation.

The second category, *intrapersonal factors*, includes factors that reflect individual, psychological/emotional characteristics of the speakers. In this case, they point to the speakers' self-esteem and racial identity. The first factor, the *HARE General and Area-Specific Self-Esteem Scale* (Hare 1985), is a 30-item, Likert-type instrument, measuring general self-esteem as well as area-specific self-esteem, according to three separate areas/subscales corresponding to peer, school, and family domains. Giles et al. (1991) suggest a strong link between psychological (and physical) well-being and accommodative behavior: specifically, that there is a reciprocal relationship between being accommodative and feeling strong, engaged, and supported (i.e., high self-esteem). Thus, it is likely that a measure of speakers' self-esteem will reflect their accommodative behaviors.

The second intrapersonal factor, the *Multidimensional Inventory of Black Identity* (MIBI: Sellers et al. 1997), specifically its *Centrality Scale*, evaluates the extent to which race is core to a person's identity. This measure was included as a means of assessing each speaker's perception of their place in the ethnolinguistic landscape and their feelings of belonging to a salient ethnic group. The *Centrality* portion of the MIBI provides a composite self-reported score, based on Likert-type responses to five items: *I live in an area with other blacks, I like my friends to be black, I like to read books about black people, I feel close to other blacks, I am similar to other blacks.* As CAT theory posits, ethnolinguistic vitality and perceived group identity are major predictors of accommodative behavior, so including this measure in a dyadic analysis of the speech of African American adolescents is appropriate. Racial identity and centrality should have an effect on accommodation in this dyadic sample.

Finally, in the third category, we have *interpersonal factors,* which assess the speakers' social skills and types of interpersonal relationships. There were four interpersonal factors included in this analysis. The first is the *Social Skills Rating System* (SSRS: Gresham and Elliott 1990), a measure consisting of four subscales with ten items each, corresponding to the factors *Cooperation, Assertion, Self-control*, and *Empathy*. We know that the adolescent years are a formative time for the development of communication awareness (Thurlow and Marwick 2005). There is also a link between adolescents' group member-ships and their social development, including their ability to communicate appropriately within a variety of contexts and intergroup encounters (Fortman 2003). As intergroup communicative dynamics are an integral com-ponent of CAT, it is relevant, then, to include this factor in the dyadic analysis. It is likely that peer accommodation will be affected by relative differences in social skills.

The next three interpersonal factors are related to the speakers' involvement and exposure to salient ethnic groups in their community. The first two interper-sonal factors have to do with the quantity/quality of ethnic contacts in each speaker's life. These were determined using a 12-item self-reported question-naire (Sellers et al. 1997). Using Likert-like responses corresponding to different number ranges, children indicated how many of their close friends, neighbors, acquaintances, and visitors were African American or White. The score for this questionnaire produced two social contact measures for analysis: *African American Social Contacts* and *White Social Contacts*. The last ethnicity-based interpersonal factor was demographic in nature: the percentage of African Americans in each child's school. As with the MIBI, all of these ethnicity-related interpersonal measures were gathered in an attempt to holistically assess the speakers' ethnic in-group or out-group involvement. Thus, like the MIBI *Centrality* score, these ethnic contacts measures are likely to be predictive of accommodation based on intergroup and ethnolinguistic dynamics.

For overall AAL usage, dyadic analysis was used to test Hypotheses 1a and 1b, and 2a and 2b. First, relative accommodation (ICC) was compared across Grades 6, 8, and 10. Next, relative accommodation was compared between dyads who chose the same partners in Grades 6 and 8, and those who did not. Third, an analysis was conducted in terms of whether the dyads were personally chosen (Grades 6 and 8) or whether peer selection was random (Grade 10).

The feature-subset/sociolinguistic salience analysis (Hypotheses 3a and 3b) proceeded in terms of whether the children knew each other (Grades 6 and 8) or did not (Grade 10). As with the overall AAL usage analysis, the feature-subset analysis proceeded by first looking at all children and then subdividing by gender.

Finally, dyadic analysis incorporating psychosocial controls (Hypothesis 4) proceeded in a grade-by-grade and a by-gender fashion, based on the grades for which there was data (see Table 6.2). Thus, each factor described in Section 6.4.4 was incorporated into a dyadic analysis for a specific gender at a specific grade. First, that factor was evaluated as to whether it had a significant effect on the dependent variable (*fpu*). If so, a pICC was calculated. Then, pICCs were compared between models *with* the addition of a psychosocial control, and those *without*.

6.5   Results

In this section we present the results of the analysis in terms of the parameters presented in the previous section.

6.5.1   Overall AAL Similarity

Dyadic analysis on the entire sample revealed that, on the whole, the children were significantly very similar to their dyadic partners. That is, the *within-dyad* similarity was significant compared to the *between-dyad* (or population) similarity. This means that the influence of a peer interlocutor had an effect on the quantity of AAL usage for all speakers, supporting Hypothesis 1a. Figure 6.1 illustrates the ICCs (accommodation) for all speakers. As the figure clearly shows, the peer effect is high and significant. Additionally, the ICCs do not change significantly across age groups for all children.

When we look at the two genders separately, we see that there are different patterns evidenced by boys and girls. Gender-specific patterns in overall AAL usage are shown in Figure 6.2. Girls exhibit consistently high ICCs within dyads across the three years. At no point do the ICCs show significant change. Boys, however, are a different story. Specifically, boys' ICCs change dramatically across time points, notably with significant downward change (i.e., decreased within-dyad similarity) at Grade 10. Additionally, the ICC at Grade 10 is itself not significant. Overall, this pattern suggests that the boys increase their accommodative affinity between Grade 6 and 8, and then lose it completely at Grade 10, where there is no difference between the within- and between-dyad AAL usage. These findings support Hypothesis 1b in a sense (that girls are generally higher than boys), but there is more to the story than that. Something clearly happens in Grade 10 that causes boys to diverge sharply from their peers, likely the fact that their peers are strangers.

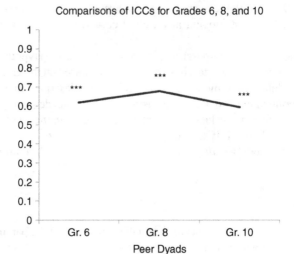

Comparisons of ICCs for Grades 6, 8, and 10

Significant ICC: *p < 0.05; **p < 0.01; ***p < 0.001

Figure 6.1 Overall AAL usage: ICCs across age groups for all dyads. From Van Hofwegen 2015a: 38

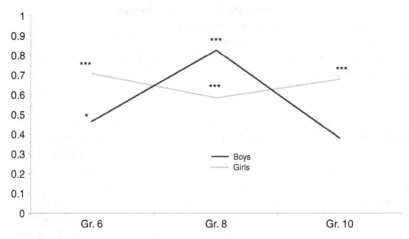

Significant ICC: *p < 0.05; **p < 0.01; ***p < 0.001

Figure 6.2 Overall AAL usage: Comparison of ICCs for Grades 6, 8, and 10, by gender. From Van Hofwegen 2015a: 38.

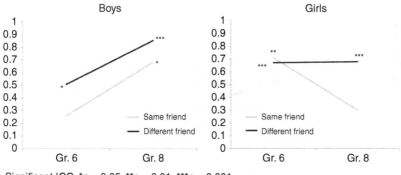

Significant ICC: *p < 0.05; **p < 0.01; ***p < 0.001

Figure 6.3 Overall AAL usage: Comparison of same-friend and different-friend dyads between Grades 6 and 8, by gender. From Van Hofwegen 2015a: 39

Peer interactions at Grades 6 and 8 show consistency; there is no overall difference in the data, findings that are inconsistent with Hypothesis 2a. At all points, the dyads show high and significant ICCs. The difference between the *same-friend* and *different-friend* dyads at Grade 8 is not significant (p = 0.09) at a 0.05 alpha level; however, a relatively low *p* value (less than 0.1) may still indicate a trend whereby *same-friend* dyads are less likely to accommodate than are *different-friend* dyads. While this pattern is suggestive, it is nonetheless counterintuitive. When we look at descriptive patterns in the ICCs of these dyads by gender, we see that the girls are driving this effect.

While dyadic analysis by gender is possible for the peer *consistency* category, statistical comparisons between categories cannot be made, due to the relatively low Ns for the *same-friend* dyads. However, ICCs can be calculated and some general gender trends can be noted. As Figure 6.3 shows, boys show an upward trend in ICC between Grades 6 and 8, regardless of peer consistency. ICC trend lines are parallel for the boys. Girls, on the other hand, show distinctly different trend lines for the two categories. *Different-friend* girl dyads have very similar ICCs in Grades 6 and 8, while *same-friend* girl dyads drop drastically in Grade 8, to the point where the ICC is not significant at all. Therefore, it is the *same-friend* girls who drastically lower their accommodative performance over the course of the two-year time span.

For the third analysis, considering dyads that are friends versus those that are strangers, we also see interesting patterns. For all youth (see dashed line, Figure 6.4), there is no significant difference between youth who know each other versus those who do not. This is inconsistent with Hypothesis 2b, where we expected to see a difference. But when we separate dyad samples

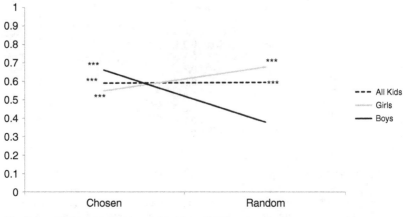

Significant ICC: *p < 0.05; **p < 0.01; ***p < 0.001

Figure 6.4 Overall AAL usage: ICCs of peer dyads who chose each other versus those who didn't (all kids), by gender. From Van Hofwegen 2015a: 39

by gender, we see that the apparent stability of the effect is largely due to the girls. Boys, it turns out, change dramatically in their relative accommodation depending on whether they know their interlocutor. In peer-chosen dyads, boys are significantly similar to their interlocutors; in randomly chosen dyads, boy dyads are not significantly similar. For individuals within randomly selected boy dyads, there appears to be next to no accommodation occurring. Findings for both boys and girls here are inconsistent with Hypothesis 2b: girls readily accommodate with their peer regardless, while boys do not accommodate with strangers.

In all, patterns of overall AAL usage within African American adolescent dyads show significant within-dyad similarity across all age points. The peer effect is powerful enough to produce high and significant ICCs for this sample. Boys and girls differ, however, in terms of how their accommodative tendencies change across the lifespan. Girls in this sample maintain consistent ICCs across the three age points, while boys show an increase and then a significant decrease in ICCs as they age. Children who choose the same partners between Grades 6 and 8 do not appear to differ in their accommodative tendencies, though boys and girls exhibit different suggestive trends. Finally, boys and girls differ significantly in terms of how they handle a peer they know or do not know. Girls show no difference in relative accommodation, while boys significantly diminish their accommodation when they do not know their interlocutor.

6.5.2   Ethnicity and Formality-Salient Feature Sets

The feature-subset analysis included specific subsets of the composite index of AAL features, those carrying *ethnic* salience (copula absence and third-person singular *–s* absence), and one carrying *formal/informal* salience (nasal fronting). For each of these feature subsets, a new *features-per-utterance* (*subset-fpu*) dependent variable was calculated for only the specific features in question. These new *subset-fpu* scores were then incorporated into dyadic analysis, testing their relative importance in explaining within-dyad variation in dyads who know each other versus those who do not. For all dyads in the sample, the ICCs for both types of feature sets and for both types of peers are always significant (though not as high as for the overall composite feature index in general). This supports both Hypothesis 3a and 3b. Again, though, when we separate by gender, we see different patterns.

As Figure 6.5 shows, boys exhibit a uniform decline in ICC for both types of feature sets – comparable to their ICC pattern for overall AAL usage – based on prior acquaintance with their peers. It is notable that for ethnically salient features in particular, the ICC ceases to be significant when the boys do not know their peers, while the formality-salient ICC remains significant. For girls, on the other hand, all ICCs are significant, but for the ethnically salient features, there is a significant increase in ICC when the speakers do not know each other. The feature-subset analysis thus shows that girls, particularly, draw upon their shared ethnolinguistic identity in their accommodative practices with strangers, as they show significant accommodation using the ethnically salient feature subset. But more nuance is needed in the hypothesis. The boy sample supports

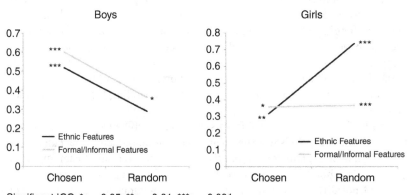

Figure 6.5   Feature subsets: ICCs of ethnic versus formality features by peer selection and by gender. From Van Hofwegen 2015a: 40.

Hypothesis 3b, in that formality-salient features are significantly accommodated in both peer selection contexts, but less so with strangers. The girl sample, on the other hand, while significantly accommodating these features (supporting the first part of Hypothesis 3b), shows no change in either context. Ethnicity-salient features, on the other hand, are no longer significantly accommodated for boys when interacting with strangers (proving Hypothesis 3a wrong), while for girls, the accommodative increase is dramatic and significant (likewise proving Hypothesis 3a wrong).

6.5.3   Effects of Psycho-social Factors

What happens to accommodative patterns when they are mitigated by psycho-social controls? Incorporating each of the dyad-specific, intrapersonal, and interpersonal factors into the dyadic analysis produced mixed results. Primarily, it was found that neither of the intrapersonal factors (the *HARE Self-Esteem Scale* and the *MIBI Racial Centrality* measure) had any significant effect on the overall variation in *fpu* (child AAL features per utterance) for any age or gender group. Thus, neither of these factors was found to play any role in the children's usage of AAE. Because they were not significant, these factors did not affect the variance controlled by the random effect of *pair*, and so no pICC was calculated for them. Contrary to Hypothesis 4, then, these factors were not significantly implicated in accommodation for these dyads.

The dyad-specific factor of *Friendship Quality* affected only one group significantly: Grade 8 girls. The pICC calculated for this factor in the model did not differ appreciably from the ICC without this control. However, for a subset of the girl dyads, the *same-friend* ones, we see that the addition of *Friendship Quality* in the model significantly improves their within-dyad similarity (see Figure 6.6). Thus, it appears that the within-dyad similarity improves for girls who have chosen the same peer for both Grades 6 and 8 when friendship quality is incorporated in the model. Given Hypothesis 4, it is surprising that this factor did not significantly impact other sub-samples in the study, suggesting that perhaps the self-reported quality of the relationship is not as important as other factors in predicting/controlling for accommodation in overall AAL usage.

Finally, for the interpersonal factors, we also see mixed and gender-specific results. As before, pICCs were only calculated for those factors that emerged as significant overall predictors of *fpu*. *White contacts* had a significant impact on *fpu* for girls at both Grades 6 and 10, but the pICC calculated for dyads at these ages did not differ substantially from the ICC without this control. *African American contacts* was also a significant predictor on *fpu* for boys at Grades 6, but not at Grade 10, and not for girls at any age. pICCs calculated for this factor for the boys at Grade 6 show no difference in pICC from the original ICC.

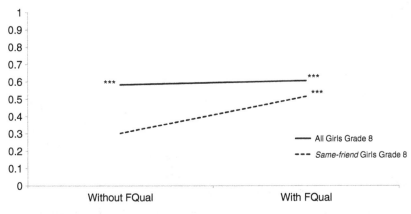

Significant ICC: *p < 0.05; **p < 0.01; ***p < 0.001

Figure 6.6 Comparison of ICCs without and with Friendship Quality (FQual) included as a control for all Grade 8 girls and for the subset of same-friend Grade 8 girls. From Van Hofwegen 2015a: 41.

Percentage of African Americans in school also significantly impacted *fpu*, but only for girls at Grade 6. The pICC, with this factor added, does not change the ICC. In all, given Hypothesis 4, it is surprising that these factors would not affect relative accommodation for any of these sample groups, regardless of peer selection method.

Grade 10 boys, however, appear to be the exception to this trend. Remember that they were the sample most affected by randomly selected peers, exhibiting striking non-accommodation in these contexts. With the addition of *African American contacts* to the model, their ICC improved to a significant margin. The same can be said for *Social Skills*, which significantly predicted boys' *fpu* at Grade 10 and also significantly improved their ICCs.

Figure 6.7 summarizes these significant interpersonal factors as well as the ICCs for the different dyad samples with or without the controls. For the sake of simplicity, only trend lines with significant ICC change are indicated in the figure.

Figure 6.7 shows that the significant interpersonal controls did not affect the girls' ICCs to any appreciable degree (they are all lowered, but are still relatively high and significant). The boys, on the other hand, show particular susceptibility to these controls at Grade 10, where we see that the addition of controls for *African American contacts* and *Social Skills* improves the ICC score to a significant level. In all, it is the randomly selected boy dyads who are consistent with Hypothesis 4. They are most affected by the interpersonal factors of social skills and quality/quantity of African American contacts.

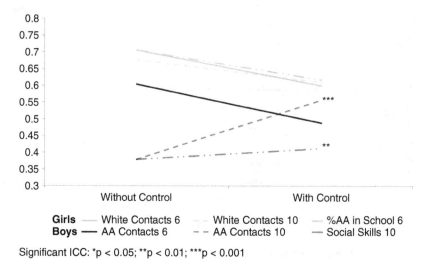

Significant ICC: *p < 0.05; **p < 0.01; ***p < 0.001

Figure 6.7 Significant psychosocial effects for boys and girls, grade indicated, without and with indicated controls. From Van Hofwegen 2015a: 41.

Controlling for these factors improves the ability of the ICC to detect accommodation between Grade 10 boy strangers.

6.6   On the Significance of Accommodation

In many ways, the hypotheses about accommodative practices among peer adolescent dyads were upheld, but with some surprises. First, we do see significant across-the-board accommodation in overall AAL usage for the whole sample. This is to be expected given Hypothesis 1a. However, when broken apart by gender, we note that the boys are strikingly less accommodative when they are paired with strangers, while the girls are consistently accommodative regardless of their partner. Girls, it seems, are quite keen on accommodating with strangers. In fact, girls show less accommodative tendency in *same-friend* dyads than in *different-friend* dyads, suggesting that knowing the interlocutor better/more inhibits rather than fosters accommodation in these individuals. Friendship quality, it appears, is orthogonal to this trend, as it is found to increase accommodation in the *same-friend* girl dyads.

Like the girls, boys are affected by the relationship with their interlocutor, but for them it has more to do with *whether they know* their interlocutor or not. If they do not know their interlocutor, then they will cease to accommodate, primarily in terms of ethnolinguistic means (i.e., through ethnically salient features). Only when the boys' social context (African American contacts) and relative social skills are factored in is accommodation improved.

While both ethnically and formality-salient features are readily accommodated, for both boys and girls, it is the ethnically salient feature subset that plays a more dramatic role in accommodation patterns. Boys who do not know their interlocutor will cease to accommodate with overall features, but will, at the same time, accommodate with formality-salient features. Girls, on the other hand, significantly increase their relative accommodation with ethnically salient features with interlocutors they do not know, while showing change in their accommodation of formality-salient features. In all, we see a striking and clear pattern in which boys and girls accommodate differently with different interlocutors, drawing upon different resources and utilizing different feature sets in doing so.

In contrast to their accommodation patterns, the lifespan development of overall AAL usage shows no differences between girls and boys. Van Hofwegen and Wolfram (2010) find no significant gender difference in terms of overall AAL usage across the lifespan; likewise Kohn (2014) finds no differences in vowel quality between genders across the lifespan. However, gender effects have been found in this population in other studies. First, Renn (2010) finds that the girls are more adept style-shifters than are the boys. That is, they are more likely to use more AAL features per utterance in informal language samples and fewer AAL features in formal contexts. Renn argues that more dramatic style-shifting in her data is evidence of sociolinguistic competence (Hymes 1974); thus, the girls can be said to be more sociolinguistically, communicatively, and socially competent than the boys. While girls may be more sociolinguistically sensitive, it is possible that this competence stems from a greater vulnerability/sensitivity to conventions dictating appropriate contexts for informal/formal speech. Thus, these differences may not be attributable to a greater *ability* to style-shift or accommodate but, rather, a greater *willingness* on the part of girls, and vice versa for boys. This vulnerability to social conventions and the exhibition of linguistic extremes has been evidenced widely in variationist work, perhaps most famously in the patterns of jocks and burnouts in Eckert (2000).

From a CAT perspective, we can think about these dynamics in terms of the *affective function* of accommodation. As Giles and Gasiorek (2013) point out, each interlocutor approaches an interaction with an initial orientation (derived from personal experience and sociocultural factors), which sets the tone for the interaction. In this context, the affective function of accommodation manages the interlocutors' concerns of social distance and personal identity. For girls, who display a pattern of relative similarity (i.e., *accommodation*) across dyads regardless of previous acquaintance, it is likely that they are initially oriented toward building positive rapport. Years of gender socialization have rewarded girls for this behavior (Eckert and McConnell-Ginet 2003), and as Giles (2008:163) says, "People will converge to others they find socially rewarding." The only context in which we found girls not significantly converging within dyads is for Grade 8 *same-friend* dyads. At first glance, this is surprising, as we might expect that dyads who presumably have been friends for longer would exhibit greater within-dyad similarity. As Giles and Ogay (2007) describe, convergence is motivated by the desire to gain approval from one's interlocutor and it also serves the utilitarian function of easing communication (i.e., it increases the predictability of utterances on all linguistic levels and thus lowers perceptive effort and processing time). When *Friendship Quality* is included as a control, the ICC for these girls improves to a significant level; thus, the mere fact of choosing the same peer in two interactions over a two-year interval cannot necessarily be an indicator of a close, accommodative friendship.

As with the girls, the boys are likely to accommodate with their peers in most contexts. The notable difference is in contexts when peers are strangers. Here, the boys exhibit a pattern of relative dissimilarity, suggesting that *divergence,* or, at minimum, *speech maintenance* is at play in these interactions. Goodwin (1980) and others have characterized same-sex boy interactions as being hierarchical and competitive, and this is likely exacerbated when boys don't know each other. Additionally, with less social import placed on politeness and building relationships, boys have less relative social reward in accommodating their dialect and thus have less motivation to do so. These findings make some sense when we consider the mitigating effect of the psychosocial factor *Social Skills,* which improved the ICC for these boys to a significant level. If social skills are a proxy for the willingness of these boys to relate effectively with strangers, then it makes sense that it would be a significant control.

The boys' relative accommodation with strangers in overall AAL usage is also improved to a significant level when their number/quality of African American contacts is taken into account. Boys more engaged within their local African American community are more likely to use their dialect as a resource for building camaraderie with a stranger. This tendency is shared by the girls, specifically for ethnically salient features, in which girls show comparatively dramatic convergence. Consistent with Rickford and McNair-Knox (1994), these findings suggest that ethnic identity is a comparatively rich resource to draw upon by these African American adolescents in the effort of building relationships with strangers. Here, it appears that ethnolinguistic vitality, coupled with gender, plays the most pivotal role in determining a dyad's accommodative patterns.

6.7   Conclusion

This study analyzes accommodation patterns in adolescent African American same-sex dyads through the use of two novel methodologies. First, it utilizes a composite index of dialect features, a *dialect density measure* (DDM), to assess a speaker's usage of canonical AAL features per utterance in a conversational language sample. A measure like this provides a snapshot of a speaker's overall language use which can then be used in large-scale statistical analysis, including longitudinal analysis (Van Hofwegen and Wolfram 2010), cross-sectional analysis (Craig and Washington 2006; Renn 2010), and dyadic analysis (this paper). Second, *dyadic analysis* (Kenny et al. 2006) has been introduced as a tool for assessing relative similarity within dyads for large dyadic samples. While dyadic analysis cannot determine a speaker's relative convergence or divergence over time in one given interaction, it can look at broad patterns over many interactions. Thus, samples exhibiting high and significant intra-class correlations (ICC) – which indicate greater within-dyad than between-dyad prediction of variance – can be said to be more accommodative in terms of the measure in question (here, the DDM) than those with low, non-significant ICCs.

Together, these methodologies provide special utility in this age of large corpora and macro-linguistic analysis. Increasingly, linguists and other scholars are turning to massive text-based corpora, many of which are publicly available at the click of a mouse. As with the FPG longitudinal dataset, often these corpora arise from studies not conceived in the fields of communication studies or linguistics. At the same time, the data within them can be of great use to communication scholars. Big data enable us to answer big questions. Overall dialect accommodation in a corpus of 201 dyadic interactions is one of those big questions.

Most importantly, though, this study has illuminated accommodation patterns for dyads in an understudied population – African American youth. Specifically, it has uncovered important gender differences in accommodative patterns that have not been revealed in other studies of the same population (e.g., Filardo 1996; Turkstra et al. 2003; Ciccia and Turkstra 2002), patterns which depend on whether peers have prior acquaintance. It has also highlighted the importance of ethnic identity and, particularly, ethnically salient features as resources for accommodation for both girls and boys, but in different ways. What the literature tells us about adolescent speech, coupled with the relatively consistent patterning for these speakers across the adolescent ages (Van Hofwegen and Wolfram 2010), makes it reasonable to conclude that accommodative findings uncovered here are still substantially attributable to the contextual factors of peer relationship.

References

Abrams, Jessica and Howard Giles. 2006. Ethnic identity gratifications selection and avoidance by African Americans: A group vitality and social identity gratifications perspective. *Media Psychology* 9(1): 115–134.

Bell, Allan. 1984. Language style as audience design. *Language in Society* 13(2): 145–204.

Bucholtz, Mary. 1996. Geek the girl: Language, femininity and female nerds. In Natasha Warner, (ed.), *Gender and Belief Systems: Proceedings of the Third Berkeley Women and Language Conference*, 119–132. Berkeley, CA: Berkeley Women and Language Group.

Bucholtz, Mary. 2000. Language and youth culture. *American Speech* 75(3): 280–283.

Chambers, J. K. 2003. *Sociolinguistic Theory.* Oxford: Blackwell.

Cheshire, Jenny. 1982. *Variation in an English Dialect: A Sociolinguistic Study.* Cambridge: Cambridge University Press.

Ciccia, Angel H. and Lyn S. Turkstra. 2002. Cohesion, communication burden, and response adequacy in adolescent conversations. *Advances in Speech-Language Pathology* 4(1): 1–8.

Coupland, Nikolas. 1980. Style-shifting in a Cardiff work-setting. *Language in Society* 9(1): 1–12.

Coupland, Nicolas. 1984. Accommodation at work: Some phonological data and their implications. *International Journal of the Sociology of Language* 46: 49–70.

Coupland, Nicolas. 2007. *Style, Variation, and Identity.* New York: Cambridge University Press.

Craig, Holly K. and Julie A. Washington. 2006. *Malik Goes to School: Examining the Language Skills of African American Students from Preschool-5th Grade.* Mahwah, NJ: Lawrence Erlbaum.

de Klerk, Vivian Anna. 2005. Slang and swearing as markers of inclusion and exclusion in adolescence. In Angie Williams and Crispin Thurlow (eds.), *Talking Adolescence: Perspectives on Communication in the Teenage Years*, 111–126. New York: Peter Lang.

Donner, Allan and Shelley Bull. 1983. Inferences concerning a common intraclass correlation coefficient. *Biometrics* 39(3): 771–775.

Dragojevic, M., J. Gasiorek, and Howard Giles. 2016. Communication accommodation theory. In Charles R. Berger and Michael E. Roloff (eds.), *International Encyclopedia of Interpersonal Communication*, 176–196. New York: Wiley/Blackwell.

Drury, John. 2005. Young people's communication with adults in the institutional order. In Angie Williams and Crispin Thurlow (eds.), *Talking Adolescence: Perspectives on Communication in the Teenage Years*, 229–244. New York: Peter Lang.

Eckert, Penelope. 1997. Age as a sociolinguistic variable. In Florian Coulmas (ed.), *The Handbook of Sociolinguistics*, 151–66. Oxford: Basil Blackwell.

Eckert, Penelope. 2000. *Linguistic Variation as Social Practice.* Malden, MA: Blackwell.

Eckert, Penelope. 2001. Style and social meaning. In Penelope Eckert and John R. Rickford (eds.), *Style and Sociolinguistic Variation*, 119–126. Cambridge: Cambridge University Press.

Eckert, Penelope. 2004. Adolescent language. In Edward Finegan and John R. Rickford (eds.), *Language in the USA: Themes for the Twenty-first Century*, 361–374. Cambridge: Cambridge University Press.

Eckert, Penelope. 2005. Stylistic practice and the adolescent social order. In Angie Williams and Crispin Thurlow (eds.), *Talking Adolescence: Perspectives on Communication in the Teenage Years*, 93–110. New York: Peter Lang.

Eckert, Penelope and Sally McConnell-Ginet. 2003. *Language and Gender*. Cambridge: Cambridge University Press.

Filardo, Emily K. 1996. Gender patterns in African American and white adolescents' social interactions in same-race, mixed-gender groups. *Journal of Personality and Social Psychology* 71(1): 71–82.

Fischer, John. 1958. Social influences on the choice of a linguistic variant. *Word* 14(1): 47–56.

Fortman, Jennifer. 2003. Adolescent language and communication from an intergroup perspective. *Journal of Language and Social Psychology* 22(1): 104–111.

Foulkes, Paul, Gerhard Docherty and Dominic Watt. 2005. Phonological variation in child-directed speech. *Language* 81(1): 177–206.

Giles, Howard. 1973. Accent mobility: A model and some data. *Anthropological Linguistics* 15(2): 87–105.

Giles, Howard. 2008. Communication accommodation theory: "When in Rome . . . " or not! In L. Baxter and D. Braithwaite (eds.), *Engaging Theories in Interpersonal Communication: Multiple Perspectives*, 161–173. Los Angeles, CA: Sage.

Giles, Howard, Nicolas Coupland and Jennifer Coupland. 1991. Accommodation theory: Communication, context, and consequence. In Howard Giles and Nicolas Coupland (eds.), *Contexts of Accommodation: Developments in Applied Sociolinguistics*, 1–68. Cambridge: Cambridge University Press.

Giles, Howard and Jessica Gasiorek. 2013. Parameters of non-accommodation: Refining and elaborating communication accommodation theory. In Joseph Paul Forgas, Orsolya Vincze, and János László (eds.), *Social Cognition and Communication*, 155–172. New York: Psychology Press.

Giles, Howard and P. Johnson. 1986. Ethnolinguistic identity theory: A social psychological approach to language maintenance. *International Journal of the Sociology of Language* 68: 69–99.

Giles, Howard and Tania Ogay. 2007. Communication accommodation theory. In Bryan B. Whaley and Wendy Samter (eds.), *Explaining Communication: Contemporary Theories and Exemplars*, 293–310. Mahwah, NJ: Lawrence Erlbaum Associates Publishers.

Giles, Howard, Scott Reid, and Jake Harwood. 2010. Introducing the dynamics of intergroup communication. In Howard Giles, Scott Reid, and Jake Harwood (eds.), *The Dynamics of Intergroup Communication*, 1–14. New York: Peter Lang.

Goodwin, Mary. 1990. *He-said-she-said: Talk as Social Organization among Black Children*. Bloomington, IN: Indiana University Press.

Gresham, Frank M. and Stephen N. Elliott. 1990. *Social Skills Rating System (SSRR)*. Circle Pines, MN: American Guidance Service.

Haggard, E.A. 1958. *Intraclass Correlation and the Analysis of Variance*. New York: Dryden.

Hannah, Annette and Tamar Murachver. 1999. Gender and conversational style as predictors of conversational behavior. *Journal of Language and Social Psychology* 18(2): 153–174.

Hare, Brian. 1985. The HARE *General* and *Area-Specific Self-Esteem Scale*. Unpublished manuscript, Stony Brook, NY: SUNY Stony Brook.

Hazen, Kirk. 2000. The role of researcher identity in conducting sociolinguistic research: A reflective case study. *Southern Journal of Linguistics* 24: 103–120.

Hecht, Michael L., Linda Kathryn Larkey, and Jill N. Johnson. 1992. African American and European American perceptions of problematic issues in inter-ethnic communication effectiveness. *Human Communication Research* 19(2): 209–236.

Hecht, Michael L. and Sidney Ribeau. 1991. Sociocultural roots of ethnic identity: A look at Black America. *Journal of Black Studies* 21(4): 501–513.

Hymes, Dell. 1974. *Foundations in Sociolinguistics: An Ethnographic Approa*ch. Philadephia, PA: University of Pennsylvania Press.

Kalbfleisch, Pamela. 2010. Gendered language as a dynamic intergroup process. In Howard Giles, Scott Reid, and Jake Harwood (eds.), *The Dynamics of Intergroup Communication*, 29–40. New York: Peter Lang.

Kenny, David A., Deborah A. Kashy, and William L. Cook. 2006. *Dyadic Data Analysis*. London: The Guilford Press.

Kerswill, Paul. 1996. Children, adolescents, and language change. *Language Variation and Change* 8(2): 177–202.

Kloep, Hendry L. and Marion Kloep. 2005. Talkin', doin' and bein' with friends'. Leisure and communication in adolescence. In A. Williams and Crispin Thurlow (eds.), *Talking Adolescence: Perspectives on Communication in the Teenage Years*, 163–184. New York: Peter Lang.

Kohn, Mary Elizabeth. 2014. *"The Way I Communicate Changes but How I Speak Don't": A Longitudinal Perspective on Adolescent Language Variation and Change*. Durham, NC: Duke University Press.

Labov, William. 1965. Stages in the acquisition of Standard English. In Roger W. Shuy (ed.), *Social Dialects and Language Learning*, 77–103. Champaign, IL: National Council of Teachers of English.

Labov, William. 1966. *The Social Stratification of English in New York City*. Washington, DC: Center for Applied Linguistics.

Labov, William. 1972a. *Language in the Inner City: Studies in the Black English Vernacular*. Philadelphia, PA: University of Pennsylvania Press.

Labov, William. 1972b. *Sociolinguistic Patterns*. Philadelphia, PA: University of Pennsylvania Press.

Labov, William. 1990. The intersection of sex and social class in the course of linguistic change. *Language Variation and Change* 2(2): 205–254.

Maltz, Daniel N. and Ruth A. Borker. 1982. A cultural approach to male-female miscommunication. In John Gumperz (ed.), *Language and Social Identity*, 196–216. New York: Cambridge University Press.

Mendoza-Denton, Norma. 1996. "Muy Macha": Gender and ideology in gang-girls' discourse about makeup. *Ethnos* 61(1–2): 47–63.

Mendoza-Denton, Norma. 2008. *Homegirls: Language and Cultural Practice among Latina Youth Gangs*. Cambridge: Blackwell.

Moore, Emma. 2003. *Learning Style and Identity: A Sociolinguistic Analysis of a Bolton High School*. Ph.D. dissertation. Manchester: University of Manchester.

Moore, Emma. 2004. Sociolinguistic style: A multidimensional resource for shared identity creation. *The Canadian Journal of Linguistics* 49(3/4): 375–396.

Palomares, Nicholas A. 2004. Gender schematicity, gender identity salience, and gender-linked language use. *Human Communication Research* 30(4): 556–588.

Parker, Jeffery G. and Steven A. Asher. 1993. Friendship and friendship quality in middle childhood: Links with peer group acceptance and feelings of loneliness and social dissatisfaction. *Developmental Psychology* 29(4): 611–621.

Renn, Jennifer E. 2010. *Acquiring Style: The Development of Dialect Shifting among African American Children*, Ph.D. Dissertation. Chapel Hill, NC: University of North Carolina at Chapel Hill.

Rickford, John R. and Faye McNair-Knox. 1994. Addressee- and topic-influenced style shift: A quantitative sociolinguistic study. In Douglas Biber and Edward Finegan (eds.), *Perspectives on Register: Situating Register Variation within Sociolinguistics*, 235–276. Oxford: Oxford University Press.

Schilling-Estes, Natalie. 2004. Constructing ethnicity in interaction. *Journal of Sociolinguistics* 8(2): 163–195.

Sellers, Robert M., Stephanie A.J. Rowley, Tabbye M. Chavous, J. Nicole Shelton and Mia. A., Smith. 1997. Multidimensional inventory of Black identity: A preliminary investigation of reliability and construct validity. *Journal of Personality and Social Psychology* 73(4): 805–815.

Soliz, Jordan and Howard Giles. 2014. Relational and identity processes in communication: A contextual and metaanalytical review of communication accommodation theory. In Elisia L. Cohen (ed.), *Communication Yearbook 38*, 106–143. Thousand Oaks, CA: Sage.

Thurlow, Crispin. 2005. Deconstructing adolescent communication. In Angie Williams and Crispin Thurlow (eds.), *Talking Adolescence: Perspectives on Communication in the Teenage Years*, 1–20. New York: Peter Lang.

Thurlow, Crispin and Alice Marwick. 2005. From apprehension to awareness: Toward more critical understandings of young people's communication experiences. In Angie Williams and Crispin Thurlow (eds.), *Talking Adolescence: Perspectives on Communication in the Teenage Years*, 53–71. New York: Peter Lang.

Turkstra, Lyn A, Angel H. Ciccia, and Christine Seaton. 2003. Interactive behaviors in adolescent conversation dyads. *Language, Speech, and Hearing Services in Schools* 34(2): 117–126.

Van Hofwegen, Janneke. 2015a. Dyadic analysis: Factors affecting African American English usage and accommodation in adolescent peer dyads. *Language and Communication* 41: 28–45.

Van Hofwegen, Janneke. 2015b. The development of African American English through childhood and adolescence. In Sonja L. Lanehart (ed.), *The* Oxford *Handbook of African American Language*, 454–474. Oxford: Oxford University Press.

Van Hofwegen, Janneke and Reuben Stob. 2012. The gender gap: How dialect usage affects reading outcomes in African American youth. Paper Presented at *Linguistic Society of America* 2012 Annual Meeting, Portland, OR

Van Hofwegen, Janneke and Walt Wolfram. 2010. Coming of age in African American English: A longitudinal study. *Journal of Sociolinguistics* 14(4): 427–455.

Williams. Angie and Peter Garrett. 2005. Adults' perceptions of communication with young people. In Angie Williams and Crispin Thurlow (eds.), *Talking Adolescence: Perspectives on Communication in the Teenage Years*, 35–52. New York: Peter Lang.

Wolfram, Walter A. 1969. *A Sociolinguistic Description of Detroit Negro Speech*. Washington, DC: Center for Applied Linguistics.

Wolfram, Walt, Caroline Myrick, Jon Forrest, and Michael J. Fox. 2016. Linguistic variation in the speeches of Dr. Martin Luther King Jr. *American Speech* 91(3): 269–300.

Wolfram, Walt and Natalie Schilling. 2016. *American English: Dialects and Variation*, 2nd edition. Oxford: Wiley Blackwell.

7   Stylistic Variation in the Early AAL Lifespan

7.1   Introduction

Speaker 1015 grew up on the more rural outskirts of Durham, North Carolina. His childhood activities included singing in his church and, later, high school choir, and he dabbled in theater as well. Enrolled in community college and studying forensics, speaker 1015 wants to work for the Durham Sheriff's office. Perhaps his early extracurriculars are part of the reason why he is so self-aware about his language use. In post-high school, he reports: "When I'm at home I speak way different than when I'm in public or somewhere like that . . . . It's just something in my mind just tells me you need to speak proper. You know, pronounce your t's and your r's and all that." At what point in 1015's lifespan did he start to pay attention to his t's and r's?

Stylistic variation appears to be a characteristic of language regardless of age, but patterns of shifting may vary significantly during the lifespan. There is obviously a range of demographic, sociocultural, interactional, and personal factors that have been observed to accompany stylistic variation, but their role in explaining style use is hardly settled and the intersection of these factors over the lifespan may certainly vary greatly. Furthermore, the social and socio-psychological covariates of style-shifting may shift greatly throughout life.

Sociolinguistic socialization in early childhood and adolescence indicates an increasing sociolinguistic awareness that may affect language-shifting. As Labov (1965) notes, while parents may be the primary influence of children's early use of vernacular dialect and shifting, peers take on a larger role as speakers enter adolescence. By the same token, different phases of adulthood status and accommodation may affect the range of and the rationale for stylistic shifting. For example, Kendall and Wolfram's (2009) study of African American leaders in small, rural Southern communities shows a surprising lack of stylistic shifting between public presentations and sociolinguistic interviews for some speakers, which they attribute to, among other factors, the relative autonomy of the demands and expectations for public presentation that exist in different communities. In an exclusively African American community, expectations for stylistic shifting towards a Mainstream English norm are quite different from a small, minority African American community surrounded by a predominant European American community. At the same time, Rickford and McNair Knox (1994) and Rickford and Price (2013) show significant change in the shifting use of African American Language (AAL) overall as well as stylistic versatility when teenagers were reinterviewed in their mid-thirties. This is hardly surprising given the social and sociopsychological factors that have changed in their lives over a couple of decades.

Longitudinally, we know very little empirically about dynamic shifting in early childhood and adolescence, the changing range of stylistic variation, and the possible factors that may covary with stylistic shift, to say nothing of the operational challenge of defining style-shift in a descriptively adequate way to begin with. Although it is possible that some of the relevant factors identified in the study of adult style-shift – for example, audience, formality, personal identity, stance, etc. – may be applied to children's style, we cannot simply assume that the relative weight of these factors will be constant, and in some cases, may not be relevant at all (Patterson 1992). Certainly, it is possible that some social and sociopsychological factors may have a greater or lesser effect as children get older. Therefore, it is necessary to ask: what are the relative influences of demographic, sociopsychological, and personal factors at different temporal points during childhood and early adolescence, and how do they intersect in their contribution to style over time?

The ability to adjust and shift linguistic styles is an inherent part of language variation, yet scholars still debate both the causes of intraspeaker stylistic variation and its role in language development. Several theoretical models have offered to describe the phenomenon of style-shifting, with no consensus as to what may be the best rationalization. Three major theories of self-stylization, the "Attention to Speech" model (Labov 1966, 1972), the "Audience Design" model (Bell 1984), and the "Speaker Design" approach (e.g., Eckert 2000; Schilling-Estes 1998; Coupland 2007), offer useful insight into speakers' use of style, but each of these models also has limitations (Wolfram and Schilling 2016).

7.2   Models of Style

The first model in variation studies that sought to explicate speakers' stylistic choices systematically was the "Attention to Speech" model initially proposed by Labov (1966). Originally intended to identify the conditions under which speakers produce their most vernacular style, this model contrasts speakers' use of various speech styles, including "casual" and "careful" speech. These two speech types are accompanied by paralinguistic cues such as differences in tempo, pitch, volume, and breathing, as well as by the use of laughter in conversation. Labov's initial investigations of style were conducted using one-on-one sociolinguistic interviews, which sought to elicit both careful and casual speech by establishing particular speech conditions during each interview. A key finding of this work was that under more formal conditions (e.g., during an interview), speakers tend to use fewer vernacular features, presumably because they are paying closer attention to their speech.

More recent work has continued to build on the notion of speech conditions as the main motivator of shifting styles. Finegan and Biber (1994:315) found "systematic patterns of register variation and social dialect variation" that were related to the linguistic environment, speaker demographics and characteristics, and the situation of use. Ervin-Tripp (2001) added to this work by showing that contrastive environments like speech versus writing, planned versus unplanned speech, and face-to-face conversation versus a speech presented to a group of people trigger style-shifts among monolinguals. Additionally, later studies conducted by Labov (2001) looked at how the interviewer's manipulation of topic during sociolinguistic interviews affected interviewees' vernacularity. In response to more typical interview questions (e.g., the interviewee's background), subjects used more careful speech; when the interviewer directed the conversation toward topics that were of "maximal interest and emotional involvement" to the subject, a more casual speech style was employed (Labov 2001:88).

Bell (1984) proposed a different impetus for style-shifting. Building upon Street and Giles's (1982) concept of a speech accommodation model, he suggested that speakers adjust their speech largely to win the approval of interlocutors. While Labov's model concentrates on contextual cues within the sociolinguistic interview situation, this "Audience Design" approach focuses on both active participants and nonparticipants (e.g., "auditors" and "eavesdroppers") in the conversation as the principal catalyst of style-shifting behavior.

A still more recent attempt at explaining style is the "Speaker Design" approach, which addresses factors that are less emphasized in the Attention to Speech and Audience Design scenarios. Proponents of the Speaker Design model (e.g., Schilling-Estes 2004; Coupland 2007) believe that the speakers' desire to project a particular identity and their relationship with respect to interlocutors are the prime motivators of shifts in speech style. Unlike the other theories, the Speaker Design approach focuses mainly on the internal motivations of speakers themselves rather than outside influences as the reason for linguistic change. This model purports that speakers aim to project group membership and personal identity through their use or disuse of certain linguistic features. A variety of critiques of the different explanatory models have been offered (see Wolfram and Schilling 2016, Chapter 9) as these models have been problematized, and the meaning of shifting variables continues to be debated among variationists (Eckert 2018).

While each theory considers style use from a different perspective, no one approach seems to capture fully, the richness of style-shifting. Clearly, the context, the audience, and the speaker's individual, interpersonal, and group identities all have an impact on stylistic choices; still, this does not explain how and why certain speakers develop the ability to shift adeptly between different language varieties, while others simply master the switching of registers. Answering these questions is especially pertinent for speakers of vernacular language varieties, who may find the capacity to move to more Mainstream American English (MAE) varieties is related to enhanced socioeconomic status. Studies of the acquisition of style may shed light on these questions.

Research that examines the processes by which style-shifting develops in child speech consider a range of questions, such as when children begin to differentiate between formal and informal tasks, the role of parental input, and the potential impact of literacy on such patterns. Evidence suggests that preschoolers and early elementary school children are still working out the details of style-shifting (Chevrot, Beaud, and Varga 2000; Díaz-Campos 2005; Smith, Durham, and Richards 2013). For example, Chevrot et al. (2000) observed stylistic differences in children of ages 10–12, but not for their younger cohorts, ages 6–7, when considering /R/ ellison in French. They attributed differences between cohorts to increased metalinguistic knowledge developed through literacy among the 10–12 year olds. In other words, know-ledge of formal spelling may lead to style-shifting between formal and informal situations. Similar patterns were found in a study of Spanish-language acquisi-tion. Díaz-Campos (2005) found that pre-school children (ages 42–53 months) showed little stylistic differentiation for intervocalic /d/ deletion across tasks, even using more informal variants in formal tasks, while a slightly older cohort (ages 54–71 months) showed stylistic differentiation reminiscent of adult populations. Yet, other studies indicate that children as young as 3–4 years old may vary the way they speak according to situation, especially for salient variables. Children may be aware that less local forms are more commonly used by parents in certain activities, such as during disciplinary moments, without having an awareness that such forms are seen as more prestigious or standard (Smith et al. 2013). This, in turn, can lead to situational variation in child speech for salient variables. Yet, as Smith et al. (2013) show, such variation does not necessarily affect all variables equally. As such, it is import-ant to analyze a range of variables to consider child style-shifting. When more than one variable is examined, evidence suggests acquisition patterns vary according to issues of salience.

It becomes increasingly important to better identify motivators for and development of stylistic shifting in light of recent work that has highlighted the impact of style use on literacy and learning outcomes (e.g., Charity et al. 2004; Craig and Washington 2004; Craig et al. 2009). Several studies have indicated that children who are better able to switch to a more standardized variety of English under certain circumstances perform better academically, on average. For instance, Charity et al. (2004) found that children who were more familiar with MAE earned higher scores on reading achievement diagnostics, independent of their memory ability. Craig and Washington (2004) found that a speaker's community influences his or her use of dialect, as well as the implementation of style-shifting behavior. In their study of 400 African American elementary school students, they compared speakers from a midsized central city (Ann Arbor, Michigan) with others from an "urban fringe" community (Detroit, Michigan). They found that approximately 85 percent of those from the midsized central city became style-shifters, alternating between AAL and MAE, while less than 60 percent of those from the "urban fringe" community shifted their speech. This result was of particular importance, given their subsequent finding that the shifters performed significantly better on standardized tests than nonshifters.

Research by Craig et al. (2009) compared the language of elementary school children in oral and written contexts to assess each child's amount of shifting. They found an inverse relationship between the amount of AAL and the children's scores on a standardized reading achievement exam. Thus, they concluded that "AAL speaking students who learn to use MAE in literacy tasks will outperform their peers who do not make this linguistic adaptation" (839). Renn (2015) examined the relationship between AAL use at the beginning of elementary school and reading outcomes in third grade.

Given the implications of such studies, it is vital to attain a clearer understanding of the speaker characteristics and qualities that are related to style and stylistic shifting skills. There is both a theoretical-descriptive and a descriptive-applied perspective that underscores the need to examine the shifting role of style over the lifespan. This chapter offers an extended perspective by considering the influence of several demographic and sociopsychological correlates during the elementary and middle school years, along with general trajectories of style-shifting.

7.3   Defining Style in a Large-Scale Study

The vast majority of studies of style in sociolinguistics have been case studies, where just a few speakers or a single speaker is examined during the course of an interactional interview, with Labov (1966, 1972) being the major exception. Even fewer studies (Rickford and Price 2013) involve changes over the lifespan, though, as mentioned earlier, there are a few studies of early childhood that do consider style-shifting. There remain major questions as to when style-shifting is initiated, the kinds of variables manipulated, and trajectories of shifting from childhood through adulthood. And, of course, there is the methodological issue of how we define style-shifting operationally. In this chapter, we consider stylistic shifting at several different temporal points – Grades 1 and 2, Grade 6, and Grade 8.

7.3.1   Language Samples – Grades 1 and 2

The data for the first temporal point ("Grade 1") were taken from language samples collected when the children were in Grades 1 and 2. Data from two different grades were used because there were no contrastive formal/informal activities in the study until the children reached middle school. Data from the seventy-three children who participated in both visits were used in this analysis.

During the "formal" Grade 2 visit, the children engaged in several narrative storytelling tasks, responding to inquiries from an unfamiliar adult examiner. The first language sample was a picture description task, in which the examiner showed the child a picture depicting a circus scene. The child was then asked to describe the picture in enough detail so that another child could draw the picture without seeing it. The other language samples were part of a narrative elicitation task, where the examiner would introduce a topic and then ask the child to share a similar experience. For example, the first story was about losing a tooth. The experimenter prompted the child by saying "I know a little girl who just lost a tooth last week. Have you ever lost a tooth?" The child was then encouraged to elaborate with questions like "Tell me what happened when you lost your tooth" or "Tell me what it's like when someone loses a tooth." Other topics of conversation were going to a basketball game, spilling juice at breakfast, and going on a trip. After each of these situations, the examiner gave two additional prompts: "Anything else?" and "Tell me more of what happened when you ... ." All of the language from each of these tasks was transcribed and combined to construct the formal language sample at the first time point.

A "mother-child interaction" in Grade 1 was used as the informal language sample at the first temporal data point. Three tasks were analyzed: a discussion planning the child's birthday party, a task where the caregiver and child played with magnets and various other materials (e.g., coins, paperclips), and a reminiscing task where the caregiver and child remembered special events like holidays and vacations that the caregiver and child had experienced together within the last year. These tasks were selected because they consisted of relatively natural speech between the caregiver and child. At the commencement of each task, an examiner entered the room to explain the activity. The caregiver and child were then left alone in the room to interact as normally as possible. All of the language from all three activities was used as the first informal data sample; speech that occurred when the examiner reentered the room was excluded.

7.3.2   Language Samples: Grade 6 and Grade 8

At the middle-school stage – Grades 6 and 8, each participant brought a friend of the same gender and roughly the same age to participate in the study. The Grade 6 and Grade 8 peer protocols were identical and included tasks that were designed to create both formal and informal peer situations. The investigators determined the formality of each task using Labov's "principle of attention to speech" (1966), which describes a formal situation as one where the participant pays more attention to his or her speech. Each pair of students (N=125 in Grade 6; N=164 in Grade 8) completed two formal tasks followed by two informal tasks.

The first formal task was a mock speech directed toward parents of children that would be entering their school in the fall. The subjects were instructed to create a five-minute speech that would describe their school and provide information and advice that would be helpful for an incoming student. They, then, individually performed the speech in front of a one-way mirror/window, pretending that they were addressing a panel of teachers who were going to choose a student to give the speech. The second formal task followed a similar procedure. The subjects were told to plan a vacation for kids in a locale where neither youth had been before. After an eight-minute planning period, the subjects were told to stand in front of a one-way window and pretend to present the vacation to an author of a book about vacations for kids. Each subject presented individually and was allotted four minutes for the speech. Transcription commenced when each subject began the speech and ended when the subject finished the speech. During both speeches, any conversation between the two subjects or between the subjects and the examiner was not considered formal speech and, therefore, was not coded for AAL features.

The first informal task was a free talk period while the subjects ate a snack. The youths were provided with a choice of snack and were then left alone for approximately five minutes. They were given no instruction as to conversation topic; the examiner merely indicated that she would return when they were finished. The subjects were recorded for the entirety of the snack period, but this was not explicitly mentioned in order to create a more comfortable environment for the participants. Only the language that occurred while the examiner was outside the room was included in the analysis. In the second informal task, the subjects were directed to discuss two issues or problems that they had selected at the beginning of the visit. Each subject was supposed to present one of his or her issues and explain why it is a problem. The other youth was then instructed to offer advice as to how the problem might be solved. The subjects alternated offering problems for discussion until the examiner reentered the room after about ten minutes. The "Issue Discussion" was coded first for all subjects because of superior intelligibility. In cases where at least one subject did not have a total of fifty utterances in the "Issue Discussion," the "Snack" portion of the interaction was transcribed until that number was attained. In these contexts, transcription began when the examiner left the room and ended when she reentered and announced the conclusion of the task.

7.4   Coding Style

Language samples from formal and informal contexts at the three temporal data points described earlier were utilized in evaluating stylistic behavior. The language samples were first transcribed orthographically using the Systematic Analysis for Language Transcription (SALT) software (Miller and Paul 1995), and then coded for the presence of forty-two morphosyntactic and three phonological AAL features (see Appendix for the complete list). All transcribers and coders underwent reliability training and were at least 80 percent reliable with the lead coder. To attain coding reliability, coders coded two previously completed transcripts. They were then compared to the same transcripts, coded by the same experienced coder. Kappas for all coders indicated substantial reliability, ranging from 0.62–0.71. An experienced coder subsequently checked approximately 75 percent of all coded transcripts, to maintain consistency.

The total number of AAL features in the coded transcripts was then used to calculate a summary variable that represented speakers' overall AAL use. Our examination of a summary variable provides a more holistic approach to the study of style-shifting across the lifespan, complementing the more common practice of evaluating a single variable at a time (see Chapter 2). The summary variables were calculated by dividing the total number of AAL tokens in the language sample by the total number of utterances. This summary measure was an adapted version of the DDM described in Chapter 2. An important consideration in calculating this measure was determining how best to account for the size of the language sample. Using either the total number of words or the total number of utterances is justifiable and has been utilized to compute similar measures, and a study assessing the vernacularity of 112 sixth graders found that the values attained from the two methods were highly correlated (r=0.96) (Renn 2007; Renn and Terry 2009). Given that utterances are used more commonly with older children (e.g., Craig and Washington 2006), this method was selected as the basis of the summary variable used in this paper.

Looking at the ability to shift one's language in formal situations in a quantitative way is vital to answering the questions posed in this chapter.

In order to study shifting behavior, it is also necessary to define "style-shift" operationally. This term is largely discussed in the literature in a descriptive way, talking about how speakers alternate their speech among multiple dialects. A definitive method for approaching the study of style in a quantitatively meaningful way has not been agreed upon, however. There are many possibly ways one might define "style-shift" operationally, just as there are variant definitions of style in the variationist literature. One recent operational definition reduces the definition to a "difference score" (Craig et al. 2009). Craig et al. conducted an analysis of the unstandardized DDM scores from oral and written contexts using the following calculation: Oral DDM − Written DDM = Individual DDM Shift Score (849). In their analysis, a positive individual shift score meant that a speaker had used more AAL in the oral context and then shifted to a lower DDM in the written context. They considered a speaker with a negative or no difference in individual shift score as a nonshifter. They found that speakers with a positive difference score, that is, those who shifted toward MAE during reading tasks, outperformed their nonshifting peers on standardized measures of reading assessment. While this work compared the use of AAL in oral and written language contexts, this type of comparison is similar to the formal versus informal dichotomy used in this study and was employed to provide a general description of speakers' longitudinal shifting patterns.

Another way to consider shifting, however, is as a ratio of two DDM scores; in the case of this work, style-shift was assessed as a ratio of the informal DDM to the formal DDM. While this method is similar to the idea of a difference score, it has some added benefits. First, a ratio accounts for the fact that a difference of ten AAL features may, in some cases, be a large difference, but in others, a small one. For example, if one speaker uses ten AAL features in formal situations and twenty in informal ones, there is a 100 percent increase in nonstandard feature use from the formal to informal context. Another speaker might use 100 AAL features in the formal and 110 in the informal context. As with the first speaker, the difference in the feature count is ten, but there is only a 10-percent increase from the formal to the informal context. In this way, a ratio offers a more precise method of capturing the extent of change in linguistic behavior.

A related benefit is that a ratio is an interpretable value that has a clear meaning. For instance, a ratio of 1.6 would indicate that the speaker used 60 percent more AAL in informal scenarios versus formal situations; thus, we can observe not only that the speaker uses more AAL in informal situations, but also how much more AAL is used. A difference score, however, is not as easily interpreted. A difference of 0.02, for example, only signifies that the speaker uses more AAL in informal contexts; it unclear whether this is a large change in language use or a small adjustment. As a result of the reasons discussed here, the ratio score was used for the statistical analyses investigating the effect of grade.

7.5   Analysis

7.5.1   Longitudinal Patterns of Style-Shifting

Table 7.1 presents the mean number of AAL features per ten utterances and the standard deviation in each grade and context. Statistical analyses were conducted to determine the independent variables' effects on language use. Since the outcome measure is a count variable (i.e., it is calculated by counting the total number of AAL features in a given speech sample), a log linear regression model was used for analyses. With this approach, the count of AAL features was the dependent variable in all analyses; it was then offset by the total number of utterances to control for differences in the length of the speech samples. The generalized estimating equations method was used to account for any correlations among the standard errors (Liang and Zeger 1986) because the data consisted of multiple observations of the same subject.

To determine the impact of context (i.e., formal vs. informal) on overall language use, the effect size of context was calculated. This was conducted by taking the difference between mean value of informal AAL use and the mean value of formal AAL use for all speakers at all time points and dividing it by the pooled standard deviation (Cohen 1988). The resulting value was $d=.34$, indicating a small effect of context on overall AAL use. Results also indicated that, overall, a significant interaction between grade and contextual shifting exists: χ^2 (2, $N=367$)=19.12, $p<0.0001$), meaning that the amount of shifting that speakers engaged in did not remain consistent over time. The major change occurred between Grade 1 and the beginning of middle school, during which time speakers increased their stylistic shifting by 60 percent ($p<0.0001$);

Table 7.1 *Mean and standard deviation of AAL features per ten utterances, by grade*

Variable	Grade 1	Grade 6	Grade 8
Formal Context			
N	73	125	170
M (SD)	1.88 (1.32)	3.23 (2.09)	2.94 (1.95)
Informal Context			
N	74	127	164
M (SD)	1.62 (0.87)	3.92 (1.86)	4.07 (2.11)

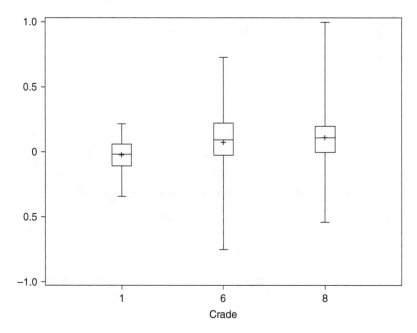

Figure 7.1 Box plot of individual shifting score at Grades 1/2, Grade 6, and Grade 8. From Renn 2011.

shifting also increased by 15 percent between Grades 6 and 8, but this difference was not statistically significant at the .05 level ($p=0.07$).

Figure 7.1 shows the distribution of the individual shifting scores at each time point. The plus indicates the mean shifting score at each grade, the line in the middle of the box denotes the median score, and the top and bottom of the box mark the values at the twenty-fifth and seventy-fifth percentile. The whiskers on the box plot show the range of values by specifying the maximum and minimum values at each temporal data point. In addition to the increase in the mean and median values over time, it is notable that the score range is fairly narrow at the Grade 1/2 time point and widens significantly in Grades 6 and 8, illustrating increased differentiation in shifting behavior among the speakers.

For each speaker, the difference score between the informal and formal DDM was calculated as detailed earlier. This difference score was then used to graphically depict speakers' use of style-shifting in varying contexts across Grade 1/2, Grade 6, and Grade 8. Figure 7.2 shows trajectories of shifting for each speaker in the sample. For the speakers who were added as peer cohorts in Grade 6, the analysis can, of course, only include the two grade levels. The

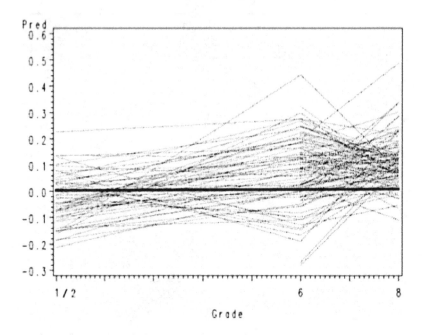

Figure 7.2 Individual trajectories of style-shifting in Grades 1/2, Grade 6, and Grade 8. From Renn 2010: 56.

difference score (i.e., Informal DDM −Formal DDM) is on the y-axis and grade is on the x-axis:

The raw data graphed in Figure 7.2 indicate several patterns in style-shifting. The first observation is that the majority of the speakers did not engage in a significant amount of shifting in Grade 1/2. This is demonstrated by the fact that all of the speakers except one have difference scores of 0.15 or less at this first data point. In fact, more than half of speakers had difference values that were less than 0; this indicates that they were using more AAL in formal contexts than informal situations. This is the converse of the usual pattern exhibited by adult speakers, who generally use more nonstandard language in informal situations. However, it does align with observations from Chevrot, Beaud, and Varga (2000) where style-shifting was not apparent among the youngest grade school cohort in their study.

There also appears to be three main trajectories of shifting behavior during elementary and middle school. First, some speakers exhibit a general increase over time, indicating that speakers are engaging in more and more shifting as they age. Second, there is also an inverted V pattern, which shows that by

Grade 6, shifting ability has increased, but in Grade 8 they are shifting less. Since these speakers are engaging in shifting behavior in Grade 6, it seems unlikely that they lose the ability to shift in Grade 8; instead, perhaps other outside factors may be influencing their linguistic behavior. Unearthing the reasons for this pattern requires extensive investigation, but they may be the result of factors like linguistic accommodation to their peer partners as discussed in Chapter 6, or changes in the speakers' goals or foci over time. While the detailed exploration of these questions is beyond the scope of the current study, the results do suggest that the speakers have developed an increased ability to shift their language in response to contextual differences by the time they reach middle school. Finally, a few speakers demonstrate a V-shaped pattern in which they shift less in Grade 6 than they do at the beginning of elementary school and subsequently exhibit an increase in shifting in Grade 8. Only a handful of speakers follow this trajectory, and it is possible that a nonshifting interlocutor may be responsible for the decrease in shifting at Grade 6.

The graph of the raw data also illustrates an apparent general increase in shifting over time, as evidenced by the overall upward trajectory in the graph. This observation is supported by the mean values at each time point. In Grade 1/2, the mean individual difference score was -0.027 ($SD=0.121$), a value that is close to, but actually slightly below zero. This indicates that, on average, children were not engaging in style-shifting, and, in fact, were using slightly more AAL in formal situations than informal ones. In Grade 6, the mean shifting score increased to 0.073 ($SD=0.245$), showing that they began using more AAL in informal contexts and then utilized fewer nonstandard forms in formal situations. This shifting behavior intensified in Grade 8, with the mean individual difference score increasing to 0.112 ($SD=0.210$) by the end of middle school. Thus, speakers not only continued shifting but increased their degree of shifting between Grades 6 and 8.

7.5.2 The Effect of Social Variables

While dozens of measures assessing the school and home environments, peer characteristics, and subject characteristics were collected throughout the longitudinal study, the examination of style focuses on five social variables. These variables are the speaker's gender; the speaker's mother's education in years, as a proxy for socioeconomic status; the speaker's African American social contacts; the demographic makeup of the speaker's school; and the speaker's self-reported racial centrality score. Some of these variables are fairly traditional and transparent, but a couple require explanation. The number of African American contacts was determined using a self-reported questionnaire (Sellers et al. 1997; Rowley et al. 1998). Children indicated the number of close friends, neighbors, acquaintances, and visitors in their lives that were African American. A response of "zero" was coded as a 1; a response of "1–2" coded as a 2; "3–4" was coded as 3; and a response of "5 or more" was coded as 4 for each contact category. The mean value of all categories was used as the overall social contacts score. The demographic makeup of the school was taken at one time point (Grade 3) to represent the elementary school value as well as at both middle school time points (Grade 6 and 8). The percentage of African American students in the school at each time point was used in analyses as a measure of racial density.

The final social variable was racial centrality, or a measure of how important race is as a component of the respondent's identity (Sellers et al. 1997). This is a self-reported score, consisting of a composite score from five items:
1. *I live in an area with other blacks.*
2. *I like my friends to be black.*
3. *I like to read books about black people.*
4. *I feel close to other blacks.*
5. *I am similar to other blacks.*
The subjects responded to these statements using a typical Likert scale, where 1 stands for "strongly disagree" and 5 stands for "strongly agree." This suggests that subjects with lower scores may consider race to be a less important part of their identity.[1]

After identifying overall and grade related patterns, the influence of each social variable was individually investigated using the log linear model described earlier. Each was considered independently since this work is exploratory rather than conforming to an existing model. To evaluate the possible contributions of each of the social variables, three outcomes were considered: a) the marginal main effect of each variable; b) the two-way interaction between each variable and the context; c) and the three-way interaction among each variable, the context, and grade. A significant main effect would indicate that the variable was related to overall AAL use; a significant two-way interaction effect would mean that there was a relationship between that variable and shifting based on context (e.g., the amount of overall shifting increases as mother's education increases); and a significant three-way interaction term would be interpreted as a relationship between the variable and context that changes over time (e.g., the difference in the degree of shifting

---

[1] It is important to note that since these data were collected, there has been a great deal of interest in the notion of racial centrality as a predictor of psychological and physical behaviors; thus, the literature in this field has grown substantially over the last twenty years. While this project utilized a segment of Sellers et al.'s (1997) Multidimensional Inventory of Black Identity to measure the degree to which speakers defined themselves with regard to race, looking at racial centrality in a quantitative way is a complex task. For example, researchers like Helms (1990) and Cross (1991) have proposed alternate methods of identifying an individual's degree of connectedness with his or her ethnic group.

related to mother's education increases over time). Each of the covariates (with the exception of gender) was sampled at three time points (Grades 3, 6, and 8) and was analyzed as a continuous variable in the regression model.

7.5.2.1 Gender Results for the analysis of the influence of gender are shown in Table 7.2. Estimates for each category are reported as the mean number of AAL tokens used per 100 utterances (e.g., on average, females in Grade 1 use fourteen AAL tokens in every 100 utterances in the informal context). The last column shows the difference in the mean AAL counts per 100 tokens in formal and informal contexts, calculated as Informal AAL − Formal AAL, to illustrate different patterns of use across context.

Tests of the marginal effect of gender on overall AAL use were not significant ($p=0.2652$), indicating that males and females used similar amounts of AAL forms, overall. The interaction of gender and context, however, did reveal a significant result ($p=0.0006$), meaning that boys and girls exhibited differing overall shifting behavior. This result is borne out in the data shown in Table 7.2. In particular, the difference values shown in the last column in the table indicate that girls tended to engage in a greater amount of shifting than boys. Finally, there were no statistically significant gender differences in shifting patterns over time ($p=0.1927$). According to the raw data, both males and females did not shift in Grade 1, actually using more AAL in the formal context in both cases, but speakers of both genders did shift in Grades 6 and 8.

7.5.2.2 The Role of Mother's Education While mother's education was analyzed as a continuous variable in the regression model, the values reported at high, average, and low levels of education are shown in Table 7.3 for ease of comparison. The mean education level of 13.57 years ($SD=2.20$), i.e., about one and a half years beyond a high school diploma, was used as the "Average" education value. An education level of 15.77 years, or one standard deviation above the mean, was used as the cutoff value for "High" education. A person

Table 7.2 *Results for gender and grade*

Grade	Gender	Informal AAL forms	Formal AAL forms	Difference
1	Females (N=40)	14/100	17/100	−3
	Males (N=39)	18/100	22/100	−4
6	Females (N=76)	39/100	29/100	10
	Males (N=49)	39/100	31/100	8
8	Females (N=101)	42/100	24/100	18
	Males (N=63)	41/100	33/100	8

Table 7.3 *Results for mothers' education and grade*

Grade	Education level	Informal AAL forms	Formal AAL forms	Difference
1	Low	19/100	23/100	−4
	Average	16/100	19/100	−3
	High	13/100	15/100	−2
6	Low	47/100	36/100	11
	Average	38/100	29/100	9
	High	31/100	24/100	7
8	Low	50/100	33/100	17
	Average	41/100	28/100	13
	High	33/100	23/100	10

with this value would have attained a level of education that is just below a bachelor's degree. An education level of 11.37 years, or one standard deviation below the mean, was used as cutoff value for the "Low" level of education. This value corresponds to a person who has started but not completed his or her final year of high school. This method of comparing high, average, and low values was also applied to investigate the continuous social variables (i.e., social contacts, school demographics, and racial centrality).

Results of the main effect of mother's education were significant ($p<0.0001$), indicating a negative relationship between the mother's level of education and overall AAL use. Thus, the more educated a speaker's mother was, the less likely he or she used AAL forms in his or her overall speech. This result is seen in the raw data in Table 7.3, where at all three time points, speakers with mothers at a low level of education used the most AAL forms per 100 utterances, and speakers whose mothers had attained a high level of education always used the fewest AAL forms. Notably, this relationship between AAL use and mother's education is evident in both informal and formal contexts.

A further look at the data in Table 7.3 shows that shifting patterns were somewhat similar in all three education groups. There was no significant shifting in Grade 1, with speakers in all three education categories using slightly more AAL in formal situations. In Grades 6 and 8, all three groups engaged in noticeable shifting behavior, so it is perhaps not surprising that a test of the interaction effect of mother's education and context was not significant ($p=0.5838$). In spite of the nonsignificant result, there is an interesting pattern in both middle school grades: children with mothers in the low education category used more AAL forms in informal situations as well as engaged in the largest amount of shifting, while children in the high education category used the fewest AAL forms in informal contexts and shifted the least.

A test of the three-way interaction was also not significant (p=0.4328), indicating that there is no variability in shifting over time as a result of mother's education. As shown in Table 7.3, all three education groups engaged in no shifting in Grade 1, engaged in a typical shifting pattern in Grade 6, and shifted even more in Grade 7. Once again, however, there does seem to be a trend in the data, with the speakers in the low education category showing the largest change in their shifting behavior, growing from −4 in Grade 1 to 11 in Grade 6 to 17 in Grade 8, and the high education group exhibiting the smallest change, from −2 to 7 to 10 over the three time points. While neither of the interaction effects was statistically significant, they do highlight some interesting patterns related to mother's education.

7.5.2.3 The Role of Social Contacts   As with the mother's education variable, the mean value of African American social contacts was compared with the values one standard deviation above and one standard deviation below the mean. Here, the "Average" value was M=3.26 (SD=0.57), the "High" value was 3.83, and the "Low" value was 2.69. Table 7.4 shows the AAL form counts per 100 utterances by context for each of these contact levels, as well as the difference between these informal and formal count values.

Once again, a test of the main effect was significant (p=0.0008), though in this case, there was a positive relationship between the social contacts score and overall AAL use. Thus, speakers who had more African American social contacts were more likely to use AAL forms, regardless of the context – a trend that can be seen at all three time points and across both contexts. The test of the interaction between social contacts and context was not significant (p=0.4126), which is consistent with the difference values in Table 7.4. In Grade 1, the difference values were very similar, ranging from −2 to −4; in Grade 6, the values ranged from 9 to 10; and in Grade 8, they were all 12. Thus, speakers engaged in similar shifting behaviors at each time point, regardless of

Table 7.4 *Results for African American social contacts and grade*

Grade	AA social contacts	Informal AAL forms	Formal AAL forms	Difference
1	Low	16/100	18/100	−2
	Average	17/100	20/100	−3
	High	18/100	22/100	−4
6	Low	34/100	25/100	9
	Average	39/100	29/100	10
	High	45/100	35/100	10
8	Low	34/100	22/100	12
	Average	40/100	28/100	12
	High	46/100	34/100	12

their African American social contacts. The three-way interaction was also not significant ($p=0.9115$), confirming that speakers' shifting behaviors did not differ over time as a result of their social contacts.

While it may be the case that a speaker's social contacts do not affect his or her shifting behavior, one possible reason for the nonsignificant findings in the interaction terms may be the way in which the data were collected. As noted earlier, the highest possible score for each category was a 4, which represented a response of "5 or more"; the mean value for the composite score was 3.26, a value that is very close to that maximum score. In addition, the standard deviation was only 0.57, which suggests that there was not much variability in speakers' responses. Many respondents therefore reported values of 5 or more, so it would seem that a value of 5 might be too low to effectively investigate this variable. A questionnaire that had a maximum response score of "10 or more" or perhaps a number even greater than that might have done a better job of teasing apart the influence of social contacts on language use.

7.5.2.4 School Demographics   The next variable looked at the potential influence of speakers' classmates on their language use. To investigate this, the percentage of African American students in the speaker's school at each time point was analyzed. Again, the mean value was compared with values that were one standard deviation above and below the mean. The overall mean value for school demographics was 47.68 percent African American ($SD=25.17$). This was set as the "Average" value; the "High" value was 72.85 percent and the "Low" value was 22.51 percent African American. Table 7.5 shows the AAL values and difference scores for these three demographic values.

The results of this variable are similar to those of the social contacts variable. The main effect was significant ($p<0.0001$) and indicated a positive

Table 7.5 *Results for percentage of African American students and grade*

Grade	% African American	Informal AAL forms	Formal AAL forms	Difference
1	Low	13/100	16/100	−3
	Average	15/100	18/100	−3
	High	18/100	21/100	−3
6	Low	34/100	26/100	8
	Average	39/100	30/100	9
	High	46/100	35/100	11
8	Low	37/100	25/100	12
	Average	43/100	29/100	14
	High	50/100	34/100	16

relationship between overall AAL use and the percentage of African American students in the speaker's grade. Thus, speakers who attended a school with a higher percentage of African American students were likely to use more AAL in both formal and informal contexts. Once again, this is seen in each grade and in both contexts, as speakers with a low percentage of African American peers used the fewest AAL forms, and speakers with a high percentage of African American classmates used the most AAL, at all grades.

As with the social contacts variable, the results of both interaction effects were not significant. In each grade, the difference values were similar: all three groups had values of −3 in Grade 1; they ranged from 8 to 11 in Grade 6; and they varied from 12 to 16 in Grade 8. Thus, there does not appear to be a relationship between school demographics and contextual style-shifting ($p=0.1439$), nor does shifting behavior vary over time as a result of the racial density of the speaker's school ($p=0.3159$). This is similar to the findings in Chapter 4 where this variable affected overall vowel use but not trajectory.

7.5.2.5 Racial Centrality   The final social variable investigated was the speaker's degree of racial centrality. As explained earlier, this score was obtained by means of a self-reported score from a questionnaire. The questionnaire contained statements related to the importance of race as a component of the speaker's personal identity. Participants responded with a score between 1 and 5, with 1 representing a response of "strongly disagree" and 5 indicating a response of "strongly agree." Higher scores indicated that race was a more important component of the speaker's identity. These values were then averaged to create an overall racial centrality score. Like the previous three social variables, high, average, and low values were compared to investigate patterns of behavior. The "Average" value was the mean score of 3.75 ($SD=0.73$); the

Table 7.6 *Results for racial centrality and grade*

Grade	Racial centrality	Informal AAL forms	Formal AAL forms	Difference
1	Low	16/100	19/100	−3
	Average	16/100	20/100	−4
	High	17/100	20/100	−3
6	Low	39/100	29/100	10
	Average	39/100	30/100	9
	High	40/100	30/100	10
8	Low	40/100	28/100	12
	Average	41/100	28/100	13
	High	42/100	29/100	13

"High" value was 4.48; and the "Low" score was 3.02. Table 7.6 provides the AAL counts per 100 utterances in each context as well as the difference values.

Analyses indicated a nonsignificant result for the main effect of racial centrality ($p=0.4092$), and again this is evident from the data in Table 7.6. In each grade and context, the count values are nearly identical in all three racial centrality categories. For example, in the informal context in Grade 1, speakers with low and average racial centrality scores used sixteen AAL forms per 100 utterances and those with high racial centrality scores used seventeen AAL forms. Similarly, eighth graders in the formal context used either twenty-eight forms (low and average) or twenty-nine forms (high). This indicates that the speaker's racial centrality score does not affect overall AAL use.

Results of the two-way interaction were also not significant ($p=0.0859$). Again, this can be seen in the lack of variability in the difference scores for each grade. In each of the three grade levels, the difference scores were almost exactly the same across all three racial centrality groups. In addition, the three-way interaction term was not significant ($p=0.7599$), confirming the fact that there is no difference in shifting patterns over time based on racial centrality scores.

7.6   The Significance of Style-Shifting in Childhood and Early Adolescence

The exploration of overall trajectories and the effect of five demographic/social variables provides a basis for a predictive model of style-shifting. Similar to Chevrot et al. (2000), we find that style-shifting does not occur among the youngest age group, but emerges sometime between the first year and fifth year of primary school. While other studies indicate that style-shifting can occur as young as ages 3–4 (Smith et al. 2013), such early patterns of style-shifting may be restricted to highly salient variables. As Chevrot et al. (2000) and Patterson (1992) suggest, school may provide models of formal/informal interactions for children, so that children become more aware of adultlike norms of style-shifting as they progress through the school system. This process may move children away from more situational style-shifting patterns for select salient variables to patterns reflecting adultlike concepts of formality. Finally, as children develop literacy skills, the influence of formal writing may impact style-shifting patterns as variants associated with written forms may come to be recognized as formal (Chevrot et al. 2000). Such factors may impact a broader swath of variables, such as those considered in the DDM, rather than the limited set that undergoes situational switching in the preschool years.

Age clearly plays an important role, with speakers shifting more as they get older, but gender also proved to be a relevant motivator for style-shift. When combining the data from all three time points, females indicated more variation in their language use, shifting to a larger extent than males on average. While statistical tests indicated that patterns of shifting over time did not differ based on gender, a closer inspection of the data reveal a trend: females tended to shift more and more with age, while males' shifting behavior remained stable once they reach middle school.

Mother's education discussed in Chapter 5 also merits consideration with respect to shifting, although it does not attain statistical significance. African American children's use of vernacular features was statistically aligned with those of their mothers from age 4 through 16, except during early adolescence. Since a mother's language plays a large linguistic influence during the early part of the lifespan, her level of education would likely impact her child's language exposure and subsequent use. This hypothesis is supported through a clear pattern in the raw data: the more educated the speaker's mother, the less likely he or she is to shift styles. While this may seem counterintuitive, the reason may be understood by more closely inspecting speakers' overall AAL patterns. Analyses did indicate a negative relationship between the mother's education and overall AAL use, suggesting that speakers tended to use more AAL if their mothers are less educated. Notably, this is true in both formal and informal contexts. On average, a speaker whose mother does not have a high school diploma used a little more AAL in formal settings than a speaker whose mother has a college degree, but he or she used a lot more AAL in informal settings. Accordingly, speakers in the "High Mother's Education" category did not shift as much, on average, because they did not use as much AAL to begin with; they are predominantly MAE users in informal contexts as well as in formal situations.

Results for the classroom demographics trend in the opposite direction. That is, the higher the percentage of African American students in a speaker's school, the larger the degree of shifting. Speakers with few African American classmates used less AAL in both contexts on average, and, therefore, shifted less than those who had a larger percentage of African American peers. Again, this finding is based only on patterns in the data, as the analysis produced a nonsignificant result for this relationship, but it deserves further investigation.

Both African American contacts and the measure of racial centrality used here exhibited no relationship with style-shifting, both in the statistical analyses and in the patterns seen in the raw data. While this may indicate that these variables are unrelated to speakers' use of style, it may also highlight a larger issue related to the challenges of data collection. For example, the structure of the social contacts questionnaire may limit its usefulness. Since the mean value for all participants (M=3.26, SD=0.57) was close to the maximum response value of 4, this measure most likely did not effectively capture the variability that truly exists for this characteristic. Setting a ceiling value corresponding to "5 or more" may have been unduly limiting, since many respondents may have had a much larger number of African American social contacts in a given category. Rethinking this measure and perhaps considering an expanded questionnaire or another method of evaluating speakers' social networks might result in different results for this variable. Similarly, the use of a racial centrality measure is somewhat controversial. A number of measures have been developed in an attempt to represent racial identity, and little consensus exists on how to best encapsulate this latent variable. In fact, the racial centrality measure used in this work is only one component of a larger measure of identity. Thus, other measures of individual identity may be needed to effectively determine whether a relationship between racial centrality and language use exists.

While this investigation provides some notable trends in the development of style-shifting in childhood and adolescence, it also underscores the inherent difficulty in studying variables that cannot always be directly measured. Nevertheless, it provides insight into some of the factors that most likely influence style use. Age and gender are clearly relevant, and the influence of parents and peers seems noteworthy, as shown in the results for mother's education, social contacts, and school demographics. Further research may indicate that factors like conversational partners and social networks are important variables in a descriptive model of style-shifting. Certainly, a lot of work remains to be done, but some of the major motivators of style and their potential effect at various stages in the early lifespan are starting to become more evident.

References

Bell, Allan. 1984. Language style as audience design. *Language in Society* 13(2): 145–204.

Charity, Anne H., Hollis S. Scarborough, and Griffin, Darion M. 2004. Familiarity with "school English" in African-American children and its relationship to early reading achievement. *Child Development* 75(5): 1340–1356.

Chevrot, Jean-Pierre, Laurence Beaud, and Renata Varga. 2000. Developmental data on a French sociolinguistic variable: Post-consonantal word-final/R. *Language Variation and Change* 12(3): 295–319.

Cohen, Jacob. 1988. *Statistical Power Analysis for the Behavioral Sciences* (second ed.). Mahwah, NJ: Lawrence Erlbaum Associates.

Coupland, Nikolas. 2007. *Style, Variation, and Identity.* New York: Cambridge University Press.

Craig, Holly K. and Julie A. Washington. 2004. Grade-related changes in the production of African American English. *Journal of Speech, Language, and Hearing Research* 47(2): 450–463.

Craig, Holly K. and Julie A. Washington. 2006. *Malik Goes to School: Examining the Language Skills of African American Students from Preschool-5th Grade.* Mahwah, NJ: Lawrence Erlbaum Associates, Inc.

Craig, Holly K., Lingling Zhang, Stephanie L. Hensel, and Erin J. Quinn. 2009. African American English-speaking students: An examination of the relationship between dialect shifting and reading outcomes. *Journal of Speech, Language, and Hearing Research* 52(4): 839–855.

Díaz-Campos, Manuel. 2005. The emergence of adultlike command of sociolinguistic variables: a study of consonant weakening in Spanish-speaking children. In David Eddington (ed.), *Selected Proceedings of the 6th Conference on the Acquisition of Spanish and Portuguese as First and Second Languages*, 56–65. Somerville, MA: Cascadilla Proceedings Project.

Cross, William E. Jr. 1991. *Shades of Black: Diversity in African-American Identity.* Philadelphia, PA: Temple University Press.

Eckert, Penelope. 2000. *Linguistic Variation as Social Practice.* Malden, MA and Oxford: Blackwell.

Eckert, Penelope. 2017. *Meaning and Language Variation: The Third Wave in Sociolinguistics.* Cambridge: Cambridge University Press.

Ervin-Tripp, Susan. 2001. Variety, style-switching, and ideology. In Penelope Eckert and John Rickford (eds.), *Style and Variation*, 44–56. New York: Cambridge University Press.

Finegan, Edward and Douglas Biber. 1994. Register and social dialect variation: An integrated approach. In Douglas Biber and Edward Finegan (eds.), *Sociolinguistic Perspectives on Register*, 315–347. Oxford: Oxford University Press.

Helms, Janet. 1990. *Black and White Racial Identity: Theory, Research, and Practice.* Westport, CT: Praeger.

Kendall, Tyler and Walt Wolfram. 2009. Local and external language standards in African American English. *Journal of English Linguistics* 37(4):5–30.

Labov, William. 1965. Stages in the acquisition of Standard English. In Roger W. Shuy (ed.), *Social Dialects and Language Learning*, 77–103. Champaign, IL: National Council of Teachers of English.

Labov, William. 1966. *The Social Stratification of English in New York City.* Washington, DC: Center for Applied Linguistics.

Labov, William. 1972. *Language in the Inner City: Studies in the Black English Vernacular.* Philadelphia, PA: University of Pennsylvania Press.

Labov, William. 2001. The anatomy of style shifting. In Penelope Eckert and John R. Rickford (eds.), *Style and Sociolinguistic Variation*, 85–108. Cambridge/New York: Cambridge University Press.

Liang, Kung-Yee and Scott Zeger. 1986. Longitudinal data analysis using generalized linear models. *Biometrika* 73: 13–22.

Miller, Jon F. and Rhea Paul. 1995. *The Clinical Assessment of Language Comprehension.* Baltimore, MD: Paul Brookes Publishing Company.

Patterson, Janet Lee. 1992. *The Development of SociolinguisticPphonological Variation Patterns for (ing) in Young Children.* Ph.D. Dissertation. Albuquerque, NM: University of New Mexico.

Renn, Jennifer. 2007. *Measuring Style Shift: A Quantitative Analysis of African American English.* UNC MA thesis, University of North Carolina at Chapel Hill.

Renn, Jennifer. 2010. *Acquiring Style: The Development of Dialect Shifting among African American Children.* Ph.D. dissertation. Chapel Hill, North Carolina: University of North Carolina at Chapel Hill.

Renn, Jennifer. 2011. Patterns of shift: Longitudinal trajectories of style shifting among African American youth. Paper presented at *the American Dialect Society Annual Meeting*, Pittsburgh, PA.

Renn Jennifer. 2015. Investigating the relationship between African American English use and early literacy skills. Paper presented at *the American Dialect Society Annual Meeting*, Portland, OR.

Renn, Jennifer and J. Michael Terry. 2009. Operationalizing style: Quantifying the use of style shift in the speech of African American adolescents. *American Speech* 84(4): 367–390.

Rickford, John R. and Faye McNair-Knox. 1994. Addressee- and topic-influenced style shift: A quantitative sociolinguistic study. In Douglas Biber and Edward Finegan (eds.), *Perspectives on Register: Situating Register Variation within Sociolinguistics*, 235–276. Oxford: Oxford University Press.

Rickord, John R. and Mackenzie Price. 2013. Girlz II women: Age-grading, language change and stylistic variation. *Journal of Sociolinguistics* 17:143–179.

Rowley, Stephanie A. J., Robert M. Sellers, Tabbye M. Chavous, and Mia Smith. 1998. The relationship between racial identity and self-esteem in African American college and high school students. *Journal of Personality and Social Psychology 74*(3): 715–724.

Schilling-Estes, Natalie. 1998. Investigating "self conscious" speech: The performance register in Ocracoke English. *Language in Society* 27(1): 53–83.

Schilling-Estes, Natalie. 2004. Constructing ethnicity in interaction. *Journal of Sociolinguistics* 8(2): 163–195.

Sellers, Robert M., Stephanie A. J. Rowley, Tabbye M. Chavous, J. Nicole Shelton, and Mia Smith. 1997. Multidimensional inventory of black identity: A preliminary investigation of reliability and construct validity. *Journal of Personality and Social Psychology 73*(4): 805–815.

Smith, Jennifer, Mercedes Durham, and Hazel Richards. 2013. The social and linguistic in the acquisition of sociolinguistic norms: Caregivers, children, and variation. *Linguistics* 51(2): 285–324.

Street, Richard L. and Howard Giles. 1982. Speech accommodation theory: A social cognitive approach to language and speech behavior. In M. Roloff and C. R. Berger (eds.), *Social Cognition and Communication*, 193–226 .Beverly Hills, CA: Sage.

Wolfram, Walt and Natalie Schilling. 2016. *American English: Dialects and Variation, Third Edition*. Cambridge/Oxford: Basil Blackwell.

8   The Relationship of African American Language and Early Literacy Skills

8.1   Introduction

Speaker 1075 moved around a bit as a kid. He started out in the Durham school system before switching over to Chapel Hill for high school. Given his personal history, he likely was exposed to many ways of speaking, both within and outside of the classroom. His attitudes about language in the classroom might very well reflect this: "If you was in English class, and you- you learning how to speak properly and ... write properly, and all that, so why talk in slang? ... Cause sometimes you talking slang, you might write ... *jumpin'* instead of *jumping*, you know?"

This position and attitude brings forth images of the Ebonics controversy from the 1990s, a cultural moment that linguists remember with dismay. More than twenty years later, the Ebonics controversy is unknown to FPG participants, but the role of language in the success of African American students is hardly settled, as it is difficult, if not impossible, to disentangle the impact on scholastic success from social factors such as standard language ideologies, structural racism, and discrimination, from potential linguistic impacts on reading outcomes. Yet, given the gravity of missed educational opportunities, we turn again to this question.

The impetus for the contemporary study of AAL in the United States was not initiated solely by linguistic curiosity. The mid-1960s, generally recognized as the pioneering period for the emergence of the field of sociolinguistics (e.g., Labov 1963, 1966; Hymes 1964, 1974; Shuy, Wolfram and Riley 1967), coincided with a growing concern for social and educational disparity in the United States initiated by President Lyndon B. Johnson's War on Poverty, the unofficial name for the legislation first introduced during his State of the Union address in 1964. Johnson proposed the legislation in response to a national poverty rate of almost 20 percent and significant educational gaps between children of poverty and those with socioeconomic resources. The Coleman report (1966) revealed an enormous achievement gap between black and white students in the United States, notwithstanding the integration of schools initiated a decade earlier through the Brown v. Board of Education case (1954). The question of language became a concern in this discussion, as linguists (Labov 1969; Wolfram 1970) hotly debated educational psychologists (Bereiter and Engleman 1966) about the linguistic status of nonmainstream varieties of English, particularly AAL. Some educators maintained that variation from socially accepted mainstream varieties constituted a fundamental deficiency in language fostered by differential family and community contexts (Coleman 1966). On the other hand, language scholars argued passionately that dialect variation was simply a matter of *difference*, not *deficit*. Shades of the debate still linger a half-century after this debate became a national educational issue in allied fields ranging from sociology (Lareau 2011) to education (Hart and Risley 1995, 2003).

Sociolinguists became interested in the role of language differences in education since AAL was linguistically dissonant with the language of education most commonly used by language gatekeepers in the schools. In this context, a number of the earliest and most well-known studies of AAL were, in fact, supported by the Office of Education rather than scientific linguistic agencies such the as the National Science Foundation. For example, Labov and his colleagues' groundbreaking work *A Study of the Non-Standard English of Negro and Puerto Rican Speakers in New York City* (1968) and Shuy, Wolfram, and Riley's *Linguistic Correlates of Social Stratification in Detroit Speech* (1967) were funded by grants from the Office of Education in the hope that these linguistic studies would lead to answers about the role of language in educational disparity.

Unfortunately, the role of language and educational inequality has not been resolved after more than 50 years of study, and the research offered here will not solve the complex issues attendant to this educational gap. At the same time, it is important to address some of the issues related to AAL and educational achievement, in this case, related to literacy. Educational success is important for all children, but African American students seem to face additional challenges with respect to academic success during childhood and adolescence (Fryer and Levitt 2006; Rampey, Dion, and Donahue 2009). Considerable evidence documents a black-white race gap even after accounting for differences in home, neighborhood, and school factors (Burchinal et al. 2011; Fryer and Levitt 2006; Hardaway and McLoyd 2009). As these factors do not fully account for differences in academic outcomes, some researchers have hypothesized that differences between the varieties of speech that many African American children use in the community and the language used in school may, in part, contribute to this disparity (Baratz and Shuy 1969; Rickford and Wolfram 2010). Understanding potential influences on early literacy became more critical as the Common Core State Standards called for shifts in English Language Arts curricula that focus on literacy, including regular practice with complex texts and their academic language; reading, writing, and speaking grounded in evidence from texts, both literary and informational; and building knowledge through content-rich nonfiction (www .corestandards.org). In order for students to meet these demands successfully, it is vital that they receive adequate and appropriate support from parents and educators.

The study reported in this chapter addresses the potential contribution of vernacular language experiences to academic success by examining whether children's use of AAL is related to their subsequent reading skills. As reported throughout this book, AAL is distinguished from Mainstream American English (MAE) both phonologically and grammatically, and the differences between the two dialects can make it more challenging for early readers to connect vernacular forms to letters and words that are presented in MAE. This work analyzes first and second grade language samples from seventy-eight African American children in the study to determine whether their use of nonstandard dialect forms was associated with three reading outcomes on the Woodcock Johnson-R in third grade, a widely used literacy evaluation tool (Woodcock and Johnson 1989). Building on studies that have shown that children who have limited early exposure to MAE, such as dual language learners or speakers of other dialect variations of English, may experience difficulty with a curriculum based on MAE (e.g., Rickford 1999; Charity, Scarborough and Griffin 2004), this inquiry examines another potential explanation for lower literacy skills among African American children in early primary school. Specifically, it seeks to investigate more fully the possibility that AAL use is a relevant factor in the early literacy outcomes of African American children by examining possible associations of language use with three different literacy subtests in order to ascertain whether AAL use might affect various components of reading ability differently.

8.2   Studies of AAL in School-Age Children

In recent decades, research in such fields as psychology, speech-language pathology, and linguistics has intensified the study of the role of AAL in children's early learning (Craig et al. 2003; Craig and Washington 2004; Green 2011; Van Hofwegen and Stob 2012). Studies of vernacular language in Georgia and Michigan, in particular, have provided insight into the impact of AAL on early academic outcomes. In the Georgia study, results suggest that kindergarten through second grade is a critical period in children's early literacy development. Terry and Connor (2012) found that while children's use of AAL forms from kindergarten to first grade was not related to letter-word reading or phonological awareness skills, changes in children's AAL use from first to second grade were significantly associated with their reading skills (Terry et al. 2012).

Studies from a sample of African American students in Michigan have shown that high AAL use is correlated with low academic achievement (e.g., Craig, Connor and Washington 2003; Craig and Washington 2004). Additional studies elsewhere have looked at the impact of AAL use in terms of style-shifting. The ability to engage in style-shifting is an important tool for speakers of non-MAE language varieties, as mastery of a more standard variety gives speakers access to the language of classroom. Connor and Craig's (2006) study of sixty-three African American preschoolers found a "U-shaped" relationship existed between the children's use of AAL features and tests of their early language and literacy skills, meaning that those with the highest and lowest levels of dialect density performed the best (pp. 780). These results suggest that the children who demonstrated high frequencies of AAL features coupled with stronger language and literacy skills may in fact be shifting between AAL and MAE, even at this early age. Craig and Washington's (2004) study of 400 African American children found that students who were dialect shifters performed significantly better on standardized tests than nonshifters. Other work by Craig et al. (2009) indicated that elementary school students who are able to shift from spoken AAL to a more standard variety of English in written tasks have better academic outcomes. These results underscore the fact that students who speak AAL at home need not learn MAE to the exclusion of their home dialect; rather, it may be important for students to supplement the language learned at home with MAE structures for the purpose of literacy.

8.3   Aims of the Study

Many earlier studies of the effects of nonmainstream language use have focused on children's outcomes in pre-kindergarten and the primary elementary school grades of kindergarten through second grade; this study, however, looks specifically at child outcomes in third grade. Third grade is often regarded as a watershed year for students in terms of the development of reading skills and academic success (Lloyd 1978; Entwistle and Hayduck 1988). According to Lloyd (1978), third grade is of particular importance because as "the last of the primary grades, the third grade is the point at which basic reading skills have been taught (and hopefully learned)" (p. 1194), and Bloom (1964) estimates that it is at this time point that 50 percent of future achievement patterns have been set, making it a crucial age to study. It is also the grade where standardized testing takes place for the first time in the school system, making it a key year in terms of educational accountability. The focus on third grade allows for a more careful examination of the association between AAL and both literacy decoding and comprehension at an age when most children have some skills in both areas. In addition, this investigation adds to the information collected from the studies in Michigan (e.g., Craig and Washington 2004; Craig et al. 2009, etc.) and Georgia (e.g., Terry 2012; Terry et al. 2012, etc.) by focusing on our unique longitudinal sample. For this study, data from the seventy-eight children who participated in the study in first and second grade were analyzed.

8.4 Measures

Data collected at each annual visit included language samples, as well as information on the home environment, the school environment, academic skills, the parents' and child's social networks, mother's background and language use, and racial identity. Participants also took a battery of standardized tests at each visit, including an assessment of their literacy and problem solving skills. The language data used in this study were collected when the children were in the first and second grades. Though multiple tasks from each time point were used in compiling the language samples, they were combined into a single dataset. Three tasks from a "mother-child interaction" in the first grade were used as the first language sample. These three tasks were a discussion planning the child's birthday party, a task where the caregiver and child played with magnets and various other materials (e.g., coins, paperclips), and a reminiscing task where the caregiver and child remembered special events like holidays and vacations that they had experienced together within the last year. These tasks were selected because they consisted of relatively natural speech between the caregiver and child. At the commencement of each task, an examiner entered the room to explain the activity. The caregiver and child were then left alone in the room to interact as normally as possible. All language from all three activities was used in analysis, though speech that occurred when the examiner reentered the room was excluded. The mean number of child utterances from the three tasks was 106.53 (SD = 36.77).

As described in Chapter 2, during the second grade visit, the children engaged in several narrative storytelling tasks, responding to inquiries from an adult examiner. The first interaction was a picture description task in which the examiner showed the child a picture depicting a circus scene. The child was then asked to describe the picture in enough detail so that another child could draw the picture without seeing it. The other language samples were part of a narrative elicitation task, where the examiner would introduce a topic and then ask the child to share a similar experience. All of the language from each of these tasks was transcribed and combined to construct the rest of the language sample. In total, each child was encouraged to tell six stories and the mean number of child utterances was 68.57 (SD = 35.51).

The language data were transcribed using the Systematic Analysis of Language Transcripts software (Miller and Paul 1995) and were then coded for the presence of forty-one features from the DDM (cf. Appendix) to calculate the composite dialect score. The language samples at both time points were aggregated as there was no significant difference in students' dialect use in the first and second grade tasks (Renn 2010). Even with the variable nature of AAL, such measures have successfully identified patterns of use in both youth and adult speakers (Craig and Washington 2004; Renn and Terry 2009). The total number of AAL feature tokens in the coded transcripts was divided by the total number of utterances to attain a value that represented a participant's AAL density. Measures of reliability in the coding as described in Chapter 3 were undertaken and Kappas for all coders indicated substantial reliability, ranging from 0.62 – 0.71.

8.5   Maternal, Child, Home, and Classroom Covariates

Demographic, family, and school characteristics were included as covariates. Two demographic variables, the child's gender (male = 0, female = 1) and the mother's education in years, were collected during the recruitment interview and maternal education was updated annually. This study used the maternal education level reported when the child was in the first grade. The responsiveness and stimulation in the home environment were collected in the first grade using the short version of the Home Observation for Measurement of the Environment (HOME) inventory (Caldwell and Bradley 1984; Center for Human Resource Research 1997). This instrument, developed for the National Longitudinal Survey of Youth, consists of a home observation combined with a parental interview and provides a measure of the quality of emotional support and cognitive stimulation in the home environment (Dubrow and Ippolito 1994). Items on the questionnaire evaluate various characteristics of the home environment, including: emotional and verbal responsivity; encouragement of maturity; the emotional climate of the home environment; access to materials and experiences that foster the child's emotional and intellectual growth; provisions for active stimulation; family participation in developing stimulating experiences; paternal involvement; and aspects of the physical environment. Each item on the scale was scored as Yes (= 1) or No (= 0). The mean of all of the questionnaire item values was used in analyses as an overall measure of the home environment.

The responsiveness and quality of instruction in the classroom were measured in the first through third grade using the Classroom Qualitative Rating Scale (NICHD ECCRN 2002). This measure is collected through direct observation and each item is scored on a scale of 1 (uncharacteristic) to 7 (extremely characteristic). Items on the scale include evaluations of classroom control, emotional climate, sensitivity and responsivity, classroom management, literary instruction, evaluation and feedback, instructional conversation, and child responsibility. The mean of all items on the scale was used to create a classroom quality rating for each grade. These values were then averaged across the three grades to attain an overall classroom quality score. Since the children were recruited at birth, they attended many schools across central North Carolina, resulting in no nesting within classrooms.

Children's reading skills were measured by standard scores on the Letter-Word Identification (ID) ($M = 97.4$, $SD = 14.9$), Passage Comprehension ($M = 103.7$, $SD = 11.7$), and Word Attack Skills ($M = 101.5$, $SD = 13.8$) components of the Woodcock Johnson-R Tests of Achievement (Woodcock and Johnson 1989) in the third grade. These tests assess different aspects of early literacy skills, with the Letter-Word ID task testing the child's knowledge of letters and words, the Passage Comprehension items assessing reading comprehension, and the Word Attack Skills section evaluating the child's phoneme/grapheme knowledge to see if he or she can apply both phonological and orthographical knowledge in order to read nonsense words aloud. Cronbach's alpha, a measure of internal-consistency reliability (Cronbach 1951), was estimated at a level of $\alpha \geq 0.90$ for all three tests (Woodcock and Johnson 1989). Reliability is considered acceptable for group comparisons when alpha is 0.50 or above (Helmstadter 1964).

8.6   Results

Data analyses focused on determining the association between AAL use at the beginning of elementary school and children's performance on measures of language, reading comprehension, and literacy skills in the third grade. First, descriptive analyses were conducted, followed by multiple regressions. Descriptive analyses included computing means and correlations. Table 8.1 provides the descriptive statistics for all of the independent and dependent variables used in analysis.

Next, the relationships among AAL use, literacy skills, demographic factors, and family and school characteristics were examined to ascertain how these factors are connected. Determining the association between nonstandard dialect use and reading and literacy skills was addressed by calculating the correlations among the three Woodcock Johnson subtests and the overall AAL use in the first and second grades. Table 8.2 shows the correlations among all of the variables in the model. The values indicating the relationship between AAL use, as measured by the DDM, and the Woodcock Johnson subtests are in italics.

As Table 8.2 shows, in the first and second grades there was a negative relationship between AAL use and all three Woodcock Johnson tests of literacy

Table 8.1 *Descriptive statistics for literacy variables and covariates*

Variable	N	M (SD)
Male	37 (47%)	
Mother's Education in Years	80	12.95 (1.99)
Classroom Qualitative Rating Scale	79	4.97 (0.63)
HOME Inventory	78	0.73 (0.08)
# AAE Forms per 10 Utterances	79	1.71 (0.90)
WJ Letter-Word ID	79	97.43 (14.86)
WJ Passage Comprehension	79	103.72 (11.67)
WJ Word Attack Skills	79	101.47 (13.78)

Table 8.2 *Correlations among all analysis variables*

	Gender	Mother's education	HOME total	CQRS total	AAE use	WJ letter-word	WJ pass comp	WJ word attack
Covariates								
Gender	1							
Mother's Education	0.05	1						
HOME Total	0.08	0.59**	1					
CQRS total	0.24*	0.19	0.29**	1				
AAE Use	−0.21	**−0.44****	**−0.42****	**−0.35****	1			
WJ Outcomes								
Letter-Word ID	0.13	.32**	.30**	0.18	−.39**	1		
Passage Comp	0.17	.35**	.42**	.28*	−.33**	.79**	1	
Word Attack	0.2	0.16	.24*	0.16	−.27*	.80**	.64**	1

Note: CQRS = Classroom Quality Rating Scale
* $p<.05$. ** $p<.01$.

and reading skills. For the Letter-Word ID and Passage Comprehension sub-tests, the correlations were moderate, with the strongest relationship existing between AAL use and the Letter-Word ID test, $r = −.39, p < .01$, and evidence of a slightly weaker association between AAL use and the Passage Comprehension test, $r = −.33, p < .01$. The correlation between AAL use and the Word Attack Skills subtest was the weakest of the three subtests $r = −.27$, $p < .05$, but it was still statistically significant.

Table 8.2 also illustrates that AAL use was related to several of the selected covariates. In particular, the bolded values in the correlation table show

Table 8.3 *Regression results for each Woodcock Johnson task including covariates*

	WJ letter-word ID		WJ passage comprehension		WJ word attack skills	
	B	SE(B)	B	SE(B)	B	SE(B)
Intercept	87.17*	20.81	60.48*	16.9	66.97*	24.05
Gender	0.3	2.98	0.67	2.42	4.17	2.98
AAE Use	−48.51*	18.11	−18.69	15.52	−24.41	22.09
CQRS Total	0.41	2.52	2.02	2.05	0.43	2.92
Mother's Ed	0.83	0.94	1.05	0.76	0.36	1.09
HOME Total	13.77	23.88	30.73	18.4	35.38	27.6
Note: $R^{2=}$	0.21		0.25		0.14	

* $p<.05$.

that children who used more AAL tended to have mothers with less education, $r = -.44$, $p < .01$, home environments that were less responsive and stimulating, $r = -.42$, $p < .01$, and classroom environments that were rated as lower quality, $r = -.35$, $p < .01$.

A multiple regression model was used to predict the students' literacy skills in the third grade. Because each subtest evaluates children's aptitude in different areas of reading and literacy, each was investigated using a separate model. In each model, gender, mother's education, and measures of home and classroom quality were included as covariates to control for their respective contributions to literacy outcomes. Results indicated that children who used more AAL scored lower on Letter-Word ID, even after accounting for these confounding home and school factors. For each additional AAL form that was used per 10 utterances, children scored approximately 4.8 points lower on the Letter-Word ID task. In contrast, AAL was not significantly related to either Passage Comprehension or Word Attack Skills when all covariates were included in the models. Table 8.3 shows the results of these three regressions.

Effect sizes were calculated for each model to further ascertain the influence of AAL use on each of the language and literacy tasks. Since the models include a number of highly correlated variables, this was another method of identifying the unique influence of AAL dialect use on children's burgeoning language and literacy skills. The effect size for each model was calculated using Cohen's f^2 (Cohen 1988). This is one of several measures that might be used to calculate an effect size for a multiple regression. It is defined as the squared multiple correlation (R^2) of the regression model divided by $1 - R^2$. The values attained for each model were: .27 for the Letter-Word ID task, .33

for Passage Comprehension skills, and .16 for the Word Attack Skills subtest. A value between 0.15 and 0.35 indicates a moderate effect size; thus, these results demonstrate a moderate association with children's scores in all three third grade subtests.

8.7   The Significance of the Results

This analysis suggests that more regular observed use of AAL in early elementary school appears to be related to the development of MAE language and literacy skills above and beyond the effects previously attributed to home and school factors (Burchinal et al. 2000; Burchinal et al. 2006; Roberts, Jurgens and Burchinal 2005). Effect sizes were notable for the Letter-Word ID, Passage Comprehension, and Word Attack Skills subtests, suggesting that differential relationships exist between AAL use and the various components assessed in these subtests. In addition, the results of multiple regression models that were adjusted for possible confounding of home and school factors found that AAL use was significantly related to lower scores on Letter-Word ID test, but not on the other two reading tests. The regression results imply that when a child encounters different language varieties at home and in the classroom, it may make it more difficult for young learners to develop decoding and vocabulary skills. This outcome supports Labov's (1995, 2001) notion that the differences that exist in the phonetic inventories of MAE and AAL may result in a misalignment in sound-spelling correspondence for AAL speakers. Such discrepancies may be confusing for those acquiring early reading skills and may heighten the "loss of confidence in the alphabet" in decoding because of structural differences like final cluster reduction (e.g., *told* becomes *tol'*) and single final consonant deletion (e.g., *seat, seed,* and *see* all pronounced as *see*) that are found in AAL (Labov 1995:45). Lexical and morphosyntactic differences between MAE and AAL may also present young children with a greater challenge in acquiring vocabulary items. For example, AAL allows for the absence of many grammatical markers (e.g., past tense *–ed*, plural *–s*, etc.) and certain forms of the verb *to be* may be deleted, which may be challenging for children trying to match their spoken language with a somewhat disparate written system (Labov 1995). Terry et al.'s (2010) study of African American students' performance on mathematical word problems in second grade also points to an interference effect of AAL on reading skills, particularly with respect to the third-person singular *–s* morpheme (e.g., *Jill eat_ a lot of ice cream*). High AAL users scored lower on mathematic reasoning questions containing third-person singular *–s*, even when analyses controlled for mathematic ability. This result may stem from the variable input that AAL-acquiring children receive, where it is present in the classroom but systematically absent in their home dialect (Terry et al. 2010). Combining these findings with the previously discussed patterns found by Craig and Washington (2004), Craig et al. (2009), and Renn (2010) suggests that children who use AAL in the home but do not learn to style-shift and adjust their use of morphosyntactic AAL features by early elementary school may experience a greater struggle with vocabulary development. The importance of investigating this issue is underscored by studies that have shown that it is essential that students who struggle with reading and literacy are identified early, as children who experience difficulties in elementary school are more likely to struggle with reading in middle school, continuing into adulthood (Scarborough 2001; Barber and Olsen 2004).

The results of this analysis also add to information garnered by studies in Michigan and Georgia. Like the Michigan-based studies (e.g., Craig, Connor, and Washington 2003; Craig et al. 2003; Craig and Washington 2004, 2006), this study used the DDM to assess children's use of AAL and investigated its relation to early academic outcomes. Both early elementary school students in the Michigan studies and in this North Carolina sample showed a decline in AAL use during the primary grades, as well as an inverse relationship between children's nonstandard language forms and reading skills. The replication of such results is important, as this suggests that these findings are less likely to be sample-specific and might well be applicable to larger populations. The patterns of AAL use in these data also parallel the declining patterns found in Terry and Connor (2012) and Terry et al. (2012), which is particularly interesting because it allows for the comparison of the DDM to the Diagnostic Evaluation of Language Variation – Screening Test (DELV-S) (Seymour, Roeper, and deVilliers 2003), a standardized screening instrument used by speech pathologists to assess a speaker's variation from MAE. A more direct comparison of the DELV-S and DDM is needed, but the fact that both studies found similar patterns in language use provides support for both assessment methods.

As previously mentioned, most of the independent variables were correlated with one another, making it difficult to tease apart the unique contribution of each one. This was particularly problematic for mother's education, the quality of the home environment, and AAL use. It is no surprise that these variables are confounded; for example, more highly educated mothers are more likely to have access to MAE. Of course, poor-quality classrooms are deeply intertwined with systemic housing segregation, along both ethnic and economic lines (Rothstein 2017). Lower success rates for AAL-speaking children cannot be separated from economic oppression and the substantial burdens and barriers that come from poverty and racism. While these external conditions present a challenge when interpreting the results of the analysis, it shows that factors like mother's education and the home environment may play an important role in promoting positive educational outcomes because they are directly related to children's access to the language of the classroom. Additionally, awareness of these high correlations is important for determining the appropriate steps to take in subsequent analyses meant to isolate the influence of nonstandard dialect use on reading and literacy outcomes.

Given the long-term nature of this study, the sample size is reasonable, but it does make it more difficult to detect a significant effect for any of the independent variables. Then again, this suggests that the significant effect of AAL use, particularly on the Letter-Word ID task, may be especially meaningful. The moderate effect sizes found for the all three Woodcock-Johnson subtests also appear more interesting when the small sample size is considered. Still, these findings only point to correlational relationships with children's learning outcomes; like many studies on this and similar topics, nothing can be determined with respect to causal relationships. These results, then, highlight the need for further investigation into the ways in which nonstandard dialect use might influence early literacy skills.

Finally, while the project collected language samples in the first and second grades and literacy data in all three grades, at least some of the children were not able to meet basal criteria on the comprehension test until the third grade. For this reason, as well as because of its importance in educational development, only literacy scores at the third grade were used as an outcome, rather than using a longitudinal approach that might examine reading skills at all three time points.

In spite of the limitations, the results of these analyses illustrate the need for attaining a better understanding of the role of AAL use in educational outcomes. Given research that has highlighted the importance of the third grade year, it is necessary to continue investigating ways in which children might attain academic success by this time point. In addition, the newly developed key shifts in English Language Arts education established by the Common Core State Standards places greater literacy demands on students; as a result, there is even greater urgency to support students who have persistently been underserved, including those who use nonstandard language varieties like AAL at home, so that they do not fall further behind their peers. While this study supports similar findings in other parts of the country (e.g., Craig and Washington 2004; Terry 2012), it is imperative to replicate this kind of work using samples of students from other areas. Additional work should employ complementary methods, like type-based tools and more qualitative techniques, as well as current standardized assessment tools like the DELV-S, to attain a more complete picture of how exactly language use influences academic outcomes. The implementation of a multifaceted approach is necessary to attain a clear view of these issues and helps determine how best to support those children who experience a discrepancy between their vernacular dialect and language of the classroom.

References

Baratz, Joan and Roger W. Shuy. 1969. *Teaching Black Children to Read*. Washington, DC: Center for Applied Linguistics.

Barber, Brian and Joseph Olsen 2004. Assessing the transitions to middle and high school. *Journal of Adolescent Research* 19(1): 3–30 .

Bell, Allan. 1984. Language style as audience design. *Language in Society* 13(2): 145–204.

Bereiter, Carl and Siegfried Englemann. 1966. *Teaching Disadvantaged Children in the Preschool*. Englewood Cliffs, NJ: Prentice-Hall.

Bloom, Benjamin S. 1964. *Stability and Change in Human Characteristics*. New York: Wiley.

Burchinal, Margaret R., Kathleen McCartney, Laurence Steinberg, Robert Crosnoe, Sarah L. Friedman, Vonnie McLoyd, Robert Pianta, and NICHD Early Child Care Research Network. 1997. Examining the Black-White achievement gap among low-income children using the NICHD Study of Early Child Care and Youth Development. *Child Development* 82(5): 1404–1420.

Burchinal, Margaret R., Ellen Peisner-Feinberg, Robert Pianta, and Carolee Howes. 2002. Development of academic skills from preschool through second grade: Family and classroom predictors of developmental trajectories. *Journal of School Psychology* 40(5): 415–436.

Burchinal, Margaret R., Joanne Roberts, Rhodus Riggins, Susan A. Zeisel, S., Eloise Neebe, and Donna Bryant. 2000. Relating quality of center child care to early cognitive and language development longitudinally. *Child Development* 71 (2): 339–357.

Burchinal, Margaret R., Joanne E. Roberts, Susan A. Zeisel, Elizabeth A. Hennon, and Stephen Hooper. 2006. Social risk and protective child, parenting, and child care factors in early elementary school years. *Parenting: Science and Practice* 6(1): 79–113.

Caldwell, Betty M., and Robert H. Bradley. 1984. *Home Observation for Measurement of the Environment Manual*. Little Rock, AR: University of Arkansas.

Campbell, Joy M., Catherine M. Hombo, and John Mazzeo. 2000. *NAEP 1999 Trends in Academic Progress: Three Decades of Student Performance. NCES 2000468*. Washington DC: U.S. Department of Education, Office of Educational Research and Improvement, National Center for Education Statistics.

Center for Human Resources Research. 1997. *National Longitudinal Survey of Youth*. Columbus, Ohio.

Charity, Anne H., Hollis S. Scarborough, and Doris M. Griffin. 2004. Familiarity with "School English" in African-American children and its relationship to early reading achievement. *Child Development*, 75(5): 1340–1356.

Christian, K., Frederick. J. Morrison, and F. B. Bryant. 1998. Predicting kindergarten academic skills: Interactions among child care, maternal education, and family literacy environments. *Early Childhood Research Quarterly* 13(3): 501–521.

Cohen, Jacob. 1988. *Statistical Power Analysis for the Behavioral Sciences*. Hillsdale, NJ: Lawrence Erlbaum Associates, Inc.

Coleman, James Samuel. 1966. *Equality of Educational Opportunity*. Office of Education Report, U.S. Department of Health Education & Welfare Report. ERIC document ED012275.

Common Core State Standards. 2014. *Key Shifts in English Language Arts*. www
  .corestandards.org/other-resources/key-shifts-in-english-language-arts/

Connor, Carol M. and Holly K. Craig. 2006. African American preschoolers'
  language, emergent literacy skills, and use of African American English:
  A complex relation. *Journal of Speech, Language, and Hearing Research* 49
  (4): 771–792.

Corcoran, Mary. 1995. Rags to rags: Poverty and mobility in the United States. *Annual
  Review of Sociology* 21: 237–267.

Craig, Holly K., Catherine M. Connor, and Julie A. Washington. 2003. Early positive
  predictors of later reading comprehension for African American students:
  A preliminary investigation. *Language, Speech, and Hearing Services in the
  Schools* 34(1): 31–43.

Craig, Holly K., Connie A. Thompson, Julie A. Washington, and Stephanie L. Potter.
  2003. Phonological features of child African American English. *Journal of Speech,
  Language, and Hearing Research* 46(3): 623–635.

Craig, Holly K. and Julie A. Washington. 2004. Grade-related changes in the production
  of African American English. *Journal of Speech, Language, and Hearing Research*
  47(2): 450–463.

Craig, Holly K. and Julie A. Washington. 2006. *Malik Goes to School: Examining the
  Language Skills of African American Students from Preschool-5th Grade*. Mahwah,
  NJ: Lawrence Erlbaum Associates, Inc.

Craig, Holly K., Lingling Zhang, Stephanie L Hensel, and Erin J. Quinn. 2009. African
  American English-speaking students: An examination of the relationship between
  dialect shifting and reading outcomes. *Journal of Speech, Language, and Hearing
  Research* 52(4): 839–855.

Cronbach, Lee J. 1951. Coefficient alpha and the internal structure of tests.
  Psychometrik 16: 297–334.

Dubrow, Eric F. and Maria F. Ippolito 1994. Effects of poverty and quality of the home
  environment on changes in the academic and behavioral adjustment of elementary
  school-age children. *Journal of Clinical Psychology* 23(4): 401–412.

Early, Diane. M., Karen L. Maxwell, Margaret L. Burchinal, Soumya Alva, Randal
  H. Bender, Donna Bryant et al. 2007. Teachers' education, classroom quality, and
  young children's academic skills: Results from seven studies of preschool programs.
  Child Development 78(2): 558–580.

Entwistle, Doris R. and Leslie A. Hayduk. 1988. Lasting effects of elementary school.
  Sociology of Education 61(3): 147–159.

Fasold, Ralph W. and Walt Wolfram. 1970. Some linguistic features of Negro dialect. In
  Ralph W. Fasold and Roger W. Shuy (eds.), *Teaching Standard English in the Inner
  City*, 41–86. Washington, DC: Center for Applied Linguistics.

Fryer, Richard G. and Steven D. Levitt. 2006. The black-white test score gap through
  third grade. *American Law and Economics Review* 8(2): 249–281.

Green, Lisa J. 2002. *African American English: A Linguistic Introduction*. Cambridge:
  Cambridge University Press.

Hardaway, Cecily R. and Vonnie C. McLoyd. 2009. Escaping poverty and securing
  middle class status: How race and socioeconomic status shape mobility prospects for
  African Americans during transition to adulthood. *Journal of Youth and Adolescence*
  38(2): 242–256.

Hart, Betty and Todd R. Risley. 1995. *Meaningful Differences in the Everyday Experiences of Young American Children*. Baltimore, MD: Brookes Publishing.

Hart, Betty, and Todd R. Risley. 2003. The early catastrophe: The 30 million word gap by age 3. *American Educator* (spring): 4–8. www.aft.org//sites/default/files/periodic als/TheEarlyCatastrophe.pdf

Helmstadter, G. C. 1964. *Principles of Psychological Measurement*. New York: Appleton-Century-Crofts.

Hymes, Dell (ed.) 1964. *Language in Culture and Society*. New York: Harper & Row.

Hymes, Dell. 1974. Ways of speaking. In Richard Bauman and Joel Sherzer (eds.), *Explorations in the Ethnography of Speaking*, Cambridge: Cambridge University Press, 433–451.

Jencks, Christopher and Meredith Phillips. 1998. America's next achievement test: Closing the black-white test score gap. *American Prospect* 9(40): 44–53.

Keenan, Janice. M., Rebecca S. Betjamann, and Richard K. Olson. 2008. Reading comprehension tests vary in the skills they assess: Differential dependence on decoding and oral comprehension. *Scientific Studies of Reading* 12(3): 281–300.

Labov, William. 1963. The social motivation of a sound change. *Word* 19: 273–307.

Labov, William. 1966. *The Social Stratification of English in New York City*. Washington, DC: Center for Applied Linguistics.

Labov, William. 1969. The logic of Nonstandard English. In James E. Alatis (ed.), *Report of the Twentieth Annual Round Table Meeting on Linguistics and Language Studies*, 1–44. Washington, DC: Georgetown University Press.

Labov, William. 1972. *Language in the Inner City: Studies in the Black English Vernacular*. Philadelphia, PA: University of Pennsylvania Press.

Labov, William. 1995. Can reading failure be reversed? A linguistic approach to the question. In V. Gadsden and D. Wagner (eds.), *Literacy among African American Youth: Issues in Learning, Teaching, and Schooling*, 39–68. Cresskill, NJ: Hampton Press.

Labov, William. 2001. *Studies in Sociolinguistics*. Beijing: Beijing Language and Culture University Press.

Labov, William, Paul Cohen, Clarence Robins and John Lewis. 1968. *A Study of the Non-standard English of Negro and Puerto Rican Speakers in New York City*: Cooperative Research Report 3288. Vols. I and II. Philadelphia, PA: U.S. Regional Survey.

Lareau, Annette. 2011. *Unequal Childhoods: Class, Race, and Family Life*. Berkeley, CA: University of California Press.

Lloyd, Dee Norman. 1978. Prediction of school failure from third-grade data. *Educational and Psychological Measurement* 38(4): 1193–1200.

McLoyd, Vonnie C. 1998. Socioeconomic disadvantage and child development. *American Psychologist* 53(2): 185–204.

Miller, John F and Rhea Paul. 1995. *The Clinical Assessment of Language Comprehension*. Baltimore, MD: Paul Brookes Publishing Company.

NICHD Early Child Care Research Network. 2002. Early child care and children's development prior to school entry: Results from the NICHD study of early child care. *American Educational Research Journal* 39(1): 133–164.

Rampey, Bobby D., Gloria S. Dion, and Patricia L. Donahue. 2009. *NAEP 2008: Trends in Academic Progress. NCES 2009–478*. Washington DC: National Center for Education Statistics.

Renn, Jennifer E. 2010. *Acquiring Style: The Development of Dialect Shifting among African American Children*. Ph.D. dissertation. Chapel Hill, NC: University of North Carolina at Chapel Hill.

Rickford, John R. 1992. Grammatical variation and divergence in Vernacular Black English. In Marinel Gerritsen and Dieter Stein (eds.), *Internal and External Factors in Syntactic Change*, 55–62. The Hague: Mouton.

Rickford, John R. 1999. *African American Vernacular English: Features, Evolution, Educational Implications*. Oxford/Malden, MA: Blackwell Publishers Inc.

Rickford, John R. and Walt Wolfram. 2010. *Formal Instruction in Oral Language (as a second dialect): National Research Council Workshop on Language Development*. California: National Academy of Science.

Roberts, Joanne E., Julia Jurgens, and Margaret M. Burchinal. 2005. The role of home literacy practices in preschool children's language and emergent literacy skills. *Journal of Speech, Language, and Hearing Research* 48(2): 345–359.

Rothstein, Richard. 2017. *The Color of Law: A Forgotten History of How Our Government Segregated America*. New York: W.W. Norton

Scarborough, Hollis. S. 2001. Connecting early language and literacy to later reading (dis)abilities: Evidence, theory, and practice. In S. Neuman & D. Dickinson (eds.), *Handbook for Research in Early Literacy*, 97–110. New York: Guilford Press.

Seymour, Harry, Thomas Roeper, and Jill deVilliers. 2003. *Diagnostic Evaluation of Language Variation – Screening Test*. San Antonio, TX: Harcourt Assessment.

Shuy, Roger W., Walt Wolfram, and William K. Riley. 1967. *Linguistic Correlates of Social Stratification in Detroit Speech*. USOE Final Report No. 6–1347. Bethesda, MD: National Institute of Mental Health.

Spears, Arthur. 2009. On shallow grammar: African American English and the critique of exceptionalism. In Jo Anne Kleifgen and George C. Bond (eds.), *The Languages of Africa and the Diaspora: Educating for Language Awareness*, 231–248. Clevedon: Multilingual Matters.

Terry Julius M., Randall Hendrick, Evangelos Evangelou, and R. L. Smith. 2010. Variable dialect switching among African American children: Inferences about working memory. *Lingua* 120(10): 2463–2475.

Terry, Nicole P. 2012. Examining relationships among dialect variation and emergent literacy skills. *Communication Disorders Quarterly* 33(2): 67–77.

Terry, Nicole P. and Carol M. Connor. 2012. Changing nonmainstream American English use and early reading achievement from kindergarten to first grade. *American Journal of Speech-Language Pathology* 21(1): 78–86.

Terry, Nicole P., Carol M. Connor, Yaacov Petcher, and Catherine R. Connor. 2012. Dialect variation and reading: Is change in nonmainstream American English use related to reading achievement in first and second grades? *Journal of Speech, Language, and Hearing Research* 55(1): 55–69.

U.S. Census Bureau. (2010). Income, poverty, and health insurance coverage in the United States: 2008. www.census.gov/prod/2010pubs/p60-238.pdf.

Vandell, Deborah. Lowe., Jay Belsky, Margaret M. Burchinal, Nathan Vanderfrift, and Laurence Steinberg. 2010. Do effects of early child care extend to age 15 years? Results from the NICHD study of early child care and youth development. *Child Development* 81(3): 737–756.

Van Hofwegen, Janneke and Walt Wolfram. 2010. Coming of age in African American English: A longitudinal study. *Journal of Sociolinguistics* 14(4): 427–455.

Wolfram, Walter A. 1969. *A Sociolinguistic Description of Detroit Negro Speech.* Washington, DC: Center for Applied Linguistics.

Wolfram, Walt. 1970. Sociolinguistic premises and the nature of nonstandard dialects. *The Speech Teacher* 19(3): 177–184.

Wolfram, Walt and Natalie Schilling. 2016. *American English: Dialects and Variation, Third Edition.* Cambridge/Oxford: Wiley-Blackwell.

Woodcock, Richard W. and Mary Bonner Johnson. 1989. *Woodcock-Johnson Tests of Cognitive Ability: Standard and Supplemental Batteries.* Chicago, IL: Riverside.

9 A Longitudinal Study in Retrospect

9.1 Introduction

The longitudinal language study conducted under the aegis of FPG has been a unique journey. Much has changed since its inception in 1990 – from the lives of the participants involved to the state of knowledge on lifespan change. At the start of this project, the study of social variation in child language took a back seat to variation in adult language, resulting in a rather limited pool of research that considered pre-adolescent age groups (Fischer 1958; Houston 1969; Macaulay 1977; Reid 1978; Romaine 1978; Payne 1980; Kovac and Adamson 1981; Martino 1982; Purcell 1984). While teens were better researched, transitions between life stages had yet to garner serious theoretical attention from linguists (Eckert 1997; Cheshire 2005, although see Hockett 1950 and Romaine 1984 for early approaches to this topic). Things have certainly changed in the past three decades.

As our colleagues were busy collecting data and as our participants were busy growing up, the field of sociolinguistics increasingly recognized that some core questions could only be answered by turning to data from younger children (Roberts 2002; Foulkes and Docherty 2006; Smith, Durham, and Fortune 2007; Smith, Durham, and Richards 2013) and longitudinal methodologies (Sankoff and Blondeau 2007; Wagner and Buchstaller 2018). This realization was fortuitous, as it has vastly improved our understanding of concerns related to how individuals modify their speech across the lifespan, how language change progresses through individuals and communities, and where children, young adults, and adolescents fit in the broader social tapestry of language variation and change. The monumental work accomplished by those involved in the study thus emerges at a crucial juncture in the field, bridging work on individual variation across distinct life stages with more traditional questions related to community variation, style, and change.

Although child social variation was a somewhat neglected component of linguistic analysis until recently, the same cannot be said for African American Language (AAL). In fact, some of the earliest examples of child and adolescent studies in the field (Stewart 1967; Dillard 1972; Stockman and Vaughn-Cook 1989), including panel studies (Baugh 1996; Cukor-Avila 2002; Cukor-Avila and Bailey 2011; Rickford and Price 2013), focused on AAL. And yet, despite the wealth of research on this variety, many of the social challenges that drove linguists to study this variety remain today: linguistic discrimination, disparities in school achievement, misunderstandings about the nature and origin of AAL, and a tendency to focus on more vernacular speakers as representative of the variety. Our work as linguists is hardly over. FPG expands previous approaches to AAL by considering the interaction between life stages, a host of social variables, and language use. Further, as the participants come from a wide variety of neighborhoods and communities, we move beyond the tradition of prioritizing highly vernacular speakers from ethnically homogenous communities (Bucholtz 2003; Wolfram 2007) to investigate the relationship between segregation and language variation. The depth and breadth of this study adds a new richness to our understanding of AAL as it relates to distinct life stages and social contexts. It also represents a more inclusive and comprehensive variationist perspective by adding to the analytical toolkit the composite dialect index that has traditionally been eschewed and dismissed by variationists in favor of myopically focused, isolated, single linguistic structures. This methodological inclusion is, of course, controversial in variationist studies, but we have offered empirical evidence and argued for its methodological utility and its theoretical validity, notwithstanding its exclusion from the canon of variation studies.

This volume brings together many allied projects born out of FPG to create a broad picture of lifespan change among African Americans through the examination of a host of linguistic and social variables. What emerges is a dynamic story of the role language plays in the social experience of growing up. Within this chapter, we bring the story together through a comparison of the various perspectives and lenses presented throughout the book. When these many perspectives are brought together, a rich picture full of nuance and variation illustrates the ways in which individual linguistic patterns morph across the lifespan. This story has been in the making for decades, but it has been worth the wait.

9.2   Unique Challenges

Work of this size and scope requires many hands. This work was born out of a collaboration crossing disciplines, ranging from speech-language pathology, sociology, and psychology to linguistics, education, and literacy, thus producing a wealth of data that presented us with both challenges and opportunities. Given the extent of the social, educational, and linguistic data available to us, it became clear that traditional variable analyses would be inadequate for generalizing patterns when working with an extensive array of variables. Our team of researchers thus began our efforts by considering the broad concerns of how to track change across multiple time points in a way that moves beyond isolated studies of individual variables. Simultaneously, we considered ways we could triangulate findings across distinct variables and subsystems of language to investigate whether distinct kinds of linguistic subsystems show disparate paths across the lifespan and when linguistic variables change in concert with each other. Our interest was in the forest, but as we pursued this broader lens, we took care not to neglect the valuable information hidden in the individual trees.

In an effort to avoid becoming data bound, we refined methods from allied fields that allowed us to capture snapshot profiles of linguistic behavior at each time point, including the use of composite indices (Oetting and McDonald 2001, 2002; Craig and Washington 2006; Renn 2007, 2010) and full vowel space measures (Vorperian and Kent 2007; Flipsen and Lee 2012). Metrics like the DDM are certainly are no substitute for traditional variation analysis, but they serve as an important complement to such studies as they provide a broad overview of language behavior. For example, vowel space measures revealed critical information about developmental patterns associated with vowel production, while the thoughtful construction of a DDM allowed us to examine the ways in which language variation correlated with the many social variables collected in this study. Such measures allowed us to perform the statistical modelling that was most appropriate for many of the questions at hand, including the use of dyadic analysis to assess peer accommodation and analyses of the relationship between AAL and literacy.

While we chose the DDM as a heuristic to capture composite snapshots across each life stage, we mindfully turned to more traditional analyses to complement this work, including variationist analyses of individual variants such as copula absence, third-person singular –s deletion, and (ING), as well as a host of vowel analyses. As discussed subsequently, a comparison of these variables reveals some general patterns among related variables, while also indicating when and where a more detailed variant-specific analysis becomes necessary. So, for example, we were able to construct two sub-DDM scores to assess features associated with ethnolinguistic repertoires and those more broadly associated with formality in Chapter 7. It has become critically apparent that the study of individual variants in isolation solves only a selective piece of the puzzle regarding the intersections between age, social factors, and language change. We thus advocate for triangulated, mixed methodologies that consider inventories as well as individual variables in the pursuit of understanding individual lifespan change in language.

9.3 Acquisition and Use of AAL across the Lifespan

The observation that children acquire a variable system in an environment rich with sociolinguistic variation has prompted researchers to examine the intersection between the acquisition of linguistic and social competence (Roberts and Labov 1995; Roberts 1997, 2002; Díaz-Campos 2005; Foulkes and Docherty 2006; Green 2011; Nardy et al. 2013; Smith et al. 2013; De Vogelaer and Katerbow 2017; Smith and Durham 2019). Such work, often focusing on the very young, illustrates the role of input, saliency, complexity, and variability on the acquisition of variable forms. Within the context of the FPG study, these factors come into play as notably complex variables, such as those associated with the tense-aspect system follow trends distinct from less complex variables like velar nasal fronting (ING), confirming patterns identified in cross-sectional data (Green 2011). So, for example, invariant *be* is largely absent from our preschool and even early elementary school data, likely reflecting later acquisition, as a result of the complexity of the aspectual properties bound up in this variable. At other times, closer evaluations of linguistic development can reveal transitions from developmental patterns to dialect-specific variation. Callahan's (2011) study is a case in point, demonstrating how constraints on copula absence shift from developmental universals to AAL-specific patterns between the ages of 2 and 4. These analyses verify patterns identified in previous cross-sectional and short-term longitudinal work on the acquisition of variable linguistic structures, more generally, and with reference to AAL, more specifically.

The theorization of life stages and their impact on linguistic behavior does not exclusively focus on trends in acquisition, many of which are nearing completion between the ages of 4 and 6, but also on broader trends in language change, across the lifespan. To that end, many linguists examine the role that institutions and social structures may have in contributing to distinct phases of language use across the lifespan, with the understanding that such structures may provide the infrastructure that leads to predictable patterns of change during childhood, adolescence, and early adulthood. For preschoolers, most research has assumed the primacy of the familial unit, marking this stage as distinct from later stages in which social institutions such as school and work impact linguistic behavior.[1] The transition from home to school institutions has thus been examined as a critical moment in lifespan change, as children gain new access to social influences outside of the family unit, creating the opportunity and social impetus for language change (Britain 1997; Eckert 2000; Kerswill and Williams 2000, 2005).

---

[1] Though, see Nardy, Chevrot, and Barbu (2014) for work that begins to consider factors such as preschool social networks on early childhood variation.

Schools provide a particularly important illustration of the ways institutional structures interact with psychosocial patterns, and, as such, have been a central consideration of sociolinguistic work on life stages and lifespan change. The institutional effect of the school environment in reducing the incidence of AAL structures during the initial years of schooling is quite apparent, though the particular agents responsible for and the structures correlated with this change may be complex. Most of this research focuses on the role schools play in allowing children to form networks beyond the influence of the family. Such newfound freedom allows children to turn to (older) peers as linguistic role models, rather than continuing to rely on parental influences. Later, the transition from a school setting to a work setting is likely to impact many individuals at similar moments in the lifespan, potentially leading to similar changes, as individuals prioritize asserting more professional identities due to linguistic marketplace pressures (Baugh 1996; Wagner 2012; Forrest 2019). Workplace structures can also influence social networks, as US workplaces are typically more integrated than US schools and have been shown to contribute to more diverse social networks post-public education (Thomas 2019). In general, the importance of transitions between institutions has formed a core component of hypotheses about when and in what ways individuals change their language as they age (Eckert 1997; Chambers 2003), particularly focusing on transitions into school during childhood and, later, transitions to work or institutions of higher education, during early adulthood (Baugh 1996; Wagner 2012).

Finally, psychosocial factors are culturally situated and variably contingent on age within communities. So, for example, the experience of becoming a parent (Woolard 2011), or the need a teenager feels to establish an identity distinct from their parents (Eckert 1997), are all experiences that potentially impact the linguistic construction of style. As most individuals progress through similar institutions and/or social roles at similar time points, these experiences may produce predictable linguistic patterns over the lifespan.

Our work clearly supports the position that psychosocial and developmental concerns intersect with these institutional experiences to produce general trends and patterns in language use over time. The predominant trajectory identified with the DDM was a roller-coaster pattern, where fewer vernacular forms were used during elementary education and the post-high school time point, while participants incorporated more vernacular variants into their speech during preschool and secondary education time points. Investigations of individual variables such as (ING) and third person singular –s absence corroborate this trend. In elementary school, children use fewer vernacular forms, perhaps due to the standardizing influences of school culture; and as individuals transition out of school, these forms similarly decline, perhaps due to linguistic marketplace pressures. As predicted by cross-sectional data as well as theories of lifespan change, broader group patterns for the use of vernacular

AAL variables indicate that adolescents do tend towards more vernacular forms, perhaps representing the importance of establishing adolescent style apart from familial norms during this time (Eckert 1997). While the direct causes of these shifts are certainly open to speculation, the fact that broader trends are apparent suggests that some shared experience of growing up influences engagement in vernacularity.

Even as the predominant trajectory of change found in the FPG study aligns with theoretical assumptions of the vernacular adolescent, the presence of a number of distinct trajectories across the lifespan is an important reminder that trends and tendencies can quickly turn into stereotypes that do not accurately represent the breadth of experiences that constitute childhood and adolescence. Nondominant trajectories illustrate that there is more than one way to grow up. Some participants refrain from vernacularity throughout their lifespan, suggesting that such individuals turn to other linguistic or semiotic resources in the construction of style. Others move away from more vernacular forms, actually decreasing their usage in secondary education, perhaps constructing a style in opposition to dominant adolescent trends (Bucholtz 1999). These observations form a conversation with more ethnographic work that highlights diverse paths in the construction of adolescent style (Habick 1993; Eisikovits 1998; Bucholtz 1999; Fought 2003; Moore 2004; Mendoza-Denton 2008). This work illustrates the ways in which language use among adolescents often takes into account locally defined oppositions, with some adolescents actively constructing identities in opposition to, or at least apart from, groups that engage in both vernacular language and culture. Thus, linguistic life-stages related to both structural and psychosocial trends do produce dominant patterns of variable AAL use across the lifespan, even as exceptions to these patterns cannot and should not be dismissed as mere noise.

9.4 Comparisons of Linguistic Subsystems: The Case of Vowels

Not all resources are equally eligible in the trajectory of change and the construction of style, a fact made apparent by the stark contrast in overarching trends found among morphosyntactic and vocalic variants. Vowels receive more attention than just about any other kind of variable in sociolinguistics, both as a result of advances in acoustic analysis and the prominence of sound changes in many varieties of English. Further, the relationship between individual and community sound change has been a central focus of studies in lifespan variation. Within this context, adolescents have been heralded as avant-garde, pushing incoming sound changes forward in the construction of style. Yet, such claims are mostly based on cross-sectional data in which adolescents are observed to use more extreme versions of incoming variants than both children and adults, resulting in a pattern identified as adolescent peaks (Labov 2001; Tagliamonte and D'Arcy 2009). The cross-sectional nature of these studies obscures whether adolescent peaks represent the advancement of sound change or simple processes of age-grading that may be reversed as teens move out of this particular life stage. Longitudinal studies become a necessary complement to cross-sectional work by identifying the extent to which such age-graded behavior is common and predictable. Such work becomes critical for interpreting what adolescent peaks may reveal about language variation and change.

In stark contrast to the patterns of vernacular dialect change found in Chapter 3, the vast majority of vocalic variables showed no group trends. The participants in our study showed no consistent evidence of age-grading for vocalic variables as they had for the morphosyntactic variables in Chapter 3. Nor did they show evidence of advancing sound change. However, as discussed in Chapter 4, this may be expected, as the incoming sound change identified among White community members has been slowing in recent years (Dodsworth and Kohn 2012), and the local AAVS appears remarkably stable across a couple of decades (Kohn 2014). Quite simply, the FPG study may have missed the window to observe incoming sound changes in the region. In the absence of a nascent sound change, teens may be less likely to display cohort-level behaviors in regard to sound variation. These findings contrast, in meaningful ways, with the adolescent panel study conducted in a community with documented ongoing sound changes (Holmes-Elliott 2018). In this panel study, group trends of vowel change across time points do emerge in the data. Further, the one salient and potentially changing sound variable considered in the FPG study, the PRICE class, did show group-level patterns for change, with incremental patterns of glide-shortening across childhood and adolescence. Taken together, such evidence suggests that children and adolescents very well may play a critical role in advancing sound change, and that adolescent peaks should not be assumed to represent simple age-graded behavior.

Clearly, age-grading does not appear to affect all linguistic systems equally. As such, it is important to consider the role that different linguistic subunits play in lifespan change. Whether these differences relate to the nature of the linguistic structure (vowels are continuous; morphosyntactic variables are discrete), or to aspects of saliency (vowel variation is typically not represented in orthography, morphosyntactic variation is), remains a fruitful area for investigation.

9.5   Parental and Peer Influences

Acquisition studies of social variation have rightfully considered the importance of input in child language variation, typically focusing on parental input in the early stages. Previous research indicates that parental influences emerge early, so social variation in early child language reflects parental input (Foulkes, Docherty, and Watt 1999, 2005; Smith et al. 2013). Unsurprisingly, this variation becomes reflected in the speech of children, creating early social patterns of language use (Chevrot, Nardy, and Barbu 2011; Díaz-Campos 2005; Smith et al. 2013).

Due to the axiom that peer models replace parental influences once children establish social networks outside of the family, few studies consider whether parental input has a lasting and/or predictable impact on the speech of a child over the lifespan (Hazen 2002). Given adolescent identity practices and observed vernacularity, linguists have hypothesized that parental speech holds little sway on child and adolescent speech once peers become available to replace parental models. Yet, it is known that not all teens embrace more vernacular forms, and the relationship between the speech of emerging adults and parents has yet to be theorized, let alone examined empirically. Further, these assumptions ignore the fact that because parents and children are typically from the same speech community, they are likely to have a lot in common, linguistically.

The FPG project provides the opportunity to examine the relationship of mother and child speech longitudinally, illustrating that similarities between parent and child speech may exist longer than previously thought, especially for some groups. Indeed, the only time when mother and child vernacularity are not correlated to some extent, within our study, appears to be early adolescence. So, the children of more vernacular mothers tended to be relatively more vernacular at every time point apart from early adolescence, while the children of less vernacular mothers tended to be less vernacular than their peers at these time points. While such correlations may not be surprising for the preschool time point, later correlations raise intriguing questions. Correlations between mother and child speech in the post-high school time period may suggest that as teens take on increasing adult responsibilities, their speech may come to align with parental models, or be subject to similar social pressures and community norms. Perhaps even more surprising, daughters of less vernacular mothers may show the influences of their mothers' speech even in high school, a time when teens are expected to orient away from or show little influence of parental models. Similar to Deser (1990), who found that Detroit teens from Shuy et al.'s (1967) study were more likely than their younger siblings to adopt their parents' Southern pronunciations, the axiomatic pattern of adolescents rejecting parental models may be an oversimplification. At the same time, the differences in vowel change based on ethnicity cannot be ignored, as a number of studies have shown that African American communities are excluded from the progression of regional vowel changes taking place in cohort European American communities (Wolfram and Thomas 2002; Labov, Ash, and Boberg 2006; Holt 2018).

Though the status of later correlations remains the subject of further investigation, it is clear that a child's language may continue to bear relation to parental language well beyond the preschool age, particularly in historically segregated African American communities. Indeed, this finding stands in contrast to all other social variables considered in this analysis, including parental relationship, poverty levels, and even whether there were additional caregivers in the home. These results strengthen the observation that familial influences deserve further attention to more fully understand patterns of life-span change.

9.6   Peer Accommodation

Even as cross-sectional evidence supports the observation that peers replace parental models after early childhood, FPG is the first project to provide a large-scale study of adolescent dyadic speech. As such, questions remain about the extent to which adolescents accommodate, under what circumstances, and with what kinds of linguistic features. Such research can grant insight into the mechanisms that underpin peer influence on adolescent speech.

Our dyadic analysis demonstrates the importance of accommodation in adolescent peer interactions, the effects of which were consistently significant across the age groups we considered. However, distinctive gendered, social, and linguistic patterns provide additional clues to when and how teens accommodate. While the boys in our study showed significant accommodation patterns with peers that they knew, they were much less likely to accommodate with peers that they had just met. Girls, on the other hand, were likely to accommodate, regardless of whether they knew their interlocutor, particularly recruiting ethnolinguistically salient variables to accommodate with strangers, all of whom were African American teens. While these patterns conform to widely held beliefs that women tend to be more accommodating in language (Giles and Ogay 2006), psychosocial factors show some nuance beneath these binary categories. Specifically, boys who rated higher on social skills were more likely to accommodate to strangers, and boys with more African American social contacts were more likely to use ethnolinguistic variants to do so. The measure of social skills, in particular, may reflect correlated factors such as cooperativeness and compliance that may be associated with the construction of gendered identities.

These results confirm the importance of accommodation in peer interactions and illustrate the utility of ethnolinguistic variables in the forging of relationships. The distinctive gendered patterns here hold intriguing implications for language change. If adolescent girls are more likely than adolescent boys to accommodate to strangers, this could provide a mechanism by which novel linguistic changes can enter a community, thus providing a possible explanation for the common pattern that females tend to lead language change. If such a pattern holds, we might expect that boys who accommodate to strangers would show similar patterns. Further research on dyadic communication and innovativeness could be a fruitful addition to social network analysis, potentially ferreting out whether accommodativeness in combination with open networks identifies individuals who spread innovative variants. In addition, dyadic analyses of other age groups and age combinations could add further context to the role accommodation plays at various distinct life stages.

9.7 Applications: Style-Shifting, Literacy, and Educational Achievement

The use of AAL by children and their ability to style-shift has been a core concern for sociolinguistic study due to the central role of standardized language in the education system (Charity et al. 2004; Craig and Washington 2006; Craig et al. 2009). A wealth of research has considered the relationship between AAL and the so-called "education gap," hypothesizing that the greater distance between vernacular and written forms may create additional barriers to literacy (Labov 1995). Our analysis aligns with previous research that suggests higher use of AAL correlates with less successful reading outcomes. Yet, as with other studies, these results cannot be determined to be causative, as it is unclear whether the use of AAL is the cause of such results or is simply collinear with other factors that may lead to the same outcome.

Despite the fact that a direct causative relationship between AAL use and reduced reading outcomes cannot be established, style-shifting is often seen as a potential panacea for the concern that more vernacular students may have less successful educational outcomes. For more vernacular speakers, style-shifting is a critical skill, as the use of vernacular AAL can result in lost educational opportunities, serious breaches of justice, and economic disadvantage (Rickford and King 2016). Furthermore, style-shifting is also a way for speakers to maintain their ethnic and cultural identities, rather than assimilating to normative whiteness. Patterns of style-shifting are particularly important to study from a lifespan perspective, given that institutional structures and acquisition patterns may influence the ways speakers style-shift at different points in their lives.

Lifespan variation in the use of style has primarily focused on preschool or early elementary children (Chevrot, Beaud, and Varga 2000; Díaz-Campos 2005; Nardy et al. 2013; Smith et al. 2013). While early work suggested that style-shifting tends to be acquired later in childhood, more recent research presents a more nuanced picture where acquisition of style-shifting is viewed as variable-dependent, influenced by factors such as linguistic complexity and saliency, as well as frequency (Smith et al. 2013). School has often been viewed as critical in introducing children to concepts of formality and register, factors that would likely influence patterns of AAL use and style-shifting, more generally. Indeed, children may be quite adept at aspects of style-shifting before school, but may simply assign different social values to tasks ascribed as formal or informal by adults. The process of learning orthography may raise metalinguistic awareness by reinforcing a connection between formality and the more conservative Anglocentric written form (Chevrot et al. 2000). School, then, becomes a place where children learn to align their concepts of formality with adult concepts of formality (Patterson 1992). As such, "there may be a magnification of stylistic differences during the school years" (Patterson 1992:185).

We considered style-shifting and the relationship between AAL and reading success, utilizing the DDM as a holistic measure of vernacularity. Likely, assessments and perceptions of formality depend on clusters of variables working in cohort. Thus, the overarching patterns captured by the DDM may come closer to how individuals perceive stylistic differences than an assessment of individual variables in isolation. Most of the participants in our study showed minimal differences across contexts at the early elementary school time point. However, by the early adolescent time points, the participants tended to use fewer vernacular variables for tasks structured to elicit more formal speech. Our data clearly align with the cross-sectional literature, suggesting that children become adept at style-shifting sometime after early elementary school, perhaps, as suggested by Patterson (1992) and Chevrot et al. (2000), due to the metalinguistic knowledge acquired through reading or socialization toward norms of formality introduced in the classroom and replicated in testing environments. While some variables may show sensitivity to stylistic contexts relatively early (Smith et al. 2013), these tendencies may be less generalized among younger speakers.

It is important to acknowledge that vernacular AAL use correlates with many other social and sociopsychological variables, making it difficult to pinpoint the exact contribution of AAL use to school success. Overall, vernacular AAL use is correlated with many external factors such as mother's education, quality of the home environment, and quality of the classroom environment (Chapter 8). These correlations reflect the socioeconomic and historical conditions that lead not only to race disparities in the US, but also the conditions that would promote the evolution of distinctive varieties of English associated with race (Labov 2010). For example, access to well-funded schools has been historically restricted, to put it mildly, for African Americans, leading to a lack of educational opportunities for mothers and a tendency for children to experience more impoverished classroom environments. These patterns are intimately related to spatial segregation, both in the form of neighborhood segregation and subsequent school segregation, due to the fact that the United States primarily assigns schools based on geography (Frankenburg 2013). Housing and school segregation also contribute to wealth inequality (Rothstein 2017). AAL use is intimately interwoven with this history, as demonstrated by correlations between segregation and participation in the AAVS and higher DDM scores (Chapter 4, Chapter 5), mother's education and higher DDMs, and social contacts and higher DDMs.

It is imperative to consider this complex sociohistorical context when evaluating school success and code-switching. Children from lower SES backgrounds tended to show larger differences between formal and informal interactions than children from high SES backgrounds, due to the fact that children from high SES backgrounds tend to use relatively few vernacular variants, even in informal situations. Code-switching is, thus, a tool for those who use more vernacular varieties of AAL, something associated with membership in communities in which more vernacular AAL varieties are found. It goes without saying, but is worth repeating, that not all African Americans speak vernacular varieties, and those who do not will not engage in code-switching, as measured here.

For those who do style-shift, our findings suggest that children require several years of exposure to scholastic norms to fully sort out the ins and outs of adultlike patterns of style-shifting, despite the fact that very young children vary their language according to context for a number of linguistic variables (Smith et al. 2013). This pattern supports Patterson's (1992) observation that young children may not assign the same social meaning to different linguistic tasks when compared to adults, or it may reflect variable acquisition processes where style-shifting patterns are acquired later for less salient, complex, or infrequent variables (Smith et al. 2013). Such concerns should be considered in scholastic and linguistic testing. When educators enter the classroom with limited knowledge of AAL and language development patterns, it can have drastic consequences. Such factors may cause educators to miss early potential and fail to foster a love of learning in more vernacular students, who, like many African American students, may be too quickly labeled as unlikely to excel (Parks and Kennedy 2007). Such early labels have the potential to persist even after style-shifting patterns have been acquired. The implicit biases of adults towards young children who use more vernacular AAL may indeed be one collinear variable that leads to lower literacy success rates among more vernacular children. These sentiments align with scholars who argue that the education gap is more a reflection of systemic racism than language use (Charity Hudley and Mallinson 2011; Young et al. 2014).

Craig and Washington (2006) note that risk factors are cumulative. Resiliency factors likely are, too. Our study replicates research that indicates declines in vernacular AAL use in the early grades correlate with reading success (Terry and Connor 2012; Terry et al. 2012). As such, style-shifting is a resiliency factor that can promote scholastic success. But due to its later acquisition, it may not be enough to prevent the impact of implicit bias in the earliest grades. With this in mind, training that addresses implicit bias and linguistic diversity may be particularly critical for early childhood educators.

9.8   Theorization of Lifespan Variation

Perhaps the most important story the FPG study can tell is that of dynamicity. Individuals continue to develop and change their linguistic behavior across childhood, adolescence, and early adulthood. When we delve into the details, we find out how truly important this observation is. In our consideration of external factors, we so often found that age became our most important variable when examining how and in what ways children changed their linguistic behavior, across the course of the study. Overall, language use may be predicted by external factors such as mother's education and socioeconomic status, but such variables are less likely to predict how and when individuals change their linguistic behavior. This may be related to the relative lack of change many of our participants experience over the course of the lifespan for certain external variables, or it may simply indicate that changes in these external circumstances did not affect the linguistic processes of growing up. So, for example, the percentage of African American students in a school correlates with involvement in aspects of the AAVS, but not shifts across time points, as students rarely experience dramatic shifts in school demographics. What remains is that cohort patterns are predominantly related to age in this study, suggesting the validity of considering the confluence of psychosocial and structural factors related to language use at distinct life stages, producing broader cultural patterns of lifespan linguistic change. In other words, it's not one variable that causes groups of children to follow similar paths through their linguistic development – it's a host of variables working in concert to produce the experience of growing up.

The exceptions to this pattern are illuminating. Growing up is not a unitary experience and not all people will follow the same paths set before them. Not all types of linguistic variables will come to be favored as a way to stand out from the crowd, just as not all teenagers will seek to draw attention to their sense of style. Not all adolescents will accommodate their linguistic behavior when talking with a stranger, even if that stranger is the same age and ethnicity as them. These patterns reveal the nuance of longitudinal studies, encouraging us to keep on pursuing ethnographic work to examine the local construction of meaning these exceptions suggest. The performance of gender, ethnicity, and style all benefit from such close and careful analyses.

Both the dominating patterns, such as when children begin to style-shift, as well as these exceptions, such as the child who stays remarkably consistent in their language use over time, provide linguists, educators, speech pathologists, and many others with a clearer picture of the role of language across the lifespan. At the culmination of the study, the participants in the FPG project were raising children, working jobs, attending college, in the military, and living their lives. While we no longer have the privilege of listening to their stories, if longitudinal research of adults has shown us anything, these adults will continue to change their language to some extent, as they build new experiences and move through their lives (Baugh 1996; Sankoff and Blondeau 2007; Wagner 2012b; Wagner and Buchstaller 2018). They have certainly changed us and our understanding of child and adolescent language with their generosity and the generosity of their families, and we are grateful to them. What they have given to the study of language variation and change over real time is invaluable and can never be replicated.

References

Baugh, John. 1996. Dimensions of a theory of econolinguistics. In Gregory Guy, Crawford Feagin, Deborah Schiffrin, and John Baugh (eds.), *Towards a Social Science of Language: Papers in Honor of William Labov*, 397–419. Amsterdam/ Philadelphia: John Benjamins.

Britain, David 1997. Dialect contact and phonological reallocation: "Canadian raising" in the English Fens. *Language in Society* 26(1): 15–46.

Bucholtz, Mary. 1999. "Why be normal?": Language and identity practices in a community of nerd girls. *Language in Society* 28(2): 203–223.

Bucholtz, Mary. 2003. Sociolinguistic nostalgia and the authentication of identity. *Journal of Sociolinguistics* 7(3): 398–416.

Callahan-Price, Erin. 2009. Childhood copula development in African American English. Paper presented at *New Ways of Analyzing Variation* 39. San Antonio, Texas.

Chambers, J. K. 2003. *Sociolinguistic Theory: Linguistic Variation and its Social Significance*. Oxford, UK: Blackwell.

Charity, Anne H., Hollis S. Scarborough, and Darion M. Griffin. 2004. Familiarity with "School English" in African-American children and its relationship to early reading achievement. *Child Development* 75(5): 1340–1356.

Charity Hudley, Anne H. and Christine Mallinson. 2011. *Understanding English Language Variation in U.S. Schools*. New York: Teachers College Press.

Cheshire, Jenny. 2005. Age and generation-specific use of language. In Ulrich Ammon, Norbert Dittmar, Klaus J. Mattheier, and Peter Trudgill (eds.), *Sociolinguistics: An Introductory Handbook of the Science of Language and Society 2nd edition*, 1552–1563. Berlin: Mouton de Gruyter.

Chevrot, Jean-Pierre, Laurence Beaud, and Renata Varga. 2000. Developmental data on a French sociolinguistic variable: Post-consonantal word-final /R/. *Language Variation and Change* 12(3). 295–319.

Chevrot, Jean-Pierre, Aurélie Nardy, and Stéphanie Barbu. 2011. Developmental dynamics of SES-related differences in children's production of obligatory and variable phonological alternations. *Language Sciences* 33(1): 180–191.

Craig, Holly K. and Julie A. Washington. 2006. *Malik Goes to School: Examining the Language Skills of African American Students from Preschool-5th Grade*. Mahwah, New Jersey: Lawrence Erlbaum Associates.

Craig, Holly K., Lingling Zhang, Stephanie L. Hensel, and Erin J. Quinn. 2009. African American English-speaking students: An examination of the relationship between dialect shifting and reading outcomes. *Journal of Speech, Language, and Hearing Research* 52(4): 839–855.

Cukor-Avila, Patricia. 2002. She say, she go, She be like: Verbs of quotation over time in African American Vernacular English. *American Speech* 77(1): 3–31.

Cukor-Avila, Patricia and Guy Bailey. 2011. The Interaction of Transmission and Diffusion in the Spread of Linguistic Forms. *University of Pennsylvania Working Papers in Linguistics* 17(2): Article 6.

Deser, Toni. 1990. *Dialect Transmission and Variation: An Acoustic Analysis of Vowels in Six Urban Detroit Families*. Ph.D. dissertation Boston, MA: Boston University.

De Vogelaer, Gunther and Matthias Katerbow, eds. 2017. *Acquiring Sociolinguistic Variation*. Vol. 20. Amsterdam/Philadelphia: John Benjamins.

Díaz-Campos, Manuel. 2005. The emergence of adult-like command of sociolinguistic variables: A study of consonant weakening in Spanish-speaking children. In D. Eddington (ed.), *Selected Proceedings of the 6th Conference on the Acquisition of Spanish and Portuguese as First and Second Languages*, 56–65. Somerville, MA: Cascadilla Proceedings Project.

Dillard, J. L. 1972. *Black English: Its History and Usage in the United States*. New York: Random House.

Dodsworth, Robin and Mary Elizabeth Kohn. 2012. Urban rejection of the vernacular: The SVS undone. *Language Variation and Change* 24(2): 221–245.

Eckert, Penelope. 1997. Age as a sociolinguistic variable. In Florian Coulmas (ed.), *The Handbook of Sociolinguistics*, 151–167. Malden, MA: Blackwell.

Eckert, Penelope. 2000. *Linguistic Variation as Social Practice: The Linguistic Construction of Social Meaning in Belten High*. Oxford: Blackwell.

Eisikovits, Edina. 1998. Girl-talk/boy-talk: Sex differences in adolescent speech. In Jennifer Coates (ed.), *Language and Gender: A Reader*, 45–58. Sydney: Australian Professional Publications.

Fischer, John L. 1958. Social influence on the choice of a linguistic variant. *Word* 14: 47–56.

Flipsen, Peter and Sungbok Lee. 2012. Reference data for the American English acoustic vowel space. *Clinical Linguistics & Phonetics* 26(11–12): 926–933.

Forrest, Jon. 2019. *A Firm-Specific Analysis of Southern U.S. English and Workplace Processes*. Ph.D. dissertation. Raleigh, NC: North Carolina State University.

Fought, Carmen. 2003. *Chicano English in Context*. Basingstoke/New York: Palgrave-Macmillan.

Foulkes, Paul and Gerard Docherty. 2006. The social life of phonetics and phonology. *Journal of Phonetics* 34(4): 409–438. Elsevier Science B.V., Amsterdam.

Foulkes, Paul, Gerard Docherty, and Dominic Watt. 1999. Tracking the emergence of structured variation realizations of (t) by Newcastle children. *Leeds Working Papers in Linguistics and Phonetics* 7: 1–23.

Foulkes, Paul, Gerard Docherty, and Dominic Watt. 2005. Phonological variation in child-directed speech. *Language* 81(1): 177–206.

Frankenberg, Erica. 2013. The role of residential segregation in contemporary school segregation. *Education and Urban Society* 45(5): 548–570.

Giles, Howard and Tania Ogay. 2006. Communication accommodation theory. In Bryan Whaley and Wendy Samter (eds.), *Explaining Communication: Contemporary Theories and Exemplars*, 293–310. Mahwah, NJ: Erlbaum.

Green, Lisa. J. 2011. *Language and the African American Child*. Cambridge: Cambridge University Press.

Habick, Timothy. 1993. Farmer City, Illinois: Sound systems shifting south. In Timothy Frazer (ed.), *"Heartland" English: Variation and Transition in the American Midwest*, 97–124. Tuscaloosa, Alabama: University of Alabama Press.

Hazen, Kirk. 2002. The family. In J.K. Chambers, Natalie Schilling-Estes and Peter Trudgill (eds.), *Handbook of Language Variation and Change*, 500–525. Oxford, UK: Blackwell.

Hockett, Charles. 1950. Age-grading and linguistic continuity. *Language* 26: 449–459.

Holmes-Elliott, Sophie. 2018. *Do Birds of a Feather Flock Together? Real Time Incrementation and Type of Sound Change*. Paper presented at *New Ways of Analyzing Variation* 47. New York: New York University.

Holt, Yolanda Feimster. 2018. Mechanisms of vowel variation in African American English. *Journal of Speech, Language, and Hearing Research* 61(2): 97–109

Houston, Susan H. 1969. A sociolinguistic consideration of the Black English of children in Northern Florida. *Language* 45(3): 599–607.

Kerswill, Paul and Ann Williams. 2000. Creating a new town koine: Children and language change in Milton Keynes. *Language in Society* 29(1): 65–115.

Kerswill, Paul and Ann Williams. 2005. New towns and koineization: Linguistic and social correlates. *Linguistics* 43(5): 1023–1048.

Kohn, Mary Elizabeth. 2014. *"The Way I Communicate Changes but How I Speak Don't": A Longitudinal Perspective on Adolescent Language Variation and Change. Publication of the American Dialect Society* 99. Durham, NC: Duke University Press.

Kovac, Ceil and H. Douglas Adamson. 1981. Variation theory and first language acquisition. In David Sankoff and Henrietta Cedergren (eds.), *Variation Omnibus*, 403–410. Edmonton, Alberta: Linguistic Research, Inc.

Labov, William. 1995. Can reading failure be reversed? A linguistic approach to the question. In Vivian Gadsden and Daniel Wagner (eds.), *Literacy among African American Youth: Issues in Learning, Teaching, and Schooling*, 39–68. Cresskill, NJ: Hampton Press.

Labov, William. 2001. *Principles of Linguistic Change. Vol.2, Social Factors. Language in Society* Malden/Oxford: Blackwell.

Labov, William. 2010. Unendangered dialect, endangered people: The case of African American Vernacular English. *Transforming Anthropology* 18(1): 15–27.

Labov, William, Sharon Ash, and Charles Boberg. 2006. *Atlas of North American English*. New York/Berlin: Mouton de Gruyter.

Macaulay, Ronald K.S. 1977. *Language, Social Class, and Education: A Glasgow study*. Edinburgh: Edinburgh University Press.

Martino, Josephine. 1982. The phoneme /θ/ and its alternative realization as /f/: A study of variation in Australian English among primary school boys, according to socio-economic background. *Working Papers in Linguistics Melbourne* 8. 39–42.

Mendoza-Denton, Norma. 2008. *Homegirls: Language and Cultural Practice Among Latina Youth Gangs. Homegirls: Language and Cultural Practice Among Latina Youth Gangs*. Malden/Oxford: Blackwell.

Moore, Emma. 2004. Sociolinguistic style: A multidimensional resource for shared identity creation. *Canadian Journal of Linguistics* 49(3/4): 375–396.

Nardy, Aurélie, Jean-Pierre Chevrot, and Stéphanie Barbu. 2013. The acquisition of sociolinguistic variation: Looking back and thinking. *Linguistics* 51(2): 255–284.

Nardy, Aurélie, Jean-Pierre Chevrot, and Stéphanie Barbu. 2014. Sociolinguistic convergence and social interactions within a group of preschoolers: A longitudinal study. *Language Variation and Change* 26(3): 273–301.

Oetting, Janna B. and McDonald, Janet L. 2001. Nonmainstream dialect use and specific language impairment. *Journal of Speech, Language, and Hearing Research* 44(1): 207–223.

Oetting, Janna B. and Janet L. McDonald. 2002. Methods for characterizing participants' nonmainstream dialect use in child language research. *Journal of Speech, Language, and Hearing Research* 45(3): 505–518.

Patterson, Janet Lee. 1992. *The Development of Sociolinguistic Phonological Variation Patterns for (ing) in Young Children*. Ph.D. dissertation. Albuquerque, NM: University of New Mexico.

Parks, Felicia R. and Janice H. Kennedy. 2007. The impact of race, physical attractiveness, and gender on education majors' and teachers' perceptions of student competence. *Journal of Black Studies* 37(6): 936–943.

Payne, Arvilla. 1980. Factors controlling the acquisition of the Philadelphia dialect by out-of-state children. In William Labov (ed.), *Locating Language in Time and Space*, 143–178. New York: Academic Press.

Purcell, April. 1984. Code-shifting Hawaiian style: Children's accommodation along a decreolizing continuum. *International Journal of the Sociology of Language* 46: 71–86.

Rickford, John R. and Sharese King. 2016. Language and linguistics on trial: Hearing Rachel Jeantel (and other vernacular speakers) in the courtroom and beyond. *Language* 92(4): 948–988.

Rickford, John R. and MacKenzie Price. 2013. Girlz II women: Age-grading, language change and stylistic variation. *Journal of Sociolinguistics* 17(2): 143–179.

Reid, Euan. 1978. Social and stylistic variation in the speech of children: Some evidence from Edinburgh. In Peter Trudgill (ed.), *Sociolinguistic Patterns in British English*, 158–171. London: Edward Arnold.

Renn, Jennifer E. 2007. *Measuring Style Shift: A Quantitative Analysis of African American English*. Master's thesis. Chapel Hill, NC: University of North Carolina at Chapel Hill.

Renn, Jennifer E. 2010. *Acquiring Style: The Development of Dialect Shifting among African American Children*. Ph.D. dissertation. Chapel Hill, NC: University of North Carolina at Chapel Hill.

Roberts, Julie. 1997. Hitting a moving target: Acquisition of sound change in progress by Philadelphia children. *Language Variation and Change* 9(2): 249–266.

Roberts, Julie. 2002. Child language variation. In J.K. Chambers, Peter Trudgill and Natalie Schilling-Estes (eds.), *The Handbook of Language Variation and Change*, 333–348. Oxford: Blackwell.

Roberts, Julie and William Labov. 1995. Learning to talk Philadelphian: Acquisition of short a by preschool children. *Language Variation and Change* 7(1): 101–112.

Romaine, Suzanne. 1978. Postvocalic /r/ in Scottish English: Sound change in progress? In Peter Trudgill (ed.), *Sociolinguistic Patterns in British English*, 144–158. London: Edward Arnold.

Romaine, Suzanne. 1984. *The Language of Children and Adolescents: The Acquisition of Communicative Competence*. Oxford: Blackwell.

Rothstein, Richard. 2017. *The Color of Law: A Forgotten History of How Our Government Segregated America*. New York: W.W. Norton.

Sankoff, Gillian and Hélène Blondeau. 2007. Language change across the lifespan: /r/ in Montreal French. *Language* 83(3): 560–588.

Shuy, Roger W., Walt Wolfram and William K. Riley 1967. *Linguistic Correlates of Social Stratification in Detroit Speech*. USOE Final Report No.6–1347. Bethesda, MD: National Institute of Mental Health.

Smith, Jennifer and Mercedes Durham. 2019. *Sociolinguistic Variation in Children's Language: Acquiring Community Norms*. Cambridge: Cambridge University Press.

Smith, Jennifer, Mercedes Durham and Liane Fortune. 2007. "Mam, my trousers is Fa'in Doon!" community, caregiver, and child in the acquisition of variation in a Scottish dialect. *Language Variation and Change* 19(1): 63–99.

Smith, Jennifer, Mercedes Durham, and Hazel Richards. 2013. The social and linguistic in the acquisition of sociolinguistic norms: Caregivers, children, and variation. *Linguistics* 51(2): 285–324.

Stewart, William A. 1967. Sociolinguistic factors in the history of American Negro dialects. *The Florida FL Reporter* 5 (2): 11, 22, 24, 26.

Stockman, Ida J. and Anna Fay Vaughn-Cooke. 1989. Addressing new questions about black children's language. In Deborah Schiffrin and Ralph W. Fasold (eds.) *Current Issues in Linguistic Theory* 52, 275–300. Philadelphia: John Benjamins.

Tagliamonte, Sali A. and Alexandra D'Arcy. 2009. Peaks beyond phonology: Adolescence, incrementation, and language change. *Language* 85(1): 58–108.

Terry, Nicole P. and Carol M. Connor. 2012. Changing Nonmainstream American English use and early reading achievement from kindergarten to first grade. *American Journal of Speech-Language Pathology* 21(1): 78–86.

Terry, Nicole P., Carol M. Connor, Yaacov Petcher, and Catherine R. Connor. 2012. Dialect variation and reading: Is change in nonmainstream American English use related to reading achievement in first and second grades? *Journal of Speech, Language, and Hearing Research* 55(1): 55–69.

Thomas, Reuben J. 2019. Sources of friendship and structurally induced homophily across the life course. *Sociological Perspectives* 62(6): 822–843.

Wagner, Suzanne Evans. 2012. Age grading in sociolinguistic theory. *Linguistics and Language Compass* 6(6): 371–382.

Wagner, Suzanne Evans and Isabelle Buchstaller (eds.). 2018. *Using Panel Data in the Sociolinguistic Study of Variation and Change*. New York: Routledge.

Wolfram, Walt. 2007. Sociolinguistic Folklore in the Study of African American English. *Language and Linguistics Compass* 1(4): 292–313.

Wolfram, Walt and Erik R. Thomas. 2002. *The Development of African American English*. Malden, MA: Blackwell.

Woolard, Kathryn. 2011. Is there linguistic life after high school? Longitudinal changes in the bilingual repertoire in metropolitan Barcelona. *Language in Society* 40(5): 617–648.

Vogelaer, Gunther De and Matthias Katerbow (eds.). 2017. *Acquiring Sociolinguistic Variation*. Amsterdam/Philadelphia: John Benjamins.

Vorperian, Houri K. and Ray D. Kent. 2007. Vowel acoustic space development in children: A synthesis of acoustic and anatomic data. *Journal of Speech, Language, and Hearing Research* 50(6): 1510–1545.

Young, Vershawn Ashanti, Rusty Barrett, and Kim Brian Lovejoy. 2014. *Other People's English: Code-meshing, Code-switching, and African American Literacy*. New York/London: Teachers College Press.

Appendix: AAL Feature Code Key

Morphosyntactic Features:

1. a. Zero Copula (*CO) = is, am, are, and other forms of the verb to be are variably included or excluded in either copula or auxiliary form

   e.g   the bridge __ out   the bridge *CO out

             they __ ugly   they *CO ugly

             because he __ cold   because he *CO cold

   b. Zero Modal Auxiliary (*MA) = will, can, do, and have are variably included or excluded as modal auxiliaries

   e.g.   how__ you do this   how *MA you do this

             when __ my dad get here   when *MA my dad get here

             maybe we __ take this off   maybe we *MA take this off

             I__ never seen it   I *MA never seen it

             they __ been do/ing that   they *MA been do/ing that

2. Subject-Verb Agreement = A subject and verb that differ in either number or person

   a. Addition of inflectional –s on non-3rd person singular subject ([P3S], coded on word)

        e.g.   we likes them   we like/3s[P3S] them

   b. Absence of 3rd person singular –s (/*3s)

        e.g.   she like_ her   she like/*3s her

   c. Leveling = is/was generalization ([LEV], coded on word)

        (e.g., we was[LEV] there, the dog/s is[LEV] in the house)

   d. Difference in number between subject and modal auxiliaries do and have ([3SA], coded on word)

        (e.g., he don't[3SA] wanna move; his wheel have[3SA] busted open)

3. Finta/(S)poseta/Bouta ([FBS], coded on word) = Abbreviated forms of fixing to, supposed to, and about to
    (e.g., she finta[FBS] backward flip; when does it sposeta[FBS] go; they don't sposeta[FBS] go; this one bouta[FBS] go in the school)

4. Ain't = Use of ain't as a negative auxiliary
    a. Ain't used as a negative auxiliary in are+not, is+not, and have+not ([AI1], coded on word)
        (e.g., why she ain't[AI1] come/ing; the car/s ain't[AI1] gonna move)
    b. Ain't used as a negative auxiliary in did+not ([AI2], coded on word)
        (e.g., he ain't[AI2] go)

5. Undifferentiated Pronoun Case = Nominative, objective, and demonstrative cases of pronouns occur interchangeably
    a. Nominative and objective pronouns are used interchangeably ([UNO], coded on word)
        (e.g., him[UNO] did and him; and then them[UNO] fall; that car ran he [UNO] over; me[UNO] don't know; and him[UNO] lose him paper/s)
    b. Use of object form for demonstrative ([UOD], coded on word)
        (e.g., them[UOD] dogs; that boy drop/ed all them[UOD] paper)
    c. Use of personal/benefactive dative construction ([BDA], coded on word)
        (e.g., you love you[BDA] some boys; I got me[BDA] a drink)

6. Multiple Negation ([NEG], coded on utterance) = Use of two or more negative markers in a clause for a single negative proposition (i.e., do NOT code he didn't do nothing, he did was always busy)
        e.g.   I don't got no brothers [NEG].
                 they didn't do nothing [NEG].

7. Zero Possessive = Possession is coded by word order alone
    a. The possessive marker –'s is deleted (/*z)
        e.g.   he hit the man/*z car
                 somebody/*z bike *CO broke

    b. The nominative or objective case of the pronoun is used rather than the possessive ([0PP]. coded on word)
        (e.g., they[0PP] house; kids just go/ing to walk to they[0PP] school)

8. Zero Past Tense
    a. The past tense marker –ed is not always used to denote regular past constructions (/*ed)
        e.g.   and this car crash__.   and this car crash/*ed.
                 they mess_ up before.   they mess/*ed up before.

b. the present tense form is used in place of the irregular past tense ([0PT], coded on word)

    e.g.   and then them fall.   and then them[UNO] fall[0PT].

            I come there yesterday.   I come[0PT] there yesterday.

9. Zero –ing (/*ing) = The present progressive morpheme –ing is deleted

    e.g.   the lady is sleep__.   the lady is sleep/*ing.

            and here/'s a lady that's   and here/'s a lady that's

            wear__ pink.   wear/*ing pink.

10. Invariant/Habitual be ([IBE], coded on word) = Unconjugated be with a variety of subjects coding habitual action or to state a rule

    (e.g., this one be[IBE] flying up in the sky; they be[IBE] messing up)

11. Zero to (*TO) = The infinitive marker to is deleted

    e.g. now my turn __ shoot you   now my turn *TO shoot you

        he was try/ing __ run after you he was try/ing *TO run after you

12. Zero Plural (/*s) = Variable inclusion of plural marker –s

    e.g. wait ten minute__   wait ten minute/*s

        two dog_   two dog/*s

        some kids got their lunchbox__ some kids got their lunchbox/*s

        and books and stuff   and books and stuff

13. Double Copula/Auxiliary/Modal

    a. Double Copula or Auxiliary ([DCA], code on word) = Two copula or auxiliary forms of the verb "to be" are used where a single form is needed

        (e.g., I'm is[DCA] the last one riding on; there is[DCA] play/ing in the snow)

    b. Double Modal ([DMO], code on word) = Two modal forms (i.e., verbs that express certain "moods" such as certainty, possibility, obligation, or permission) for a single verb form

        (e.g., I might could[DMO] go there; you oughta mighta[DMO] take that)

14. Regularized Reflexive ([RRF], code on word) = Reflexive pronouns himself and themselves are expressed using hisself and their/theyselves or their/theyself

    (e.g., he stand/3s by hisself[RRF]; everybody stop and hurt theyself [RRF]; they *CO skate/ing there all by theirself[RRF].)

15. Indefinite Article ([INA], coded on word) = Use of a regardless of whether the first sound in subsequent noun is a vowel or a consonant

    (e.g., a boy is giving his friend a[INA] airplane)

16. Appositive Pronoun ([APP], coded on word) = A pronoun that is used in addition to a noun or a second pronoun to signify the same referent
    (e.g., the crossing guard she[APP] *CO whistle/ing to him; this one he [APP]/'s down on the ground)

17. Past Form for Participles ([RPF], coded on word) = Substitution of the regular past tense form for the past participle; this should be coded when the speaker is referring to an event that has completed before another past action
    (e.g., I had went[RPF] down there for SAE "I had gone down there"; he may have took[RPF] the wagon for SAE "he may have taken the wagon")

18. Preterite had ([HAD], coded on word) = 'had' + verb in past tense form where Standard American English would use the simple past form (e.g., My mama, she was about to go to Bible study, and on the way back there her car had[HAD] stopped. And then she had[HAD] called the house because somebody let her use the phone. And then she had[HAD] called the house, and then I said, "Hello. Who's this?" for SAE "My mama, she was about to go to Bible study, and on the way back there her car stopped. And then she called the house and because somebody let her use the phone. And then she called the house, and then I said 'Hello. Who's this?'")
    **Note that in the above example, the car stopping does not occur BEFORE going to Bible study. (In Standard American English the use of "had stopped" would require the stopping to have occurred before going to Bible study.)
    **When coding this feature, be sure to record at least the immediately preceding and following sentences in the "Notes" column.

19. Regularization of Irregular Past Tense Form ([IPT], coded on word) = Substitution of regularized past tense form for an irregular verb
    (e.g., everybody know/ed[IPT] he was late; they throw/ed[IPT] out the old food)

20. Zero Relative Pronoun (*RP) = Absence of the relative pronoun when it is refers to the subject of the sentence
    e.g. that/'s the man __ come here   that/'s the man *RP come here
          that/'s the dog __ bit me   that/'s the dog *RP bit me

21. Uninverted Direct Questions ([UDQ], coded on entire utterance) = Formation of a direct question without I-to-C inversion
    (e.g., Why I can/'t go [UDQ]?)

22. Inverted Question without if/whether (INQ, coded on utterance) = Inversion of elements in a question without a complementizer whether/if
    (e.g., she ask/ed could she go [INQ]?)

23. Existential it or they ([XIT], coded on word) = The use of it or they to denote the existence of something (equivalent to Standard English there is) (e.g., it[XIT]/'s a doughnut in the cabinet; it[XIT] ain't no spoon; they [XIT]/'s a good show on TV)

24. Regularized mines ([MIN], coded on word) = Regularization of the possessive pronoun mine to mines, through analogy with yours, his, hers, etc. (e.g., mines[MIN] is nice; that book is mines[MIN])

25. Remote past "been" ([RPB], coded on word) = been is used to mark action in the remote past; in such cases the word been is always stressed (e.g., he been[RPB] had that job; I been[RPB] bought her clothes)

26. Completive done ([DON], coded on word) = done and did are used to indicate a completed action and are in a preverbal position (i.e., they are not the main verb) (e.g., he done[DON] fall down; they did[DON] fell)

27. Double Marking = Multiple agreement markers are used for forms
    a. Multiple agreement markers for irregular plural nouns (i.e., addition of plural –s on irregular form) ([DMN], coded on word) (e.g., then the peoples[DMN] in the car is smashed)
    b. Multiple agreement markers for pronouns ([DMP], coded on word) (e.g., what/'s thems[DMN] doing?)
    c. Multiple agreement markers for irregular verbs (i.e., addition of past tense –ed or plural marker for number on irregular form) ([DMV], coded on word) (e.g., a boy was hurted[DMV] on the floor; they fells[DMV])

28. Zero Preposition (*PR) = Prepositions are variably deleted
    e.g. what happen/ed __ the tree?   what happen/ed *PR the tree?
         I play __ home   I play *PR home
         he got runned over __ a car   he got runned over *PR a car
         the boy fell out the car   the boy fell out *PR the car
         the boy he got __ an accident   the boy he got *PR an accident

29. Zero Article (*AR) = Articles are variable included and excluded
    e.g. I/'ll set them up in __ minute   I/'ll set them up in *AR minute

         police officer/s and __   police officer/s and *AR
         ambulance was there   ambulance was there
         can you push it into __ bottom   can you push it into *AR
         for me   bottom for me

Phonological Features:

1. Nasal Fronting ([NAS], coded on word) = Substitution of /n/ for /ŋ/
   (e.g., and this boy *CO get/ing[NAS] ready to fall: "getting" = [gɛtIn])

2. Prevocalic Cluster Reduction ([PCR], coded on word) = Word-final consonant cluster ending in a stop is reduced, even when followed by a word
   beginning with a vowel (Note: Do not code and &just for this feature)
   (e.g., best[PCR] apple)

3. Labialization ([LAB], coded on word) = Substitution of /f/ for /θ/ and /v/
   for /ð/
   (e.g., everybody had they mouth[LAB] open: "mouth" = [maUf];
   let the other cars: "other" = [ʌvər])

Potential Feature Codes:

1. Copula Use ([XCO], coded on word) = Use of the copula where it could be
   deleted under the rules of AAE grammar.

   **This should be coded wherever the copula could be contracted in
   SAE (e.g., *What his name?* should be coded because it could be
   What's his name? in SAE; *I don't know where he is* should not be
   coded because **I don't know where he's* is ungrammatical in SAE.
   **Cases where only the phonological environment precludes contrac-
   tion in SAE should be coded (e.g., *His nice* should be coded even
   though **His's nice* does not exist in SAE for phonological reasons).
   **Do not code first person singular cases (e.g., "I/'m")

2. Lack of Nasal Fronting ([XNA], coded on word) = Use of /ŋ/ in a multi-
   syllabic word
   (e.g. "going" = [gowIŋ]

Miscellaneous Codes:

1. No Feature ([OOO], coded on utterance) = No AAE feature within a
   particular C-unit

2. Fully Unintelligible ([UNI], coded on utterance) = More than 20% of a
   particular C-unit is unintelligible

3. Partially Unintelligible ([PUN], coded on utterance) = Part of a given C-unit
   is unintelligible, but it is 20% or less of the entire C-unit

4. Elliptical Response ([ELL], coded on utterance) = The speaker's utterance is not a complete C-unit, but it is in response to a question)

   (e.g., yes, uh-uh, pizza, after school – as response to a question)

5. Abandoned Utterance (>) = The speaker abandons an utterance, even if it contains a complete clause.

   (e.g., when he was marooned on an island with all shark he>)

6. Interruption (^) = The speaker abandons an utterance because he or she is interrupted.

   (e.g., I was on my way to the store when^)

7. Filler ([FIL], coded on utterance) = Words like "OK", "yeah", "uh-huh", etc. that are not in answer to a direct question and are used as a space filler

8. Casual Article ([[CAR], coded on word) = When the subject omits an article because he is reading a list, not because of a vernacular feature. Be sure to not the difference between this and the "Zero Article" feature

Index

CPSIA information can be obtained
at www.ICGtesting.com
Printed in the USA
LVHW020849260121
677450LV00017B/487

9 781108 798983